LONG ROAD HOME

LONG ROAD HOME: A CHINA JOURNAL

VERA SCHWARCZ

YALE UNIVERSITY PRESS
NEW HAVEN AND LONDON

Published with assistance from the foundation
established in memory of William McKean Brown.
The author wishes to acknowledge the assistance
of Hannah Sokal-Holmes, who prepared the map
of China.

Designed by Sally Harris
and set in Palatino type.
Printed in the United States of America by
Vail-Ballou Press, Inc., Binghamton, New York.

Library of Congress Cataloging in Publication Data

Schwarcz, Vera, 1947–
   Long road home.

   Includes index.
   1. China—Description and travel—1976–
2. China—Intellectual life—1976–   . 3. Schwarcz,
Vera, 1947–   .   4. Students—United States—
Biography.   I. Title.
DS712.S378   1984   951.05   83–16657
ISBN 0-300-03009-6

The paper in this book meets the guidelines for
permanence and durability of the Committee on
Production Guidelines for Book Longevity of the
Council on Library Resources.

10   9   8   7   6   5   4   3   2   1

For my friends in China, in gratitude for their company along the way

CONTENTS

ILLUSTRATIONS

ACKNOWLEDGMENTS

Three years ago, as I was leaving China, this book was about to die before it was born. It seemed too personal, too laden with risk for Chinese friends. At that point, a group of loyal, critical readers emerged who helped me weather repeated waves of doubt and fear. They became midwives to a work I was able and willing to stand by. In the first year after I returned from China, my American friends—Chris Gilmartin, Janet Luongo, Jan Willis, Jeannette Hopkins, Gloria Stern, Jason Wolfe, and Elisabeth Young-Bruehl—took turns reading the journal. Their concrete suggestions and support saved me repeatedly from the temptation to abandon the project. At the same time, colleagues in the China field, especially John Fairbank, Paul Cohen, Irwin Hyatt, Jonathan Spence, and Frederic and Carolyn Wakeman, gave me reason to believe that such a book might be useful to a broad range of readers. Without their reasons, I might have never discovered my own.

In the next couple of years, as I moved toward publication, the manuscript benefited greatly from suggestions by Jerome Grieder, Maurice Meisner, Marilyn Young, John Israel, and Anne Greene. In the final stretch of this long road, my editor at the Yale University Press, Charles Grench, more than kept his word to mix moral support with tough-minded criticism. Without his vision and confidence, this would have been a far tamer book, if a book at all.

A NOTE ON ROMANIZATION

Throughout the book, I have used the *pinyin* system for the trans-literation of Chinese names. Developed on the mainland, this system is currently becoming standard around the world. Thus, even for familiar names such as Chou En-lai and Mao Tse-tung, I have used the slightly more novel forms Zhou Enlai and Mao Zedong.

Unless otherwise indicated, all translations are my own. I have, however, kept the old spelling for China's capital. Although I lived and worked in what is now known as Beijing, the city that became my home over the sixteen months described here cannot be called by any other name but Peking.

INTRODUCTION

I have felt it essential to take a long road home to China . . . to sense the shape of China by observing how a Western dichotomy does not fit Chinese thought. We need the West in mind in order to keep it in mind and out of the Chinese picture—and thus to be able to trace the picture's outline. Joseph R. Levenson, "Will Sinology Do?" Journal of Asian Studies (1964)

On February 23, 1979, fifteen years after Joseph Levenson warned that we could never see China except through Western eyes, I arrived in Peking. A member of the first group of officially sponsored American exchange scholars, I thought that I understood what Levenson meant and was ready to start tracing my own China picture. But I was wrong. An outline would emerge only much later. The long road came first. Before I could see anything of China, I had to come to terms with my own many-layered preconceptions about the country that had been the object of my study for a decade. This journal describes the slow process of peeling away those notions. It shows how long it took to see anything of Chinese life, how much longer still to see things through Chinese eyes.

The West I carried in mind was a mixture of America and Europe. I was born and raised in Romania. Calling itself a socialist republic since 1944, Romania proved to be an inadequate model for what I would find in the post-Mao People's Republic. Although my Chinese hosts often pointed to Romania as an ideal for economic modernization, I sensed that they used my birthplace as a code word for their own goals of a more efficient, somewhat freer society. Still, we had a common reference point. That made the long road just a little bit shorter.

The languages I had studied back home—Romanian, Hungarian, Russian, French, and German—did not bear directly on China. And yet these, too, helped. They opened my ears to the many ways people have of expressing the same thoughts, the same feelings. Long before I went to live in China, I had learned to look for meaning between words. As an immigrant to the United States in 1962, I had had to learn to cope in an English-speaking world without previous exposure to its conventions, to its slang. When I went to Vassar College four years later, my language base was still unformed. I learned to speak and write in complex terms before I had grasped the meaning and the beauty of simple words. Living in China, writing this journal, I began to make English my own. Away from home, I became a writer in the language of my adopted country. I became more American in China.

I also became more Jewish. My parents, survivors of the Holocaust, had tried to share some of their history with me. Withholding its horrors and their own doubts, they hoped I would not cut myself off from the Jewish people. I didn't. But the terms of my belonging had to be defined and redefined over and over again. In China, among a people intensely aware of history, tradition, and the rituals of daily life, I grew more comfortable with my own questions about Jewish identity. I created and observed Jewish rituals. Friday nights especially became a way to stop worktime, to shape it into something else. A time to rest, to reconsider things, to catch my breath in an otherwise hectic week. Often, I wrote my journal in a Shabbat mood.

The China knowledge I had gathered before China was also part of the "West in mind" that I had to learn to keep out of the picture. This knowledge—or rather, this informed ignorance—was the hallmark of a generation of specialists trained during the Cold War years, when there was no possibility of going to the People's Republic. Beginning graduate study at Yale in 1969, I finished my degree at Stanford in 1977, with a year's interlude in Taiwan. My teachers, colleagues of Joseph Levenson, had also been cut off from the mainland. But Levenson's generation of China scholars had been made modest by their lack of contact with the area of their study. My generation, on the other hand, had taken distance as a license for conjecture. We had joined the field during the Vietnam War. The late 1960s were also the years of the Cultural Revolution. We were, in no small measure, inspired by it. Those of us involved in antiwar activities, especially, looked to China as a potential alternative to the Soviet Union's bureaucratic communism. We took seriously Mao's notion of "uninterrupted revolution" and hoped it would really "serve the people." We discounted news of violence in China along with untruths about Vietnam.

In China, for sixteen months I heard an uninterrupted stream of horror stories about the Cultural Revolution. Unable and unwilling to shut my ears, I had to rethink many of my previous views about China. The result, for a while, was confusion. Not unexpectedly, that confusion was more humbling, more difficult to bear than what I anticipated when I applied for one of the first fellowships for prolonged study in the People's Republic.

In the fall of 1978, after President Carter's science adviser, Frank Press, came back from China, the recently formed Committee on Scholarly Communication with the People's Republic of China announced the first exchange program. We had to apply by November and be ready to leave in February. I was already on leave from my university and was thus in a position to take advantage of the sudden opportunity. When I applied, friends and colleagues familiar with the work of the committee warned that we were to be an experimental group, that neither the Americans nor the Chinese knew what to expect of the exchanges. I liked the challenge and was willing to put up with the uncertainty. By December 1978, I had been selected for this trial run, along with six advanced graduate students. Our moderate competence in Chinese, the feasibility of our respective research projects, and some positive assessment about our ability to adjust to Chinese bureaucracy persuaded the committee to choose us from some one hundred fifty applicants.

Then, on January 1, 1979, a further announcement: United States and China would normalize their diplomatic relations. Having prepared to go as officially nonofficial students, we were now swept up in the public drama of normalization. On January 29, the morning that China's new leader Deng Xiaoping arrived for a state visit in Washington, two students from our group, myself and Tom Gold, were interviewed on the "Today" show. We were asked for the first time the media question that was to inundate us during our initial months in China: "What do you expect China to be like after years of book study?" I tried to say something about China being different from what we expect. But I didn't know how different it would really be. It was a moment, after all, when America was ready to believe that China was almost like us, or about to become what we wish it were. Russell Baker, in a column on January 28, tried to poke fun at these expectations as well as at Chinese eagerness to buy American things and borrow American ideas:

> Modernized China begins for a tourist at Peking's Richard M. Nixon Airport, a vast concrete-and-glass airopolis on the Mongolian border, some 120 miles from the capital. . . . Here are all the amenities that make O'Hare and Dallas-Fort Worth airports cherished homes away from home for the busy traveller—infinite distance, shops full of Gothic Manchurian novels, computerized lost luggage service, plastic seats individually equipped with small television sets and Muzak. Or as it is called in China, Maozak.

Was "Maozak" all that was to be different in China, then? I didn't think so. But how could we prepare to notice something other than what we were looking for? I decided to write to a few of my oldest and closest friends across the United States and ask them what they would like to know about China, how they would want to use my eyes and ears there. I had shared parts of the long road with them before, from Taiwan in 1974–75, from my three-week China study-tour in 1977, from Israel in 1978. A California friend wrote back a letter which I carried with me to China and tried to mull over during the next sixteen months:

> It occurs to me that reporting on China has been so strange that it jogs people to realize that a flesh and blood American is actually going to live and study and do research for a year, living in a dorm. Such normal activities. In a place that isn't mysterious or inscrutable in the old sense, but just isn't known. . . . So I guess what I am most interested in is how people relate to their families, at work, in playgrounds or in school, at the conference table. There is a wonderful children's book called *What Do People Do All Day?* by Richard Scarry. And that's about what I need on China. . . .
> Then, there is the question of institutional pressure. Does ideology of the "imposed sort" play a more dramatic role

than here? For example, pictures of cultural or political heroes give me the creeps. They would be torn down in America, of course. (Even Jimmy Carter would laugh at a poster of himself put up somewhere. Someone would stick a flower in his mouth!) The nature of pressures (as well as encouragement) on scholars would also be important to know about. We have our funding and narrow professional problems. What about them? Can a scholar sit in his own backyard or on her sunroof and have an "idea" in the social sense of ideas? . . . Without care for finding similarities and differences, there will be no communication. . . .

I am glad you are better prepared than Montesquieu's Usbek in the *Persian Letters*. You might think of the *Persian Letters* when contemplating your correspondence, which could have an important effect (whether obvious or immediate or not). It is really a wonderful opportunity for you, as well as for all of us.

True, I was going to China somewhat better prepared than the eighteenth-century fictional Persian used by Montesquieu to make critical comments on his own society. But not much better. Usbek's quest for something beyond the familiar informed my own effort to go beyond the West, through the West, to China and back. Usbek's first letter home echoes the mood of my own departure in February 1979: "Nous sommes nés dans un royaume florissant; mais nous n'avons pas cru que ces bornes fussent celles de nos connaissances, et que la lumière orientale dût seule nous éclairer." (We were born in a properous realm, but we did not believe that its boundaries were those of our knowledge, nor that the light of the Orient [for me, the Occident] should alone illuminate us.)

So, I kept this journal as a way to carry on mental conversations with friends back home, something that could not be done through the mail, which apparently was opened on both sides. Reflections on day-to-day events I recorded more sketchily in a diary. Then, every week or so, I would distill in the journal some of my main concerns, some of my more unsettling encounters. I did not try to write a Chinese equivalent of *What Do People Do All Day?* I couldn't have. Many print and television journalists were already in place trying to do that, claiming that they had gotten the real scoop on the real China. Their haste, and not infrequently their arrogance, led me to be suspicious of superficial impressions too easily passed off as representative of daily life in China. Also, during the first few months our group was in China, momentous public events blurred any view of the real China. So, I focused on marginal details and, over time, hoped to glimpse something of what was going on at the core of Chinese society.

The sixteen months I spent in China, from February 1979 to June 1980, were a time of transition in world affairs, as well as in Chinese domestic policies. Because of China's invasion of Vietnam on February 18, the international situation became tense on the eve of our arrival. The Vietnamese invasion of Kampuchea (Cambodia) and the expulsion of ethnic Chinese from Vietnam were given as proximate causes of the war. Neither was affected by it. But the Chinese press did report 20,000 soldiers killed in the February–March war. At this time, too, the American Liaison Office became the official United States Embassy. On March 1, Chief Representative Leonard Woodcock became the first American ambassador to China since 1949.

During much of 1979, the Carter administration tried hard not to "play the China card." It tried to maintain a policy of détente with the Soviet Union while improving business ties with China. By December, this policy was overturned in the aftermath of the Soviet invasion of Afghanistan. In January 1980, after a four-day visit to Peking, Secretary of Defense Harold Brown declared that the United States would now send arms to China "to bolster China's military position so it could assist the West in a war with the USSR."

Throughout the spring of 1980, the Iranian hostage crisis occupied our attention as Americans, even though we lived in far-away Peking. How all that was going to affect U.S.-China ties was not clear. We all breathed a sigh of relief when presidential candidate Ronald Reagan declared that he had abandoned his previous plan to break with China and reestablish diplomatic relations with Taiwan.

Inside China, in the meantime, the reevaluation of the legacy of Mao Zedong continued. For a while, it looked as if a de-Mao-ification movement, not unlike the de-Stalinization that took place in the Soviet Union after the death of the dictator, was about to take place. After the war with Vietnam, criticisms of Mao's military policies and his vision of guerrilla warfare were heard in high places. By June, his pictures, his sayings, and some of his statues were being dismantled in the capital. But by October, as the People's Republic celebrated its thirtieth anniversary, a more cautious tone had set in. Mao Zedong was declared to have been wrong in the political assessment that led to the Cultural Revolution, but nothing more. No longer a god, he was still enshrined as a sage and founder. But he was not alone. In March 1980, Mao's archenemy during the Cultural Revolution, Liu Shaoqi, was also rehabilitated posthumously. Liu was another sage, founder, this time of the pragmatic policies being followed by the regime of Deng Xiaoping.

A loud "Four Modernizations" program was launched with much fanfare in 1978. It was designed to transform China's agriculture, industry, national defense, and science and technology. It, too, suffered a severe setback during our time in China. By April 1979, the government was telling its American, Japanese, and West German friends that estimates for the rate of growth and the amount that China would borrow to upgrade its industries would have to be scaled down considerably. To many Americans at home this came as a shock and provoked the first wave of disenchantment with China. A year later, Chairman Hua Guofeng was resigning his position in favor of Sichuan party chief Zhao Ziyang, a close follower of Deng Xiaoping. Although Hua Guofeng took on himself the blame for the overly ambitious modernization program, it was not clear whose fault it really was. Corruption and autocracy seemed more widespread.

The subject of bureaucratic corruption and political bad faith was discussed most actively in posters put up on Peking's Democracy Wall. In January 1979, this outcry was still sanctioned by the highest authorities. They saw it as a "citizen's forum" to air views about the hated "Gang of Four," (Jiang Qing, Mao's wife, and three of her leftist followers). But by March, it became clear that the criticism on Democracy Wall was not limited to the past. It aimed at present injustices as well. Deng Xiaoping's first counterattack came in a March 1979 speech criticizing Shanghai youths who took to the streets to demonstrate their impatience with officials who failed to bring them back from the countryside (after forcible resettlement during the Cultural Revolution) and who failed to find them jobs. Shortly after Deng's speech, prominent leaders of the Democracy Wall movement were arrested in Peking. Among them was Wei Jingsheng, one of the editors of an unofficial magazine called *Tansuo* (Exploration) and Fu Yuehua, a young woman leader of out-of-town petitioners.

In October, when Wei Jingsheng was sentenced to fifteen years in jail as a "counterrevolutionary," I experienced my own most intense political crisis in China. The government's attack on "bourgeois liberalism" and "bourgeois democracy" made me suspicious of its earlier propaganda in favor of "emancipation of thought." It also made me realize that freedom of thought and speech and legal due process—all of which were being attacked as products of "bourgeois" revolutions like the American Revolution and the French Revolution—were, for me, universal values. I believe these values to be more beneficial to people across time and culture than do the ideologues who condemned Wei Jingsheng's quest for a fifth modernization: democracy.

While these upheavals went on in the public world, I was privileged to have a quiet, private place from which to observe, into which to retreat for reflection. For all of the sixteen months in China, I had a single room in a student dormitory, first at the Peking Language Institute, then at Peking University. In this room I spent many hours alone, listening to music, reading poetry, having private lessons in Chinese, writing this journal. Although my room was devoid of the comradeship (and censorship) of a Chinese roommate, its privacy enabled me to invite many different Chinese friends for leisurely talks. This would have been, at first, more awkward on the streets or in their homes.

It was a year of very slowly ripening intimacies. Chinese culture is not as flamboyant or as outgoing in its psychological manner as the cultures more familiar to me. So I had to learn patience and learn not to blame authorities for thwarting friendships that would develop after months of germinating trust. My travels outside of Peking, especially the summer trek through thirteen provinces from Mongolia to Xinjiang, from Sichuan to Zhejiang, brought me closer to my Chinese friends. Corresponding with them, in Chinese, from China, made my return to Peking more intimate than I expected.

That homecoming changed the shape of the journal. I wrote much less in the last two-thirds of my time in China than in the first five months. Opportunities for scholarly conversations increased in the fall of 1979. New source materials also became available about the subject of my research: the May Fourth movement of 1919. Some of the intellectuals who participated in that event and their friends and disciples began to move to the center of my concern at this time. Their thoughts, impressions, life stories fill much of the second half of the journal. The gnawing feeling of being an outsider confined to the outskirts of Chinese society diminished at this time, as my language skills improved and my circle of friends broadened.

I became less of an outsider as I learned more about history. In fact, it would not be an exaggeration to say that I became an historian in China. Although I arrived with a Ph.D. in Chinese history, I spent much of my time unlearning or relearning what I thought I already knew. The May Fourth movement was a constant thread in this process. A patriotic student protest at first, it grew into a broad cultural movement to introduce ideas from the West, to make Chinese thought more scientific and more democratic. In China, I came to see how the May Fourth legacy has been repeatedly used and abused to bolster political goals inimical to the aims of the original movement. I realized that so much of its agenda remains yet to be fulfilled.

Getting to know participants in the May Fourth movement and their students and followers was the most unexpected, most precious breakthrough of my time in China. The sixtieth anniversary of the movement provided general sanction for frank discussions about the role of intellectuals in history, and in the Chinese revolution in particular. These discussions might have remained abstract, and become frustrating in time, had they not been matched by the willingness of survivors to engage me more personally. The first of those who did was Zhang Shenfu, a philosopher who was eighty-seven years old by the time I met him in October 1979. Although I met others of his generation in the spring of 1980, Zhang Shenfu remained my most loyal conversation partner. We met regularly at his home, and there he shared with me the details of his life and his thoughts. Those details provided the foundation for a broader research effort that still goes on, and will, I hope, result in a reassessment of Zhang Shenfu and his times.

Octogenarian survivors of the May Fourth era were not my only intimates in China, though they consumed much of my time and interest. Over the months recorded in this journal, I made other friends as well. Most of them are intellectuals, many of them over forty. They, too, are survivors, survivors of the Anti-Rightist campaign of 1957 which had labeled them as "rightist deviationists" and of the Cultural Revolution which had attacked them as the "stinking ninth," more odious in the eyes of their Red Guard persecutors than traitors, landlords, capitalist-roaders and other "evildoers." My friends often used the Holocaust as a parallel when they told me of their public humiliations, their beatings, their forced labor and their exile. It was hard to listen to these stories. Harder still for me because they cut so close to the painful experience of my parents. It took me a long time to see how these survivors are so different from my parents and from other Jews I know in the United States and Europe. Their lack of bitterness, their enduring commitment to socialism, their willingness to forgive the party its excesses and respond again to its call to help China—this time through their academic specialties—took me aback over and over again.

And yet I remain worried about my friends. The persecution of the recent past weighs heavily on their memory, and on mine. Therefore, in publishing this journal I have decided to withhold most of their names and to change the identity of some. I have, however, kept the names of all my informants over age sixty-five, both because they gave me permission during our interviews and because historians of the future might find these ruminations useful.

This journal, then, is an offering to friends, both Chinese and American. It is my attempt, retrospectively, to make more mutual a process which was often marked by lack of mutuality, and not infrequently marred by misunderstanding. I confess that the outline of the China picture drawn here is merely my own. But perhaps, by its very partiality, it will provide yet another building block in a more truthful understanding of China and of the West.

Such an understanding, I know, is nearly impossible. Why try, then? Because, as Paul Valéry wrote in his preface to the French-language autobiography of the May Fourth poet, Sheng Cheng:

> It is unfortunate for humankind that relations among peoples always begin through contacts by individuals least suited for

searching out common roots, for discovering shared sensibilities.

At first, people reach out to each other through their toughest, greediest men, or those most determined to impose their doctrines without receiving. . . . These men take on the task themselves, often sacrifice themselves to it, the task of doing unto others what they would not have done unto themselves. . . . At the beginning, there is always contempt. No ease for reciprocity, no time to let it grow. [*Ma Mère et Moi à Travers la Première Révolution Chinoise*]

Genuine reciprocity with China remains elusive. But a lessening of contempt is long overdue. If this journal breaks down some of the divide between what Valéry called "the maggots," those who prefer to know nothing beyond their own culture, and the "foreign devils," those who force others to live according to their own values, I will be quite satisfied.

March 16, 1983
Middletown, Connecticut

LONG ROAD HOME: A CHINA JOURNAL

CHAPTER 1

MARCH 2 *After one week in China*

The peace of Friday night descends in Peking. We've been here seven days. Behind my back the sun pours into the room. Miracle of miracles, I have a single room. Two other American women are sharing the room next door. To my right, a small solid bookcase. It is marked with characters saying, "For Public Use at the Language Institute." The wooden top is softened by the color and texture of two plants: a pink and red cyclamen and a dense miniature fern. The cyclamen, a tribute to the coming of Shabbat and a gift to myself for having passed the language exam. This ordeal over, I will be able to transfer to the university immediately.

The fern is set off by its simple blue square ceramic pot. The shape of the pot recalls the classical style of the Song dynasty but for its white clay legs, which display the mass reproduction skills of the People's Republic. I acquired both plants yesterday at the downtown foreigners' Friendship Store. An Australian physicist of Cantonese background helped me pick them. "You see," he explains, "they have a hint of potential rather than manifest exuberance."

I ask the physicist about his thoroughly un-American patience. Why wait for rather than grasp at opportunity? He answers that it is a Chinese habit, that it makes his people healthier psychologically than Westerners. I'm tempted to concede his broad, nearly racist, generalization. True, the people we see in buses and on the street appear to laugh more readily, seem not to mind long periods surrounded by many others. I find my own edginess

1

about crowds almost embarrassing. Yet I suspect that my impatient, more turbulent transactions with the world point toward a kind of personal, perhaps Western, creativity. At what cost?

On my left, the iron bed looks menacingly institutional, but its simple double cotton mattress is comfortable. The large, enveloping quilt is another reminder that I now live in China. Half an hour after our arrival we signed a sheet entitled "Usable Property Acknowledgment." Each of us received two sheets, two pillows, two pillow covers, a quilt with cover, one summer blanket, one tin washbasin, one large thermos water bottle. These things are ours for the duration of the year. We will take them along to any institution that we are transferred to in China, and will return them when we leave the country.

These few possessions mark our commonality with Chinese university students. When, as often enough it is, all else is different—our food, stipends, intellectual liberties—these basic provisions signal our welcome into the local culture. Nothing so simple, so efficient in its daily ordinariness, seems available to foreigners coming to America for study or for work. Back home, we fret over necessities and allow luxuries to hold dominion over our imaginings.

Here, reflectiveness seems crowded out by media-mongers unleashed upon a scene of instant historic significance. The end of Mao's revolution, the formal opening of the American Embassy, the renewal of scholarly exchanges after a thirty-year halt. Just now news reports verge on the histrionic. CBS descended rudely and mercilessly upon us during our tense written-language exam Tuesday afternoon. ABC in turn, with Bernie Kalb in an outrageous rabbit coat, followed us through a frozen morning walk in the Forbidden City. They're all hankering after pontifications about the meaning of normalization in trite, contrived settings. Too little time to pay attention to lasting differences between us and the Chinese at this moment when American reporters proclaim the end of the revolution from two-minute shots in Peking beauty parlors. How or why curly hair can be taken as an index of mass political transformation I do not understand.

On my desk, two invitations: part of the public clutter to get past, before there is time for more personal reflection. The first came the night of our arrival, hand-delivered from the Embassy (then still the Liaison Office). I delight to see my name spelled

为欢迎首批美国留学生来华学习，谨订于一九七九

年二月二十四日晚六时在国际俱乐部仙鹤厅举行招待

会，请出席。

周培源　　李　琦

Invitation to our first reception, signed by Zhou Peiyuan and Li Ji: "To welcome the initial group of American students coming to study in China, you are cordially invited to attend a reception at the International Club on February 24, 1979, at 6:00 P.M."

Official photograph at the International Club reception. I stand second from the left, flanked by Dr. Mary Bullock (*2d row, first from left*), head of the Committee on Scholarly Communication with the People's Republic of China, and Karen Gottschang (*third from left*), a friend and fellow student from the University of Michigan. In the center (*sixth from left*) is Zhou Peiyuan, President of Peking University and head of the Chinese Academy of Science. Kneeling in front of him is Linda Bell, another friend, a graduate student from U.C.L.A.

correctly after its misspelling so many times at home. Inside, red Chinese characters in two simple rows over a dash of yellow flowers. I read: "To welcome the initial [the Chinese connotation includes some primacy of excellence] group of American students coming to study in China, you are cordially invited to attend a reception at the International Club on February 24, 1979, at 6:00 P.M." It is signed by Zhou Peiyuan, president of Peking University and chief of the Chinese Academy of Science, and Li Ji, vice-minister of education. Beneath their names, the traditional seal of Zhou Peiyuan in soft yellow. It echoes the yellow flower in the classical manner used by traditional scholars to indicate their bond with the world of amateur painters.

The evening was momentous without being intimidating. Our importance is dramatized by the presence of important Chinese dignitaries. Zhou's speech is short, informal, warm. An American senior scholar responds to the welcome speech. He is mindful of his words using the occasion to thank our hosts, as well as to remind them of academic requests not yet settled to our satisfaction. Our student representative gives a well-received talk in Chinese.

For me, the nicest surprise is a long personal chat with Zhou Peiyuan. Almost a legend in the United States, in person he turns out to be open, alert, interested. Once I relax a bit in the presence of this contemporary of the subjects of my historical research, I bring the conversation around to the May Fourth movement— the patriotic demonstration Zhou had joined as a high-school student in 1919. He tells me that a special conference is planned by Peking University and the Chinese Academy of Social Sciences this year for the sixtieth anniversary of the May Fourth movement. Then he introduces me to the chairman of the History Department of Peking University. In just a few minutes he sows the seeds of scholarly discourse, which promise to be quite substantial. Perhaps the cumbersome title of our fellowship granting agency—the Committee on Scholarly Communication with the People's Republic of China—may be literal after all. In the wave of excitement since that talk with Zhou, my audacity goes so far that I write to him asking to be a foreign observer at the spring conference.

Next day: my first spring outing in Peking, a ten-minute ride to the ruins of Yuan Ming Yuan (the Garden of Perfection and Light) on a borrowed bicycle. I'm surprised to pass farmhouses with elaborate terra-cotta chimneys—seemingly the only aesthetic indulgence in the hard life of Chinese peasants—so near the university. Entering the muddy paths of the park, I leave behind the noise and flurry of the city. The space inside is both imperial and antique in its dilapidation. History and time collaborate in softening this landscape. I happen upon an unostentatious commemoration of culture.

As my path turns, a full view of the ruins appears, strangely European. The park was part of the Qian Long Emperor's summer palace, built in the 1740s by two Jesuits, Castiglione and Benoist, a period of rather safe interest in Western oddities. Qian Long had indulged himself with European music rooms, ornamental pools, aviaries. That palace was sacked in 1860 by English and French troops, who looted it in the name of Queen Victoria and Napoleon and burned what could not be carted away. What remain are five or six columns and a huge floral arch gently fallen against a carved stele.

Climbing up on the hill toward the columns, I spot a young man painting on a small canvas. Back home, an art historian lecturing at Harvard had denied there was any curiosity about modern Western art among Chinese youth. The canvas I see in front of me is skilled, though tentative. The painter's tools strike me as primitive, his colors are few, he uses a stick instead of a brush. His image conveys alien, graceful ruins as seen by an alert observer of decay.

I start a conversation. The young man is a student at Peking University, living in dormitory number 26, next door to where I will probably be. He tells me how baffling Western art was at first sight. He has taught himself how to paint with oils. Now he needs some guidance, some further help in approaching impressionist and abstract art. I offer to share recently acquired insights from a New York painter friend along with some postcards of twentieth-century art I had brought along just in case someone was interested. Our relaxed conversation is a hint of what is now possible in China after decades of official orthodoxy. I wonder why so few of these subtle, quiet rhythms of cross-cultural contact ever make it into media presentations of China's current "Westernizing madness."

On the path in front of me, I hear the cadence of English words, indistinct in their Chinese recitation. Around the corner, in a huge marble cornucopia, lying in the late winter sun, is another student. I catch his voice memorizing the passage, "We will build a strong socialist motherland." His sloganeering English words are belied by the decayed European setting and his mandarin recitation style. Perhaps youths like this student might yet build "a strong socialist motherland," because they are reaping the benefits of a peasant revolution and because they witness both the new and the decrepit West. Corners of quiet reflection on a Saturday afternoon will, no doubt, help as well.

I walk on, looking for a stele that I heard is good for rubbings. I come upon two huge marble turtles, well preserved among the ruins. A voice behind me asks in urgent Chinese: "So what does it make you feel like? What do you make of our rich tradition and paltry subsistence today?" I turn to find another Peking University student. He begins to talk about the unsettling contradiction between the cleverness of the Chinese people in the past and the backwardness of the Chinese economy in the present. I sense a conflict between cultural pride and material shame, an intense, naive haste to catch up with the West. As I say goodbye to him I ask myself: Who will be the guardians of Chinese culture in the coming period of transition?

The last sight in the park: workers with wooden shovels and wooden barrels engaged in quiet restoration. One starts humming a loud, deep melody reminiscent of Paul Robeson's music, which is still popular in China. I ride my bicycle peacefully into the chilly dusk.

MARCH 4   *Coping on a Sunday* The description in the fellowship
afternoon: laundry, toilets   application had stated that dormitory conditions in China would be "spartan." I wake up around 8:00 A.M., spared from the usual 7:00 A.M. blast of "The East is Red" over the loudspeakers and from the daily news in loud, indistinct Chinese. Graced though the day is by its silent beginning, it has an ordinary, seasonal grayness. I had read before about the ashen colors of late winter in North China. I now understand what the Senegalese woman

had in mind in the shower room last night when she said "Six months here can be like an eternity."

For out-of-town Chinese students who spend the weekends at school, Sunday is laundry day. I imitate their housekeeping. The wash takes nearly the entire day. My tape recorder plays "The Harder They Come" as I try to mend the shoddy, expensive winter underwear I bought at a fancy sporting goods store the day before I left. I have to go down three flights of stairs to the boiler room for hot water. The trip is repeated five times before I finish the last load with the dirty blue jeans. In a fit of homesickness, I use a drop of perfume in the rinse. I doubt that Yves Saint Laurent has been put to such mundane use before.

In the course of many soakings, scrubbings, and rinsings I have a chance to savor the strength of my karate-trained fingers and wrists. A Chinese girl sings alongside as she does her own wash. Her high, lilting notes soothe my spirit. They are so unlike the jarring Peking opera blaring from newly "emancipated" radio stations. With a rag from the well-supplied Peking Hotel bathroom, I start to wash the mud off my boots and running sneakers. Half an hour later, I realize the wisdom of a Canadian's advice last week: "Wear local shoes, the cotton kind. They are cheap and you can throw them away."

It must be something in my nature or perhaps in my Romanian temperament that thrives on coping and relishes hardship. At home, this part of me had become a source of despondent introspection. Here it is an effective mechanism for cultural adaptation. I am convinced I know too little about the social layerings of the psyche. How do different cultural settings alert us to the arbitrary conventions of our own?

Coping in China is not only necessary but dignified. An example of coping takes place daily in our toilets. These are floor-level bowls. So one must squat above an elevated ridge of porcelain. Some members of our pioneering group equate squatting with squalor. Yet in these toilets a scrupulous Chinese modesty prevails. The cubicles are separated from each other by wooden walls just high enough so that the person relieving herself is not seen by another entering the room. Eye contact happens only after we have finished and stand up. In those few moments of necessary lingering, our eyes meet. Essential functions simply performed.

MARCH 6   *Back-door privileges:*   The expression *houmen* (literally
jazz, disco, and the cleaning girls   "rear gate") has come to have
a very negative meaning in
Chinese during the past decade. Once used to damn party cadres
for their reliance on political status to acquire special favors, it
has grown to encompass all means that help circumvent and, by
implication, subvert official channels. All around us, there is an
endless griping against and clamoring for *houmen.* Sometimes in
newspapers, mostly in private conversation, we hear stories about
university study opportunities provided for the children of Peking
intellectuals, about rare books acquired by aesthetically indulgent
Shanghai bureaucrats, about special foods transported to the private dwellings of Cantonese factory managers.

Clearly, there is a back door to get anything if one has sufficient
standing at the "front gate." To find a *houmen* is to get away with
something. But to get privileges is perhaps less precious than the
bit of nonconformity a back door affords. What makes one important is not to have to abide by rules that apply to everyone
else.

As I walked through the Forbidden City's front gate with our
delegation last week, I remembered my rushed visit here in 1977.
It had been my first trip to China. I remember that the most serene
gardens, the most delicately artful places, were near the rear gate,
in the private quarters of the Qing emperors. There the bedrooms
of the concubines and the study chambers for the scholars proliferate. Now, I wish that our minibus would park by the rear
entrance so we could enter directly into the courtyards named, a
touch playfully, "Cultivation of the Self" and "Perfection of Character." Instead, we have to go through the imposing front entrance and past the golden lions so that the CBS crew can film
our official role in the normalization process.

For an hour or so we endure being photographed as we walk
through reception halls. We try to bear up under interviews about
"What is it like to know China in the flesh after years of studying
it through books?" Whatever insights the questions might have
evoked are drowned out by the slightly obscene insinuations of
the questioners. They're unprepared to hear about differences that
exist and will remain between us, our notions, and Chinese realities. Eventually, I take off from our group and hurry toward the
back palaces.

There, among the kneeling elephants, the sun shines warmly and trees twist among once carefully arranged mosses. Even in their present disarray, these courtyards recall the tastes of sequestered women and the indulgence of their guardian eunuchs. This area around the *houmen*, now as before, touches me with its intimate scale. In this still "revolutionary" society, I wonder if anyone else is tempted by the life style of traditional courtesans? For me, the lure of their domain remains undiminished by recent political concerns.

Later that night, back at the dorm, I had a furtive conversation with a Chinese fellow student about our ambivalent response to a disco party sponsored by African students on a Saturday night. It left me shaken to glimpse how fast China could Westernize without modernizing: Chinese women were shoved around, handled on the foreigners' dance floor. Shyer, lazier Chinese men, drunk, watched them. At one point, I caught the look of one young man; it moved up and down my own body, with furtive, aggressive intent. Still too naive in my notions of cultural and political differences, I didn't expect to find that here.

The Chinese girl and I whisper while we retell all this. We're washing clothes in the cement sink. The running water provides comforting cover for her "incorrect remarks" about the "bad working girls" at the dance. "I hated their tight red sweaters the most, you know." It also muffles my own complaint about drunken, lascivious male students. Our intimacy is short and covert—a psychological *houmen*. Certain forms of personal expression seem to be the true back-door privilege in present-day China.

Another muted sign of the "emancipation of the mind" that is unfolding along with the official Four Modernizations program: an encounter with a Chinese jazz pianist from Shanghai. I meet him at the home of the Canadian journalists John Frazer and Elizabeth McKinnon. This musician, in his sixties, had been silenced for thirty years. Suddenly he is blooming again, infusing old melodies with new virtuosity. In a foreigner's living room, he takes off his cotton jacket and, with his worker's cap still on, plays intensely "When Smoke Gets in Your Eyes." Later, his young twenty-four-year-old wife dances with the foreign host. She amazes us with her graceful dignity. We are surprised, not only because we cannot imagine a Chinese woman who could dance as she did, but also because many of us remember the prostitutes of

Taibei, Bangkok, and Tokyo. They, too, knew Western dances, but looked grotesque when they had to sell themselves by performing. This Chinese couple, on the other hand, radiates a *houmen* quality. They are accepted, condoned, but certainly not appreciated in their own society.

I am reading Marilyn French's *The Women's Room.* It is a raw, bitter, quintessentially American novel. Here in China it becomes my own *houmen* out of the cheerful, official line about love and marriage. I try to prepare for the upcoming International Women's Day celebration on March 8, but find I'm unable to put aside the personal rages and hurts I carry from back home. French's book doesn't help, so I turn to some poems by Guo Moruo, a poet who celebrated political revolution and Western romanticism in the 1920s.

Before retreating from Marilyn French into Guo Moruo, a word about an encounter in the shower. I had heard around the dormitory that Western women have never seen their Chinese roommates undressed. Though there is no word for privacy in Chinese, there is a pervasive shyness about bodily revelation among these gregarious but discreet students. Tonight, in the bathroom with five half-enclosed shower stalls, a tall woman comes right up. Without a towel and holding only a plastic stick to fix her flood of black hair in place, she introduces herself as a worker at the institute, a cleaning girl on the morning shift. I rush into the shower, hurried along by the line forming behind me. By the time I come out, it becomes clear that three of the cleaning girls have shared the shower next to me with great hilarity and much pleasure. Two, still naked, come up to me, nearly breast to breast, and start a long conversation about where I learned my Chinese, how long I am going to be at the institute, what work I do, etc. They laugh, beam. I enjoy their warmth but feel taken aback by their open sensuality. Such a difference between the students here, educated, aspiring intellectuals, and these laboring, wage-earning women. I leave somewhat in a hurry. My pretense at cultural adaptation is wearing thin. China keeps breaking through.

> Ladies and Gentlemen, you have become tired of
>   living in this fetid gloom of the dark world.
> You surely thirst for light.
> Your poet, having dramatized so far, writes no more.

> He has, in fact, fled beyond the sea to create new
>   light and heat.
> Ladies and Gentlemen, do you wait for the appearance
>   of a new sun?
> You are bid to create it for yourself.
> We will meet again under the sun.

This is the last paragraph from Guo Moruo's 1919 poem "Rebirth of the Goddess." As I finish reading it, my moodiness lifts. Thoughts about literature as a locus of critical thought sharpen in turn. My gratitude to the writers of the May Fourth period grows deeper and deeper. They continue to nourish my mind with their literary testaments. Even when their metaphors remain alien to me (for example, Guo Moruo's excursions into Daoist cosmology), I recognize in them a thoroughly familiar, Western urge for self-expression.

Some questions that have been with me for half a decade of China studies: How has self-expression been distinguished from selfishness (the self-indulgence which we know so well from our own culture) during China's modernizing revolution? How has literature, woven out of the word-skills of an intellectual elite, come to be China's most persistent weapon of attacking, analyzing, and even resolving political and social problems? These questions are not answerable yet. But a few incidents of the past week convince me that I am in the right place at the right time for this inquiry: A "new" opera is the rage of Peking these days. Called *Hai Rui Dismissed from Office*, it is, in fact, the work of literature that sparked the Cultural Revolution in 1965. Written by another May Fourth intellectual, Wu Han, it is set in the late Ming dynasty. But Mao saw it as an attack on his own swift, unjust dismissal of a loyal general, Peng Dehuai, in the late 1950s and set out to suppress its author and the criticism. Now, with Mao dead and Peng Dehuai posthumously rehabilitated, the play is once more at the heart of the capital's cultural scene.

The night I saw it, the audience was mostly old people, looking even more worn because of their hardworking lives. They were greatly thrilled by the sumptuous costumes of silk and brocade. The display of color and texture was matched by a superior performance of traditional music and singing. (To my ears Peking opera still sounds shrill and discordant. Once in a while, when cymbals subside for a minute or when the stylized laughter becomes truly outrageous, I'm enchanted too.) The climax comes when the virtuous Hai Rui is asked to give up his official seal because he has transgressed the conventions of mandarin corruption. He shouts, on behalf of the viewers, "You blood suckers who live off the people, you'll surely pay for your crimes." This line echoes contemporary rage against the Gang of Four. It also could be heard as a warning to the present regime to make good on its promise to improve the people's livelihood.

A few days ago I spent a morning reading posters at Democracy Wall. I find a wide scattering—poems about how hard it is to stand up alone against the authorities, stories about unwanted pregnancies, declarations against China's current invasion in Vietnam, songs in blood by rusticated youth, confessions of sexual fantasies by overseas Chinese. Again, literature is the dominant form of protest. And yet, unlike Wu Han's script, these quests for self-expression are beside the point for most of the Peking citizens who hurry past the Wall.

I have also been scanning recent scholarly publications in my room at the Language Institute. I have decided to specialize in literature at Peking University. History is still mired in ideology.

MARCH 8   *Cultural Revolution survivor: Wang Guangmei*   I had expected that China would be emotionally exhausting, especially now with so many people willing and eager to tell their stories of hardship and suffering during the Cultural Revolution. I had heard from Chinese-American friends about difficult family visits, filled with the most recent version of "speak bitterness" sessions—not unlike those early 1950s tales told by poor peasants about the cruelty of landlords. Except this time it's mostly intellectuals who are unburdening their souls about their sufferings at the hands of vicious young Red Guards in the years 1966–69. None of my forebodings, however, prepared me for the passionate reemergence of those shoved out of recent history.

Invited to the Great Hall of the People for the International Women's Day celebration. Over fifteen hundred women in attendance from all over the world; this is a decorous, official afternoon. Our small American group is made up of Karen Gottschang, Linda Bell, and I. We're all excited by the opportunity to enter this hallowed place in Chinese public life, glad too that the event concerns women and, thus, ourselves. We arrive with camera in hand, ready to take pictures of the hall, of each other, and perhaps, having started our own rumor, to witness the official rehabilitation of Ding Ling, China's foremost woman writer, harshly disgraced during the Cultural Revolution.

Inside the hall, I find some unsuspected resource of audacity and follow a Chinese television crew. I end up close to Deng Yingchao, Zhou Enlai's widow and the most venerated revolutionary in China today. A socialist heroine in her own right, by virtue of her long history of struggle against the Guomindang (KMT) and the Japanese in the 1930s and 1940s and her thorough analyses of the predicament of women. She appears today more like an aged queen. Officially she is called "older sister Deng." Yet she evokes and accepts an extraordinary degree of attention and privilege savored by few others besides Mao and Zhou.

When she arrived today, there was a sudden flood of camera lights, and much ceremonial bowing. This small lady sits surrounded, almost overwhelmed, by waiters bringing her towels, arranging her jacket, organizing the crowds around her. In my mind, the scene echoes Jiang Qing, Mao's widow, who, although currently despised for her Empress Dowager manners, remains nonetheless the paradigm for powerful women in high public office.

I met Wang Guangmei, the widow of the foremost victim of the Cultural Revolution—Communist Party leader Liu Shaoqi— nearly by accident. I had moved up toward the front of the hall through hundreds of tables during the rather trivial show staged for the occasion (awkward Chinese ballet dancers stiffly performing a Spanish romance). I start a casual conversation, in Chinese, with women sitting at the second head table next to Deng Yingchao. Suddenly, a woman is introduced to me as "Madam Wang," a woman of striking beauty with fierce eyes. She stands up, grips my hand, having heard that I am part of the first group of American scholars to come to China officially.

She speaks her own name proudly, Wang Guangmei. Still holding my hand tightly, with her eyes unflinching, she asks: "Do you know who I am?" I fumble, aware that I am in the presence of some dignitary. I search the faces of the other women around the table. Their muted whisperings spur me on to risk, "Are you Liu Shaoqi's wife?" I use the Chinese word for spouse, "loved one," because I am unable to remember how to say widow in Chinese. I remember a rumor heard in Washington the week before I left that Liu's widow was coming back to public life again. Everybody was surprised. Her husband had been the archenemy, the "revisionist devil," during the long decade of the Cultural Revolution.

Madam Wang nods in assent. I fall silent, embarrassed by my ignorance and shaken by the suddenness of our encounter. She grips my hand harder, hugs me, tells me that she wants to become friends. This overused word is somehow charged with new emotion. I can't quite grasp its meaning but trust it has a kernel of truth. I mumble something about inviting her out to Peking University, ask for her address. She tells me, "My destination is not decided yet." (She does not yet have an approved Peking residence because of her long exile in a commune in the northwest.) I joke back, "I'm not settled either." She asks for my name. I write flustered, stumbling over the many strokes in the middle character of my Chinese name ("Shu Hengzhe," chosen in memory of another woman writer-educator, who was trained at Vassar in the 1910s and returned in 1920 to become the first woman professor at Peking University). Madam Wang takes her pen and writes on a napkin in fine, bold calligraphy, "Long live the friendship between Chinese and American women, 1979.3.8."

Later I bring Karen and Linda to meet her. She holds all of our hands at once in her own, and keeps saying, "We must become better friends." We leave her, aware that she values us as Americans. Her own new freedom is somehow a result of the thaw inside China that is accompanying the new openness toward the U.S.

Even more striking than her response to us are Wang Guangmei's encounters with other Chinese women. An unending succession of tears, hugs, handshakes, with words from young and old alike: "It's been too long since we've seen you! We have missed your brave and helpful presence." She stands in the midst of these passionate outpourings, matching each in intensity. It is hard for me to fathom how one person can sustain and reciprocate so many intimate expressions of others' sufferings. Then, I realize

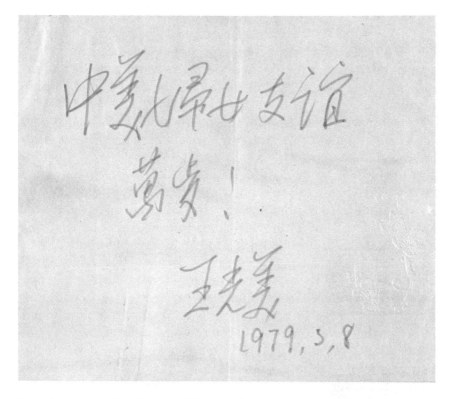

"Long live the friendship between Chinese and American women." Napkin signed by Wang Guangmei on March 8, 1979.

that she must have achieved a unique inner victory. She was not broken by persecution but strengthened by it. I gather that her support of her husband was neither blind nor naive. She remained his rock of strength on principle. Their solidarity was not unlike that of some Jews during the Holocaust.

The Holocaust is a historical precedent much in use among Chinese intellectuals to describe their own lonely and alienating survival into the current period of exuberant modernization. I hope we will get to know Madam Wang better. Maybe that's impossible. No matter; my day has been graced by her powerful dignity.

Back in the dorm, I feel tired, drained. Again, as often already in these two weeks, I feel inadequate. I fret about the limitation of my language skills. Just when I need to hear connotations, to grasp what must be left unsaid in spite of newly legitimated talkativeness, I find I hear less and less. I feel weighed down also by a sense that I am not strong enough, not experienced enough or clear-minded enough to be an appropriate receptacle for this experience. Yet, I know that in time I will be able to create some meaning.

I am left with one "lesson" from Madam Wang—that it's all right if we become strong and insightful after the need for strength and insight has passed. This calls into question my own relationship to the history of the Holocaust. I keep trying to avert the past by a desperate effort to become strong before disaster hits my generation. I keep hoping that if I build up my capacity for endurance I will somehow outwit the forces of destruction. But now that strikes me as both impossible and simple-minded.

I try to learn from Chinese survivors. Unlike Jewish ones, they are not burdened by a sense of unprecedented suffering. They have experienced many revolutionary upheavals and contradictions. Each change in party line created as many unmentioned heroes as there were demons to be exorcised through mass movements. In the West, unfortunately, we hear so much about the demons that we are unprepared to recognize the heroes. Here in China, however, they are too moving, too pervasive to be overlooked.

MARCH 12   *Moving to the university: a nightmare, some Chinese and Jewish "types"*   I moved to Beida (the shortened name for Peking University) on Saturday. The decision to enlist in the Literature Department makes sense still. Rush to my first class this morning, Monday. Nowhere to be found. I ask fellow students, "Has Classical Chinese moved?" Their nods are terse and negating. The idea that such a course could be taught at all in China after the recent attack on all aspects of traditional culture is a vulnerable novelty.

Yesterday I bought some new plants for my room. A grassy fern is already dusty. My improvised sprayer, an impotent tool against Peking's proximity to the Gobi desert. In the fit of optimism which accompanied my talks with the Literature Department last week, I also bought a brown succulent that promises spring flowers. There are glimmers of possibility that I may be allowed to do archival research. Also, a slightly veiled promise

Front gate of Peking University. Our dormitory, No. 25, is the first building visible on the right.

of opportunities for an oral history of Peking University. The expectation of genuine "scholarly communication" is intoxicating. It does not, however, develop the kind of patience, humility, and skills in circuitousness that I will need to endure the frustrations of Chinese bureaucracy and not become undone by the bitter envy of other foreign students. We are the first American group, and we arrived at a particularly fluid moment in Chinese intellectual life. We have been greeted by surprisingly accommodating Chinese hosts and resentful fellow foreign students. Just this morning, however, the ice feels thin and my own stride is cautious.

Last night's dream, the first vividly remembered dream since our arrival: I am visiting an aquarium with Jan, my closest friend from home, and Tom, a fellow American in China. We pass by the tank of a goldfish, striped and fat, with bulging eyes. I am admiring its beauty when it leaps up menacingly. I sense with a wave of dread that its leap was somehow directed against me. But Jan assures me that I am being foolish. We are off next to look at the big open tank, recalling the aquarium with the dolphins I visited in Mystic, Connecticut, shortly before leaving. Here, large, flat fish are swimming. Suddenly one of them jumps straight up into the air, makes an amazing curve, and heads toward me like a huge flying knife. I duck on impulse, and its perfectly executed murderous dive fails. It splashes down in outraged failure. I flee in terror. I pass another goldfish tank and a fish leaps out of the tank, like a sharp arrow pointed at my neck. I run out in absolute panic, and wake terrified by the feeling, "Why me?"

Two nights ago, I had my first long talk with other American women here about being unfree in China. One conjectured persuasively that an overseas Chinese student at the Language Institute might really be a spy. Another, shaken by her proximity to a sinologist jailed in China in the early 1950s, shared a detailed scenario of all the troubles to be visited upon us this year.

I know our mail is being read and that the authorities here have much information already about our varied vulnerabilities. I also know that our fears are excessive, the product of certain gloomy moods. Still, I find myself scared for the rest of the dream night. I have also been worrying about classes at the university. I dread some unmasking of my linguistic and, by association, scholarly pretensions. I have some vague, muted vision of public humiliation. Other frustrated foreigners are full of menacing, jealous warnings: "It will happen to you, too; they will get to you," or "How come you Americans are getting everything? Single rooms? Private tutors?"

The morning after the dream: I am listening to Bach. Outside my window the flow of Peking's morning traffic: trucks, mules, and bicycles divided by a wall from the university track field where students run, memorize English lessons, and practice *taiji chuan*. My vantage point now is one of tension-filled in-betweenness. I hear the clanking of truck engines as I watch the measured movements of the martial artists. I catch a glimpse of working girls with permanented hairdos getting on the bus outside the university wall and see pigtailed intellectuals inside poring over Stendhal in the original French. But I have yet to touch or be touched by either side with any sense of lasting intimacy. The bits of Chinese I speak and understand just serve to remind me of the periphery to which Westerners have been shunted in China for so long.

Today, while mopping my dusty cement floor, I look up and meet the eyes of "An Armenian Jew," a photograph taken on Ellis Island in 1924 which I brought to China with me. The image focuses on the face of a bearded young man in his early twenties. I feel close to him. We share the experience of exile, a we-ness known through layers of otherness. Perhaps that is why there are so many American Jews in China studies, perhaps that was the reason behind the longing of a friend back home. Not a sinologist, he wanted to come to China so that all of his assumptions might be questioned anew. The Armenian Jew is a powerful image precisely because he is a familiar type—much as the engraving of the young Zhou Enlai on the opposite wall of my room is, for Chinese, an image of valor and revolutionary foresight. Somewhere between these, I hope and expect to find some new meanings for my personal and scholarly endeavors.

"Types" proliferate in Chinese society more rapidly than anywhere else I have been—from pictures of model workers on postcards and lovely engravings of national minority dancers on calendars for foreign consumption to the formal warmth extended to us as American "friends." The solicitousness I receive here, I feel, comes to me more as a "pioneering American scholar" than to me personally as a May Fourth researcher.

I wonder how much of this codification of relations is a matter of survival in a mass society like China. Living among nine hundred million people, each individual is always surrounded by more "significant others" than anyone could possibly encounter with any degree of intimacy. Perhaps we Westerners have something to learn from China about the art of gracious mediation, about how to endure and benefit from contact with many unknown others. This skill in withholding the self and in patient attention to the type embodied in another is strikingly absent from the insistent eyes of the Armenian Jew.

Last night I had a fine dinner at the home of the brother of a colleague back home. He lives in a beautiful old private compound in an alley behind the "Northern Sea," the imperial playground that was once the boundary of the Manchu palace. He is a composer, his wife is an artist, their eighteen-year-old daughter is studying for the college entrance examinations, and a son is in

Shanghai getting ready to go to the United States as an undergraduate. The evening is full of a graciousness I had imagined but never expected to be able to experience in China, which still restricts contacts with foreigners.

There are more than ten dishes prepared by a live-in older woman, kindly called *ayi* (aunt). We drink tea and wine from heirloom porcelain and silver goblets. The evening is filled with muted talk and the calm well-being of the well-to-do. Leaving on the trolley after dinner, I savor the surprising ordinariness of being simply a resident of Peking. Tired, I return to my dorm room among other residents going home.

MARCH 18–20   *Arrested at the boundary: living as a foreigner in China*   In Chinese the word for boundary is *jiexian*, which means world-divider. I came to China prepared to accept certain limits that are meant to exclude. Perhaps my experience as an immigrant from Romania to America in the early 1960s made me excessively skilled in the "I can't be one of you, so I will define myself against you" mode of cross-cultural survival. In any case, I seem to hover around world edges, perennially tempted to break out or to enter in, inevitably pained when I am stopped. Great as the hurt of thwarted crossings might be, however, I am always surprised and grateful that crossings are possible at all.

Yesterday afternoon, I took my first ride on my newly acquired bicycle, bought at the Friendship Store for $100 U.S. The bicycle is as much a freedom machine as the yellow Datsun I owned at home. I have been anticipating the mobility it will offer, the promise of back-alley adventures, a more intimate encounter with Peking than the crowded buses or sequestered taxis allow. With my hair tied back and covered by a silk scarf to protect against the pervasive desert dust, wearing my sunglasses and parka, I take off for the Summer Palace—the most natural and lyrical of Peking's imperial indulgences.

At the front gate of the park, I come upon a dozen buses that have just poured dozens of American tourists into this no longer forbidden splendor. Feeling myself to be a resident more than a passerby and having come here to soothe my spirit by the lake-

One of the many "Out of Bounds" signs that surround the city of Peking. The more recent signs (this among them) carry an English inscription as large as the Russian. On those put up in the 1950s, Russian is far more prominent.

side, I go on to look for the back gate. *Houmen* by now are my favorite entrance route to Peking's ceremonious and cluttered monuments.

I ride around the wall of the palace and ask a little boy where the rear gate is. He answers in that broad-mouthed flurry of r's and w's which is the fun of Peking dialect: "Around the bridge up somewhere ahead." I glide smoothly down a hill and turn into a street that hugs the outer hills of the Summer Palace. Suddenly a People's Liberation Army soldier in his early twenties, his harsh voice augmented by a menacing pistol, stops me. Our exchange is gruff:

"What nationality?"

"American."

"Identification?"

"My passport."

"Hand it over."

I take it out, watched by thirty local residents who had gathered in less than a minute.

My insides tremble with the unexpectedness of the arrest. I remember vividly a run-in with Peking police in 1977 during another adventure off the beaten track. Then the charge was not directed at me but against the Chinese-American in our group who was making an unauthorized search for relatives. From the aggressive beginning and mild outcome of that encounter, I know not to get too frightened. China is not (yet?) like the Soviet Union, after all.

The soldier and I talk for five minutes. Two phone calls later, he lets me know I am being detained for "going beyond the boundary." He points to a sign a few yards away, on which it is written in bold Russian with a small English subtitle "No foreigners beyond this point."

I start to defend myself. "I was just looking for the back gate of the Summer Palace, the sign was too indistinct as I rode off the bridge, I will find my way back just fine, thanks, I am a student at the University—" All of this in halting Chinese. Suddenly I feel dumb, incompetent, powerless because I cannot grasp the words of my interrogator and the hilarities of the by now one hundred onlookers.

After the third phone call, another slightly older soldier appears. "You are looking for the gate to the Summer Palace? Well, it is on the other side of the bridge. This area of the street is out of bounds to foreigners." He hands me my passport. There is general relief all around, and the younger soldier says: "Sorry for the inconvenience. You sure speak good Chinese." I climb on the bike in a hurry, trip over the kickstand, and pedal away from where I am not wanted.

Across the bridge, around the corner, I find the back entrance. Stopped again: "No foreigners allowed in this way." I ride away sad, angry, aware too that we foreigners are in China now, as foreigners were two hundred years ago, on thin sufferance indeed. Yes, the current modernization drive depends on our aid, but we as individuals interested in this culture and in the society are seen, at best, as irritating and ridiculous.

Pedaling back toward the front gate I am intensely aware that I look and am different from the masses around: my scarf, glasses, coat, face all give me away. I am beginning to feel defiant about that foreignness. The other strong emotion is the desire to conform. I wonder how soon I can get cotton shoes, a padded jacket, a worker's cap. Maybe then.

I realize how subtle and deadly these normalizing pressures have always been in China's mass culture. I remember how well, how bitterly the writer Chen Jo-hsi had captured this pressure to conform in her stories about the Cultural Revolution. In *The Execution of Mayor Yin* she dared to reveal how traditional habits of gossip, mutual surveillance, and cowardice were not only undiminished by the new revolutionary culture, but actually pressed into its service. Thinly disguised "progressive personages," like the old harpy who spies on young women or the local bully who forces neighbors to take down the washing racks during Nixon's visit, are coming alive to me now as I live in China.

Back at the front gate, it is almost 5 P.M. Droves of Americans are pouring out—older than I, probably rich, most likely gullible. They seem to be what the Chinese prefer these days, prefer over jittery scholars like me, tampering with the well-guarded uniqueness of Chinese civilization. I park my bike in the open square, defiant and despondent about finding the "proper bicycle parking area." I walk into the now almost deserted palace park through lovely courtyards where miniature trees are sprouting tentative buds, and find my way to the large lake. Underneath a pagoda I sit looking at marble bridges, temples, hills, painted walkways. The serenity of the landscape calms me. From time to time, I am aware of and disturbed by groups of Chinese youths. No one seems to go for a walk alone here. Good times always require a crowd (in Chinese the word for good times, *renao*, means literally the heat generated by many). Again I feel the foreignness in my desire for privacy. There is no word in Chinese for this concept at all.

On the way back, a quick, warm exchange with a worker from Shanxi province who is on a visit here. Not from Peking, he seems more relaxed, more open about contacts with us aliens. Our exchange so unlike the bureaucratic wariness that colors social intercourse in the capital.

Trying to get into the back gate of Peking University, rushing to return to the one place in the city that seems to want me to be part of it, I am stopped again:

"Where is your school badge?"

"I don't have it yet; we Americans just arrived a few days ago."

"Be sure you get it soon and wear it at all times."

I get ready for dinner, sullen about the thorough typologizing that is the hallmark of Chinese life—a slot for everyone, everyone in a slot. Except that I am not certain what my slot will be, and I bristle at this pigeonholing as well.

The rest of the evening, a marvelous surprise, a reaffirmation of how *jiexian*, world-dividers, do not merely exclude, but also delineate. Some boundaries not only limit but invite a savoring of internal variety. As I sit to eat in the foreigners' mess hall (dejectedly defiant about being a privileged American who can afford food many times more expensive than the rice and fatty pork served to Chinese students), I meet Bridgitte, an American lady in her seventies. She fought her way into China fifteen months ago. At that time there was no embassy yet, no "proper channels" to come here to work for the Chinese government. Now she teaches English at the university. Tough-spirited, she remains troubled by her role in training new elites. She successfully challenged Chinese authorities to let her live in a student dorm rather than in the safety of a hotel reserved for "foreign experts." She challenged the English Department to let her teach some courses on American literature and history, rather than just drill students in correct, dull, and dulling sentence patterns about how to buy a pair of shoes. Her husky voice, dim eyes, gaunt strength attract me. Here another kind of American, so different from the tourists invited on expensive tours these days.

In the shower a good talk with a woman from Sri Lanka. She is going home for the first time in four and a half years, bent upon not rushing into marriage, and determined to get a job that will keep her in contact with China. Our conversation in the shared shower cubicle is in Chinese and echoes so many others. Almost all foreigners whom I have met, who have stayed here for over a year, want to find a line of work that is somehow China-centered. Some have even said, "I want to work for China." All have left me aware that China does not exclude. In the end, it also invites us to know ourselves better, to bring that knowledge to bear on China's unfolding modernity.

After dinner I am off to the first dance party at the newly official U.S. Embassy. I still feel, gloomily, "Ah well, I am seen as just another American anyway so I might as well indulge." I remain filled with rancor that China does not appreciate the differences between those of us who want to learn about this country on its own terms and those who want to change it according to a Western, capitalistic paradigm of modernity.

The Saint Patrick's Day affair at the embassy is full of lonely businessmen and young State Department personnel. Most are midwesterners, not unlike their predecessors who had been equally drunk and equally comfortable in Shanghai in the old days. I am much relieved when I meet some fellow students from the Language Institute. The two women, Linda and Karen, especially are quickly becoming good friends of mine. Our paths had crossed in and around Yale, years earlier. We are finding each other's values and experiences congenial. All of us have been divorced, pained, and are now tenuously successful.

On the periphery of our fun that night are two Chinese-American men eager to dance. Linda and I take turns responding to their offers. In that crowd of wealth, conservatism, and relative ignorance about China, we feel rather estranged. One of our dance partners is a short, thin engineer. With his head thrown back, he is undulating, grinning broadly. The other man is shy, younger, with a strong athletic body, skilled in disco steps. Linda is a broad-hipped woman. With black boots, she is tapping out a strong audacious call. I also wear black pants and vest. Thinner now than when I arrived in China, and less frightened by a body I am coming to move in more easily. Back "home" at the university by 3 A.M. I feel tired, happy. Perhaps China frees us, teaches us much more than it forbids or limits or denies.

Two days later another *jiexian* challenged, overcome. Seiji Ozawa conducts the Boston Symphony and the Peking Central Philharmonic Orchestra in front of a capacity audience of twenty thousand in the Capital Athletic Stadium. Tickets for our group are provided by the Embassy. The only question is the number of these precious commodities, since each one of us has at least one Chinese friend who would want to come.

On stage, Ozawa swoons and heaves and charms the mass Chinese audience. The program is tame, conventional, yet effective in introducing various Western instruments and displaying the virtuosity of Chinese musicians: Mendelssohn's Violin Concerto in A Minor opens the concert in a mood of noisy, ceremonious settling-in. In the aisles pass talkative soldiers, workers, high-school students who have gotten tickets late by patient waiting in endless lines. On the floor of the stadium a truly international media pandemonium: less than one foot away from concert violinist Joseph Silverstein is a swarm of Chinese, Japanese, and American TV cameramen. By the time the second piece, Verdi's Overture to *La forza del destino*, begins, the scene calms down enough for me to engage in a conversation with the Chinese roommate of one of my American fellow students.

Yang Jisheng, in his mid-thirties, is a thoroughly professional, experienced archeology graduate student. The faint wrinkles around his eyes and his historical sophistication make me want to call him "Mr." ("xiansheng", literally "first-born" in Chinese, a title once ostracized and now slowly regaining currency). Yang is the first colleague here that I felt awkward calling either "comrade" or "fellow student." We get involved in a long explanation of the meaning of the word *destiny*.

We agree that the Chinese translation of the title of the Verdi piece, although literal enough, is wrong. It conveys the meaning of fate, "flowing with a force greater than, other than, oneself." The Chinese word hints at some natural, uncontrollable force with which the individual has to come to terms, or learn to fathom through meticulous discipline of the inner self. Verdi on the other hand, we feel, is expressing something that cannot be said in Chinese: the possibility of a person choosing, shaping his or her own destiny. Outrageous as it sounds in Chinese, perhaps even triumphing over the unpredictable.

Next, the Chinese piece for the evening, Concert for Pipa and Orchestra, by a contemporary Chinese composer. The ancient Chinese instrument is a fine match for the virtuosity displayed earlier by the violin—no doubt a *yin-yang* echo consciously chosen by Ozawa. The mood of the whole piece, however, is insipid. Lilting Western instruments provide an awkward counterpoint to the pipa as they seek to imitate China's rivers, mountains, lakes.

During Beethoven's Fifth, Ozawa has his joint Boston-Peking musicians and the audience in total, majesterial control. Each time his baton slashes down, during each swirl of his Asian black, American-length hair, one can feel the force of thousands listening. I take photographs of an older man and a little girl. Their intense concentration, their self-forgetfulness is a sign to me that *jiexian* can be crossed. Their faces show them taken out of, beyond, Chineseness into some realm of universal beauty.

MARCH 23 *Chinese acquaintances: a doctor, two professors, a woman at the zoo* Yesterday afternoon, while shopping for silk downtown, I was caught in snow flurries. Along with thousands of others, I scurry along, half surprised, half delighted. By the time Christine, a Dutch friend, and I get back to the university around 11:30, the campus lies hushed in a cover of snow. We are too thinly dressed to move about "appropriately"—a very Chinese concept of harmonizing behavior with circumstance. On this day, clearly that would call for a walk around the lake. I woke up this morning to snow-covered trees outside my window. The sun is high, a soft, penetrating yellow that has not vanquished but has at least graced with some luster Peking's gray spring.

I have been watching with rising anticipation the buds abandoning modesty throughout the week. The oncoming spring mirrors my optimism about beginning research at the university, the novel pleasures of settling into my daily life in China. I lie in bed a long time—savoring the space for rethinking that the snow has engendered. Warm under the quilt, I stretch, roll, sit up, look at the Lu Xun calligraphy on one wall, the Matisse cutouts on the other, a red Romanian hand-woven cloth straight ahead. I feel better than I have allowed myself to feel for years. Not lonely, not sad, not hurt, not longing, not scared, not performing, not producing, not winning, not losing, neither touched nor touching. World enough and time . . .

Time to think over my initial impressions of current Chinese "emancipation," especially as it affects my old ideas among new intellectuals. Clearly a new elite is afoot in China, a social counterpart, a grounding for the idea of freedom of thought. I haven't been able to reflect upon any of this too clearly because of a profound ambivalence: On the one hand, the Cultural Revolution of the 1960s has been a powerful, positive influence on my own political ideals, and on the other hand, in China today I am met with such open friendship and personal consideration precisely because some of the strident egalitarianism of those days is now being abandoned. I also know that I cannot go through this China year with politics on the back burner even if all the Chinese around me seem to be in a retreat from political action and thought.

All this brings me round about this morning to Deng Xiaoping and Simon Leys. Both, I feel, are wrong and yet have to be heeded. They provide a good starting point for thinking about changes in China today.

> Deng: It doesn't matter if a cat is white or black,
> as long as it catches mice it's a good cat.
> Leys: China is best known during the winter, when
> shadows are stark, deepest social truths
> known best unadorned by foliage of ideals.

On this late winter morning I ask myself, what difference does it make if an intellectual, scientist, or student believes in socialism? How do these beliefs affect research in modernization? It seems to me that Mao's ideals remain very much part of the structure of social life in China—not superstructural niceties, but embedded everywhere in people's lives, in what they wear, in how they address each other on the bus.

Some recent encounters: a rusticated surgeon, an aged diplomat, an outspoken literary critic, a meticulous linguist, and two different kinds of Peking University students—the older group of worker-peasant-soldier students and the new examination candidates. The variety of my recent encounters hints not merely at sociological complexities but also at a range of political contradictions that coexist here today. Perhaps now that I don't need China to confirm my own values so intensely as before, I will be able to observe more, better. It is too soon to tell.

Last Thursday afternoon, a visit from Dr. Sheng and his wife, relatives of a friend in the United States. Both are short, somewhat plump. He comes dressed in his fine gray cotton "Mao suit," really a Sun Zhongshan (Sun Yat-sen) uniform. She wears a simple black rayon shirt over cotton trousers. They had written to say that they would visit me at my dorm around 2:30. I prepare some Ovaltine from home and bring to my room our dining room's finest Western-style pastry. They walk in, full of warmth and openness, knowing that I had been sent by "family," which is the most direct entrance to Chinese intimacy anywhere in the world. First we look over wedding pictures I brought from a niece they've never met. Her husband is an even more puzzling unknown. Yet Dr. Sheng and his wife have little difficulty with it all. Both are delighted by the new family member.

The conversation begins with home news, their niece's beauty, their new son-in-law's skill in foreign languages. I eagerly share details of my friends' lives back home. These bits of information so novel and precious to this uncle and aunt poring over their first close-up of relatives far away. We agree to try to get the young couple to visit China. Now, since it is officially allowed, they could stay in the relatives' homes. I look forward to witnessing my friends' initiation into a history that could not be claimed personally earlier.

Having talked intimately about those far away, we turn to the circumstances of their own lives. Dr. Sheng was sent down to the countryside in 1973 and is still living in that village. Overworked with patients, training other doctors, he still tries to respond to the increasing health demands of peasants in this period of emancipation and modernization. His wife works in a factory, comes home around 6:00 to shop and cook dinner for four, including her twenty-four-year-old daughter and new son-in-law. Yes, they would like to get back to Peking, but it is still hard to arrange. Also, the countryside needs much more medical attention because of its poverty and backwardness.

They sound honest, thoughtful about their feelings, as they talk of adjusting to life in the village. Peasants' gifts there enable them to refuse gifts of food from me. My American friends had asked me to get them anything they need from the Peking Friendship Store. They sound convinced and convincing when they say they have all they needed, that life is good even if hard. They invite me to visit them as soon as the weather warms up, to see life in the countryside. I hope to see them again soon. Their lives are marked by a combination of privilege and commitment I want to know more about. They promise to come back and get me with the car the hospital makes available to Dr. Sheng for official business. Later I see the car—a jeep with a weather-worn peasant driver. I apologize to the driver for unknowingly having kept him waiting. His handshake is firm, forgiving—neither haughty nor supplicating in the face of a "Western scholar."

That same night, I take a cab to the Peking Hotel. It is the center of all foreign activity: business, flirting, bargaining, flaunting, scrambling, the cutting edge of China's love affair with the West. Here, in the oldest, pre-1949, part of the hotel, lives Dr. Li Tie-zheng, a friend of a Chinese colleague back home. He was one of China's diplomats to the West under the Nationalist regime, stayed in the United States after '49, wrote his book *Tibet: Today and Yesterday*, taught at the University of Hartford. In a fit of patriotism he returned to China in the 1960s. Now, he is a sort of national treasure. He travels to the West frequently, has been given privileged accommodations with his lady friend, a one-time ballerina. I had heard that he was urbane, gracious, fluent in English, highly connected, and generally a precious if not always available source of current Chinese views of the world.

I arrive for our 6 P.M. dinner with a gift for him from his American friend, a recent spy novel. He greets me most decorously. A tall, slender man in his seventies, he wears an elegant gray pinstriped suit, a tasteful yet audacious orange woolen vest, and a perfectly coordinated silk tie. The sitting room of his apartment is large, fancy in the People's Republic style with gray cotton-covered lounge chairs, a refrigerator, and some paintings on the wall from noted contemporary artists. We have dinner with his son, one of his eight children (four of whom live in the U.S.), a travel agent in San Francisco. Fine food is served to us in the private dining room of this otherwise overcrowded hotel. Our conversation ranges from China in the 1930s, to the Middle East Peace Treaty, to marvelous bits of criticism about how the Peking media keeps its populace in "the dark ages" about world events. Mostly I listen. Dr. Li is alert, his conversation broad in scope and unorthodox.

I leave wondering how China can contain such erudite, privileged luminaries. Something about the nation's new, bold entrance into the world scene depends on men like Dr. Li, from old, wealthy families, rather eccentric in their personal habits of loving and living. They not only legitimate the regime symbolically but somehow contribute to its internal resiliency as well. I'd like to talk to him more before he takes off for the United States on his yearly visit with that part of his brood. Here at Beida I met one of Dr. Li's twenty-four grandchildren, a student from Radcliffe. She shares some of her mother's reservations about this flamboyant man, who seems to have given to China and to the world more readily than he chose to give to his own family.

At the university, encounters continue. I attend two lecture courses, which are mobbed by students because they are rumored to be taught by the "best professors" to surface in this period of intellectual emancipation. Yuan Liangjun teaches modern literature. He looks as I imagine the literati must have looked in their moments of inwardness and sincerity: thick glasses, a traditional overcoat, blue or gray with a high Chinese collar and covered buttons. His red Beida professor's badge is a sign of modernity, yet it echoes symbols of office worn by officials of earlier dynasties. Then, he starts talking: the most conscious, critical, humorous Marxist I have met up to now. Full of quips about Mao's fallibility, about how rage against the old order had better be couched in skilled literary form, how history matters in the unfolding of consciousness.

His lectures are a self-consuming marathon, his intensity lightened somewhat by an undulating voice that rises for humor and drops into soft questions at crucial points in his analysis. Two-hundred-odd listeners (all Chinese except me) are on the edge of their seats most of the time—unsure if they can or should follow this man's iconoclastic reasoning. Still they come eagerly because they hear the depth of his commitment to a revolutionary heritage they can only read about these days. They sense that he might be the last of the radical intellectuals in this new period of materialist sobriety.

Liu Baiyong, a visiting researcher from Wuhan University, is here for one semester of advanced work in linguistics. He also teaches classical Chinese to a hundred or so literature majors. He always wears cadre clothes, a blue or gray four-pocketed jacket, once a woolen hat, another time a gray worker's cap. (It is very cold in these classrooms: no heating and many broken windows.) He is soft-mannered, speaks very slowly. Each line of classical poetry or traditional philosophy is read out loud, with obvious delight, in mandarins' language forbidden to be taught during the Cultural Revolution because it was deemed too "feudal." His explanations are clear, thoroughly innovative, based upon erudition and theoretical rigor. He exudes calm competence.

I watch and wonder: what did he do during the Cultural Revolution? Did he attend many criticism meetings? Was he quiet, uninterested, and uninterrupted in his studies? Did he use his calm voice to indict others who were more feverish? I'm not sure I trust him but somehow I like him. I am learning more about Chinese language from him than from anyone in my past years of assorted training.

I have an appointment with Yuan Liangjun next week to discuss one of his articles, which I read and found to be a positive example of historical criticism in the guise of literary criticism. I will visit Liu Baiyong in his dorm. He has asked students to come by for chats and clarifications.

Two groups of students here are startlingly different. This is the last year when Beida has students who were sent to the university after labor experiences in factories, communes, and the army. It is also the first year for the first group of students who were selected in national examinations, the winning competitors in a frenzy of preparation for tests in English, math, history, geography, etc.

These two groups look, act, sound different: the first is much older, clothed in simple cotton jackets and trousers, their faces worn by work. They listen in classes with a relaxed, autonomous smile. "Worker-peasant-soldier" students don't talk much to others or to each other. They know themselves to be the end, perhaps the unwanted end, of a revolutionary experiment in education. Still, they don't seem anxious or insecure. Many are going back to work in the units they came from. In those factories and communes they hope to find support, and maybe further opportunities, for part-time study.

The younger group, mostly sons (and a smattering of daughters) of high-level cadres, is dressed well in woolen, tailored jackets, colorful padded coats, notebooks with fancy covers. They walk around with tape earphones in their ears, muttering English. They approach us foreigners whenever they can to practice English. They are gleeful participants in weekly dances here, confident that high positions await them when they graduate. They are a self-conscious group. Having passed very competitive exams, they don't hide much of their sense of being somehow "better." Their conversation is studded with snickers about China's backwardness and unabashed curiosity about life in America. I feel drawn to and yet alien from the first group and generally put upon by the fawning attention of the latter. I wonder how the year will unfold in friendships.

Today ended on a rather sad note. It started out fine. This means I was in a good mood, gliding on my bicycle relatively unnoticed and expansive. I ride into town along wide, tree-shadowed boulevards, effortlessly blending into the day of other Sunday riders. There are couples taking time to talk after a busy, other-oriented week of work. Down by Democracy Wall a crowd, milling about

Major intersection to the left of Democracy Wall in Peking. The large placard carries a quotation from Chairman Mao: "In industry learn from Daqing, in agriculture learn from Dazhai. The people of the whole nation learn from the People's Liberation Army, the P.L.A. learns from the people." Pasted at the bottom of this quotation is the poster challenging Mao's denunciation of Liu Shaoqi.

new posters. The only one that catches my eye, because the rows of readers are at least five deep, is entitled "Was Liu Shaoqi a Man or a Monster?" The wall poster goes on in a righteous but reasoned tone to call into question some of the indictments against this "chief capitalist-roader" during the Cultural Revolution.

It ends with bold proclamations that Mao (Liu's chief accuser) was not a saint but just a man like Liu—a conclusion thoroughly in keeping with the present official view that all leadership is fallible. This is also a convenient explanation for the return to power of Deng Xiaoping—thrice-deposed, thrice-arisen revolutionary leader. Some Western tourists drive by and take pictures of these "radical" phenomena. Unable to read a single character, they will probably convince themselves and their eager listeners back home that antigovernment sentiments are well and alive in China. I buy some of the hurriedly sold "underground

newspapers"—another example of the officially sanctioned periphery of criticism. Mostly stories, poems, these journals are well
within the bounds of accepted sniping at authoritarianism and
bureaucracy.

I lunch in an alley noodle shop, enjoying some moments of
aloneness and rest in the midst of ordinary Chinese people. I
slurp my delicious meatball soup along with the rest of the cus-
tomers. Silently I watch a gathering of three women in their late
forties. They seem to be sisters meeting each other after some
time of separation. They are composed, unadorned, attentive to
each other, yet each with a solid apartness that seems nurtured
by hard work and a hard-won position of responsibility elsewhere.
I am drawn to this older generation. They too are sharing in
freedom brought about by the new winds of modernization. Yet
freedom for them does not mean that they can now finally curl
their hair or brighten up their clothes. They are merely finding a
more leisurely way of being whatever they have become. I stop
to shop a bit in a locally renowned department store. Intending
to buy some jacket to go to classes with, I end up getting a rather
fancy traditional-style blouse. I keep meaning to buy the common,
more practical garb of Chinese people, and instead I walk out
with silks and mandarin clothes.

I ride back to the university against the wind, uphill. I stop on
the way at the zoo to see how ordinary Chinese people spend
their Sundays. I take lots of pictures of families crowding around
the pandas, who have been let out for the spring. I delight at
these masked fruit-eaters. I stop to rest against the pavilion, as I
had seen other tired walkers do.

A woman slides over and begins to talk with me. Her face is
very open, startling after the furtive side glances from others. She
asks me my age. It turns out both of us are thirty-two. She has
an accent, so I ask where she is from. A hasty, jumbled tale about
being around the train station for days, in from the country to
protest something about lack of food and housing. "Nothing is
being resolved," she complains. Her story is frantic, she looks
disturbed. I gather she hasn't eaten for a while. By now (all this
in less than five minutes), a crowd of no less than a hundred has
gathered around, sullen, watchful, sensing in this woman's outpouring to a foreigner a momentous transgression.

With stomach rising in anxiety, I decide to keep talking. She asks my name, wants to be friends. I tell her that I'm an American exchange student. She asks if America is full of white people. "Are there any Chinese like me?" She presses on: "Do you really understand my words?" "Don't worry," I answer her worried query, "I understand enough of what you say." The crowd grows in size, its fears and antipathy palpable. To the side, a woman in her fifties looks official, a bit angrier than the rest. She finally asks the young woman, "Who are you? Are you alone? Why are you babbling at one who can't make out your words?" My friend answers, agitated: "She understands. Yes, I'm alone." (The worst thing, it seems, in Chinese society, which depends on mutual aid and mutual surveillance.) She starts off again, even more agitated about her tale of the railroad station. The older woman is getting restless, grabs my friend's arm, and pulls her off. I smell danger, don't interfere, just say "Goodbye, take care." My friend leaves dutifully, but is not contrite.

I sit a little longer, and watch with hatred the immense, dense gathering around me. They say nothing. Their unresponsive mass is a strident call to the attention of worried officials. After the crowd disperses, I get up and walk out, fighting back tears. Why would only a "crazy" person dare talk to me so openly in China? What must have been her story for her to want to tell it to me so much?

I rage silently as I walk toward the bicycle parking lot. I notice her standing by a bus stand. I shake her hand. Her eyes are open, with tears like mine. I hold her hand for a moment longer. She asks my name again. I repeat it (glad just then that in Chinese my surname, Shu, means comfort), and try to leave before she is noticed again. Just a few steps ahead, an ice-cream vendor. I ask for two ice creams, walk back, give her both, and say my last goodbye.

I ride away on my bicycle in a hurry. China, again, seems closed, furious, superstitious. I know this is my own rage, my impotence at not having understood more of what the woman at the zoo was saying. Still, I wonder: why was Nie Yuanzi, the female instructor who started the Cultural Revolution at Peking University, supposedly put away a few weeks ago? Why was Fu Yuehua, the woman who had organized support for out-of-town petitioners, put away in haste and damned as "prostitute and counter-revolutionary" by Deng Xiaoping himself?

This society does not hate women, exclusively. I just tend to respond to that more. I see a clear line of descent in modern Chinese literature from Lu Xun to Chen Jo-hsi: he blasted murderous Chinese conformism in the 1910s; she catalogued its outrages during the "proletarian revolution" of the 1960s. I turn into the side street which leads to Peking University, exhausted, dejected, knowing that there are many harsh truths I have yet to grasp. Next to a bus stop, a mother slaps her daughter across the face. Another breach in China's painstaking orderliness.

MARCH 31 *Intellectual history: among Chinese intellectuals* Settled in my Peking life: ran out of home-brought coffee and found my first cup of "Shanghai Instant" quite tasty. The cyclamen plant I bought a month ago is at the peak of its bloom, all its bulby potential manifest in nine pink-white blossoms with purple centers. This flower, much admired by my Chinese visitors, strikes me as thoroughly oriental. Its upturned petals suggest butterflies, the blossoms seem ready to lift off from watery green leaves. Yesterday, a literate guest could not think of its Chinese name. We looked it up in the dictionary and it turned out to be transliterated as *xiankelai*, meaning literally "celestial guest arrives." My asparagus fern is called in Chinese "reed of culture" or "misty reed." Both sets of characters are simple, common, and layered with connotations of classical poetry.

And yet what seems never quite is in China. What one expects to find is an acceptable beginning. But perceptions must constantly be revised. So I ask myself: Had I had fewer notions about China and Chinese history beforehand, would I be relearning so much so fast? Were my questions less "mine," would I hear the answers differently? Would I do justice to what is "theirs," distinctly Chinese, rather than a vaguely cosmopolitan "ours"?

I came to China, among other things, to continue a study of intellectuals and revolution. The focus of my work has been the May Fourth movement of 1919, which was the catalyst for a revolution of consciousness in China. It encompassed an attack on Confucian values, a great excitement about Western modernity, an elaborate experiment with vernacular literature, free love, class analysis, the birth of the Communist movement, and much, much more. I sense that the 1919 "Enlightenment movement" is some-how the foundation for the "emancipation of thought" proclaimed all around us in China today. What the connections are I do not yet know. I wonder if there are any at all. Enforced echoes, after all, are not historical connections. I did not expect to be able to express my interest in the theme of enlightenment overtly. Back home, the topic seemed too Western, too elitist, to be researched in the People's Republic. Again, what seems never quite is. But it remains a good foundation for rethinking both China and ourselves.

Last Thursday I was taken for a visit to Professor Wang Yao, a noted literary historian at Beida and a member of the Chinese Academy of Social Sciences. Our meeting was a prompt and sur-prisingly generous response by the Beida Literature Department to my interest in the history of the May Fourth intellectuals. Back home, I had read a copy of Wang Yao's famous book *An Outline for a History of Contemporary Literature*, written in the 1950s.

I arrive at Wang Yao's house with the academic adviser assigned to me, Yue Daiyun, a fine, open-minded woman in her late forties. I have carefully prepared questions about the impact of social violence on the self-perceptions of literary intellectuals in the 1920s. Wang Yao's house lies behind other faculty dorms. Unlike those recently built, multistoried cement blocks, this is an extended family compound out of the eighteenth-century novel *Dream of the Red Chamber*. Past two tiny former servants' pavilions, a muddy footpath, then the big red gate where we park our bicycles.

We open the high, rusty brass handles and are greeted across the courtyard by Professor Wang. He is a man in his late sixties, with long white hair, dressed in a finely tailored gray wool jacket. He extends his arm in a courteous greeting, made even warmer by his smiling eyes. He takes us to a sitting room, surprisingly traditional. "You have obviously never seen a Chinese professor's house," remarks my adviser. Behind the couch from which Pro-fessor Wang speaks is a wall-to-wall antique bookcase: square shelves covered with wooden blinds, on which are carved four gold characters in the ancient, square style of the Han dynasty. All around us, glass-covered bookcases filled with horizontally arranged classical texts and a few vertical, modern sources.

Professor Wang Yao, modern literature specialist, and his wife at home, on the Beida campus.

Yue Daiyun, my adviser and colleague in the Literature Department at Beida.

Faced with one of China's most eminent cultural critics, I stumble a bit in getting my questions out. At first Wang Yao, too, seems awkward. It is his first prolonged meeting with a Western scholar, I gather. But soon enough we are leaning toward each other—he, animated; I, alert and comprehending. We talk of his friends, the aged and dying luminaries of the League of Left-Wing Writers. This was a Marxist group, founded in Shanghai in 1930 to criticize the policies of the Nationalist (KMT) government. Wang Yao explains to me how the lectures that Mao Zedong gave in 1942 to set down the Communist Party policy on literature and art developed out of ideas about the popularization of culture already championed by May Fourth intellectuals in the 1930s. He nods approvingly at my criticism of Western scholars who subsume May Fourth under previous modernizing movements. The May Fourth movement remains, we agree, an epoch-making event with significant implications for the present.

Often in our conversation Wang Yao leans back laughing at some particularly subtle point of his own, his brown and broken teeth a contrast to his skillfully chosen words. He speaks with a heavy northwest, Gansu accent. As we leave, I ask if he has lived in this house for long. "No, just moved in recently. Too many upheavals in China during this past decade." Back in the dorm, a Chinese student mentions, as an aside, "Wang Yao was one of the most badly beaten professors at Beida. He was locked up for months in the cow pen (a holding shed for 'stinking intellectuals') during the Cultural Revolution, you know."

A Western friend taunted me a few weeks ago: "Let me know if you ever meet a Marxist in China." Well, I did. Yuan Liangjun, the instructor who teaches the crowd-gathering modern literature survey, came to visit me yesterday. I had read one of his articles and found it to be a fine piece of critical analysis. I want to translate parts of it for an essay introducing contemporary Chinese scholarship to American sinologists. He arrives exactly at 2:30 P.M. as we had agreed, sits down comfortably on the bed, which also serves as my guest couch. There is no ceremony, although for him, as for Professor Wang, this is the first prolonged conversation with a Western scholar.

The son of poor Shandong peasants, Yuan had written many essays for newspapers before the Cultural Revolution. Now he is emerging as one of China's most prolific, contentious literary critics. He takes Lu Xun as his mentor, not merely as the object of

Talking with Yuan Liangjun in my room at Beida. Photograph courtesy of Karen L. Gottschang.

his scholarly studies. I ask the questions I prepared after reading his articles. How does he think intellectuals become Marxists? How did offspring of the gentry, like Lu Xun, come to be revolutionaries in the late 1920s? He answers with a keen sense of the ambivalences and fears that intellectuals have to conquer within themselves before they can become activists in the social movements of their day.

His conversation is focused, his voice loud, strong. He jots down key phrases in Chinese which he realizes I have difficulty grasping. We talk at length about China's current modernization drive. He is openly critical about the youth's waning faith in socialism. When he tells me China is "backward" he does not mean its people are somehow unworthy, which seems to be the connotation of this phrase on the lips of other cadres I have talked to. Rather, he is pointing to the problem of material scarcity, which he believes is holding back the development of Communist consciousness in China. He is a party member. He knows little about America but doubts the veracity of its portrayal as "heaven-like" in the Chinese media. He asks me hard questions about class distinctions in the United States. I look forward to learning from him, with him.

CHAPTER 2

APRIL 4   *Rumors of a "crackdown"*

Something has been afoot in China for the past week or so. I wake up Sunday morning and go out to get hot water from the boiler room. Unlike at the Language Institute, it is not in the basement of our dormitory but down the street. It is 8 A.M. or so. Several hundred neighborhood people pour through the university gates. They each carry a stool or a little bench. The throng is heading toward the campus auditorium, where many political meetings have been held during and since the Cultural Revolution. They seemed engaged in something at once habitual and new: political meetings on a mass scale used to be frequent until a year or so ago. Since then, public life has become routine, dutiful. "Oh sure, the government moderniza-tion program is great stuff. But let's all wind down from the frenzied social-mindedness of the Mao era." All this is muted, of course, but not far below the surface.

Then, the apolitical suddenly becomes politicized again: the "liberating dances" of two weeks ago are now officially con-demned as "prostitution markets." About this time, too, we begin to notice more Chinese women lingering longer with African stu-dents. Then come the rumors of ordinances that prostitution will have to "be cut down." There are new regulations at the Language Institute, ostensibly for foreigners' safety and Chinese students' morals. Westerners here are wondering if this means a "turning off the faucet" of Chinese-foreign contacts in general. Are we being watched, isolated? Is the honeymoon with the West over?

These questions would not be so pressing had illusions about the "tide of Westernization" been less pervasive in the Western media. All those reports about chic hair styles, dissenting wall posters. If only they could be just like us! I don't usually feel prey to such wishful thinking. And yet I feel deeply affected by this "something afoot" here.

Just now I am preparing a two-hour lecture in Chinese about American approaches to modern Chinese literature. An avalanche of contacts and talks with Chinese scholars this week. All this when contact is supposedly being cut off by word passed down through that hidden but thoroughly efficient party network. Recently, Mr. Lu, a distressed intellectual in his sixties, intelligent, perceptive, was wringing his hands as he talked about the idealism of Zhou Enlai, about the crisis of faith among youth. Tonight, surprisingly, the political administrator of the History Department brought a woman professor in her fifties to my room. She teaches world history and is especially interested in American-Chinese relations in the nineteenth and twentieth centuries. I feel at once delighted by the spontaneity of the visit but concerned that it may be part of a surveillance.

The pace of public meetings is increasing all around us. My Friday lecture was postponed until Tuesday so the Literature Department could have its own political meeting to discuss Deng Xiaoping's latest, still unpublished directive. Everybody knows the topics to be discussed, which are based on the crucial points of last week's "Shanghai Public Security Department Announcement." The announcement stridently reasserted "socialist discipline": No lying down in front of trains, no dissent against higher-ups, no wall posters in other than designated areas. The implication is that "democratization" will lead to "counterrevolutionary tendencies." Those who talk about "the salutary effect of the Shanghai announcement" focus on the "need to do something about sellers of pornographic photos in back alleys."

Somehow, I sense the announcement is something much, much bigger. Newspapers are featuring more conspicuously political articles, on topics such as "How does a revolutionary view the future?" I feel at once energized and edgy. Off tomorrow to Tian An Men Square for the commemoration of the April Fifth movement of 1976, a mass outpouring sparked by the death of Zhou Enlai which turned into a demonstration against the Gang of Four.

Not much happened in the
square, some milling about by a
crowd of several hundred while
security police announced regulations against "improper" expressions of political opinion. Their magnified voices are a reminder
that something might have happened here were it not for the
prompt word sent down through all channels the past week that
no demonstrations were to be held this year. Still some groups
come with ceremonial salutes, wreaths, traditional white paper
flowers of mourning. What is being put to rest here is not only
the memory of Zhou Enlai, but the mass movement of 1976 itself.

Most of those milling about the heroes' monument are vaguely
looking for "action." Foreigners with cameras around their necks
always a magnet for Peking's impulsive flow of humanity. An
American friend, Linda, is caught in a corner with a rapidly gathering crowd, laughing nervously. Her voice is shrill with vulnerability in the centrifugal pull of the crowd. As I come down the
stairs to help relieve her tension, I recall Lu Xun's descriptions of
the deadly lethargy of Chinese spectators.

There are others in the square as well. Young men and women
in their late twenties, around the periphery of the roving onlookers. These youths might very well have been the impassioned
poet leaders of 1976. For them, we foreigners are extraneous—
recent arrivals and therefore of no interest. They seem to prefer
to watch their own countrymen with their serious eyes. Has their
struggle accomplished anything? That hard, awful question that
every revolutionary must ask: "What has changed, after all?" They
know that the answer is "much." But also "little," when compared to the initial hopes, the initial ideals of the activists who
raised their voices against autocracy in April 1976.

The "action" is not where it was supposed to be. So, Linda and
I turn the day into a personal savoring of our Peking life. We keep
wondering why we always chase the news in China. News is not
reported on the radio or on the TV. What is known is only what
people create, an elusive prospect in this huge society. Yet, this
is liberating, too, intimate and concrete in an unexpected way.
Not able to be creators that day, and refusing to be either spectators or objects to be spectated, we become buyers, fingering
silks and looking at art.

Linda's quest for spring color is gratified by lush green silk.

Later in the alley of officially sanctioned antique stores, we indulge some more. I ask to seek works by Shi Tao, a seventeenth-century genius who chose madness as a form of resistance to the Manchu invasion. His traditional literati landscapes became harsh, angular, as his political despondency deepened. I found a nineteenth-century reproduction of a Shi Tao sketch: cliffs towering over windswept pines. No sage walking on a mountain path, no mist, no greens, merely stark blue-gray. The mood is at once rugged and vulnerable. It suits me well.

Something is definitely afoot. I sense it in the arrogant flick of the wrist with which a young political hack visiting me throws the wrapper of the chocolate I offer him on the floor of my room. He and other cadres of the Cultural Revolution era are staging a comeback among frightened, aimless, older intellectuals. Yet, he is neither symptom nor cause. Just a rigid ideologue with acceptable answers to old questions. More subtle is the flurry of meetings about socialist discipline and a socialist future, a rising tide of concern about the political demoralization of the young.

Weeks before the Shanghai announcement and Deng's talk, my conversations with older Chinese friends inevitably drift toward criticism of the post-Cultural Revolution generation. Some frank doubts are voiced about the youth's commitment to socialism and some bitter questions asked about the rosy portrayal of capitalist America in the Chinese media. It could be that when Deng rails against the slackening of "political work" among youth, he is, in fact, giving voice to criticisms, sentiments rising from below. This filtering of opinion from bottom to top is at once a slow and covert process in China, nothing so eye-catching as the lonely, marginal cries on Democracy Wall. I try to listen harder, to see more patiently than before.

It is not that China was becoming "Western" during this past year, but rather that we Westerners were somehow center-stage. So, until recently, paying attention to ourselves here sufficed for a somewhat truthful impression of Chinese realities. Now China is turning inward. Is it away from "us"? Why do Westerners always feel betrayed when China turns to Chinese concerns? Its own problems have been spreading. The shoving on buses could be and is seen by many as a symptom of a more widespread quest for selfish comfort. "What is modernization for?" is the question now asked from the top. The range of answers from below might well become bewildering and untenable. I am trying to hear more just when less is being said.

My lecture in progress continues to worry me. My language skills seem to be slipping. I feel as if I were stammering in the face of a large and hostile crowd. A part of me knows that I am suited well enough to give this presentation on American views of modern Chinese literature. Also I know that my colleagues in the Literature Department are eager and generous. And yet my nights are restless again. Old, old worries about being imprisoned by inchoate words well up from my days as an immigrant in Vienna and New York. Then, not only did I lack words, but I was filled with impermissible thoughts. Reluctant to mouth the anti-communist slogans I was supposed to express in my "flight to freedom," unable to see myself as a refugee from "behind the Iron Curtain," I longed to be articulate. If only I could make my points more reasonable, I used to believe, my unconventional ideas would be somehow more acceptable.

It is an old movie indeed. As I wake in the middle of the night, I enjoy letting old anxieties drift past like ghosts in a Chinese opera. In some deep, deep way, I feel safe in China, safe as a quester among a questing people. I know enough about their tradition and their revolution for them to consider my opinions seriously. Also, I happen to be here at a time in my life when I can enjoy, rather than worry about, my own strengths, however limited.

So, I walk around tense but observant. Today I noticed wall posters at the University commemorating the April Fifth movement. Having looked for action afar, in Tian An Men Square, I am delighted to find it nearby. A host of poems on a cafeteria wall: tame, official in spirit and tone, praising party leadership and the Four Modernizations. Some, however, dare to reveal some questions and fail to mouth "correct" answers. A poem on democracy asks whether freedom can be grasped as readily as "Coca Cola can be imported." It goes on to warn that unless China remains "of the masses" there will be no country left to be "democratized" at all. This is a striking rejection of Western stimulants by the very constituency, China's educated youths, whom foreign businessmen hope to ensnare most readily. They still might succeed, to be frank.

Another satiric poem parodies the contemporary mood: "Politics no longer turns me on./ Only with materialism do I get my kicks./ Yeah, revolutionary slogans are a matter of the past./ Only harsh realism truly satisfies my longings." Yet another poem is a long letter addressed to "My Beloved." It turns out to be a sentimental allegory about the relationship between Zhou Enlai and his wife, Deng Yingchao. What is remarkable is that love, too, can be expressed, indirectly but nonetheless profusely, in public.

So, the changes in China seem delicate, manifold, subtle. To fret about my language limitations now is simply to dull my eyes and ears. I try not to worry, try just to be thankful to China for demanding the improbable. Outside, the first creatures of spring, a fat frog and a furry moth, both sighted tonight.

APRIL 17 *Visit to Xian: imperial and revolutionary traditions* Tonight I returned from a twenty-four-hour train ride through three provinces: Hebei ("North of the Yellow River"), Shanxi ("West of the Sacred Mountains"), and Shaanxi (untranslatable literally) and its capital Xian, "Western Peace." I came back in time for our Tuesday night gathering of American students. Tonight, as during our last few times together, the evening turns into a gripe session. There is a general discontent in the air, a desire to lash out, to get tough with someone, somewhere.

I try to hold on to the fullness of heart and mind that this first journey in China as a resident of China brings to me. It's not difficult just now. I have, after all, more material security than many foreign students. I have more money for travel, a teaching job back home. So, my purpose is firmer. Materialism in China is not a matter of theory. Students—Chinese and Western—are worrying about money, peasants about land. For a privileged idealist like me, who tends to invest ideas with the weight of deeds, it is chastening to be in China.

On the train to Xian, I traveled "hard-class sleeper." Six persons share an open cubicle provided with sheets, blankets, and pillows. I am assigned the "best" bunk, the middle one, neither in the busy bottom nor in the claustrophobic top. Below me, a man and two young boys. He is fortyish, with a rasping cough and a worn face, a cadre who had come for a meeting in the capital and is now accompanying a friend's sons back to their mother in Sichuan. The boys are seven and three, amazingly well-behaved during the twenty-four hours I spend with them in close quarters. The youngest is a baby, hardly talks, wears baby clothes with split crotch pants. As he urinates repeatedly in a tea cup throughout the trip I see his enlarged testicles, probably swollen because of the cold. The busybody amateur psychologist in me wonders what happens to adult sexuality in China as the result of this prolonged exposure of vulnerable maleness during early childhood. This surely calls into question some of the norms about maturation and identity so freely conjectured about back home.

Throughout the night, the man coughs and coughs, sitting between the sleeping children. Awakened once by what I am sure are his dying sounds, I see him catch his breath, lean over the younger boy, shake him gently, and awaken him enough to pee. The rest of the time for the entire day we are together, he is feeding, hugging, talking, wiping, minding the boys. Where else in the world would a tired, sick man take on, be asked to take two small kids, not his own, across several thousand miles? A "favor" for a friend.

In the dining room on the train a group of people from the same danwei, or unit, that all-important economic and affective focus of contemporary life. They, too, are returning from a meeting in the capital. Four men in their forties sit at one table, next to them two men and a woman in their early twenties. Everybody is jovial with food and drink. Hilarity rises as the group talks, all at once, no one listening much to specifics, offering each other beer and various dishes. Then, the young woman with flushed cheeks and long, long braids walks over to the older men's table with a bowl of noodles to share. They break out in a flurry of jokes. Their teasing is personal, direct, yet without a trace of an intent to demean. The jokes are addressed to her as their coworker and are not about her. Neither her age nor her sex seem to be a source of vulnerability in this society.

Again I ask myself, where else but in China? I realize how swiftly, smoothly I have benefited from China's peculiarities. To come on this journey, alone, but thoroughly safe, is a new kind of freedom for me. After all, for three decades such journeys had been forbidden for foreigners in China. Also, as a woman in the

States, I had spent almost no time alone out in the streets after dark without a conscious fear of attack, of being injured, or of casual insult.

Too often we take this liberation which China offers for granted. Too often we search frantically for more obvious kinds of freedom of self-expression. Too often, we forget that a self must be nurtured and allowed to blossom first before freedom for self-expression can bear any fruit. In the West, we are more used to a self which bursts, at once, aggressively and defensively upon the world, an "I," based on a notion of the Creator. This obsession with the power of creation which resides in the self comes from His image. What are we to make, then, of ancient Chinese civilization which lacked creation myths? Which was "mired" (in the eyes of certain Western critics) in earthy tales about wondrous occurrences? Happenings, not feats, seem to be the stuff of Chinese life and imaginings.

As the train travels through the provinces west of the bend of the Yellow River, I see loess hills, still full of cavehouse villages. The red, fertile mud can be as easily leveled for fields as dug up for dwelling. At first sight it appears primitive, after the capital where cadres' talk is obsessed with China's "backwardness." And yet, as my days in Xian continue, I take rides (on a rented bicycle) into villages four or five hours outside of the city, sit for tea with peasants resting from hauling wood or grain, and I glimpse something else. China is poor to be sure, and often barren, but not primitive. Consider the skill involved in designing the simplest contraption to put eight homemade wooden trunks on a bicycle to be taken to the local free market. As the architecturally balanced bicycle suggests, new means are constantly invented here to deal with old needs. There is wisdom here, if not exactly "creativity" in that Western sense of invention out of nothing. In our own frenzied quest for something absolutely unprecedented, we do not see that we are often reduced to less in our drive for more. China, on the other hand, is crafty, minimalist, repetitive.

In Xian, I ran into an American tourist group led by David Kressner, director of the Asian Collection of the Pasadena Art Museum. We talk about the scarcity of motifs in Chinese art. He begins his explanation/critique as we pass by an exhibit of Neolithic pottery in Wanbo Museum, site of a six-thousand-year-old village. On the vases exhibited, he points out "the fish motif, the embodiment and carrier of all ideas at that time. At first you will note one big, easily recognizable fish, next comes the double-fillet fish motif, then two sets of fish facing each other, finally an abstraction—a small square with diagonals and dots in the side triangles. The only traces left of the fishes are the lingering eyes. Like all Chinese abstractions, rooted in a living, simple thing, this repeats over and over again."

Kressner writes articles about the human-mask imagery in Chinese art and collects Ming-period furniture. I delight in borrowing his eyes for a morning of Chinese art gazing. I share with him, in turn, some of my theories and questions about the Chinese idea of repetition, of reenactment of tradition—an idea that created the greatest civilization in the world. Something important here about cultural layerings appreciated for their very accretion. Layers of the past are not seen as obstacles to be forgotten or overcome.

Foreign visitors come to Xian mostly for the tombs. The city was established as the capital by China's first emperor, Qin Shi Huang, in 221 B.C. and then of the two great dynasties, the Han (202 B.C.–A.D. 9) and the Tang (A.D. 618–907). The land is dotted with imperial remains, layers consciously and elaborately deposited over time. These layers are excavated today in the same spirit. Emperors used to spend months or years finding the right configuration of mountains for their own burial sites. (I wonder what part of ancestor worship in this imperial manner is autonecrophilic. In Chinese, this thought/question cannot be quite articulated. Can it be grasped better in Western tongues?) Emperors commissioned artists for their own wall paintings, their own casket engravings, their own monumental stones, as well as for miniature clay sculptures to decorate their tombs. The results must have been as costly then as they are impressive today.

Most awesome today is the mausoleum planned for himself by the First Emperor, the maniacal, visionary barbarian who rose up in the western steppes beyond the bend in the Yellow River. He had a wild notion of a unified China and brutally conquered all China by 221 B.C. What he provided for himself underground was as unprecedented as the name he chose for himself above. This paradigmatic "Son of Heaven" and "Ruler of All Realms" fell as quickly as he rose. Twenty years to make and less than twenty to lose the Empire. Nonetheless, he bequeathed a pattern, an idea of a unified empire, which was to be imitated by all Chinese rulers from 221 B.C. to A.D. 1911.

At the site of the Qin Shi Huang excavation in Xian: several football fields of half-buried clay figures of soldiers, horses, chariots. In the exhibition hall stand large statues: generals, literary officials, archers, servants, horses. All slightly bigger than life, at once shy and assertive, not unlike the manner in which the actual figures must have thrived before they were buried by this harsh unifier. The figures are erect, rigid in demeanor, with slight smiles fluttering on most lips. These were conquerors who knew themselves to be wielding unprecedented means, unprecedented cruelty, and were anxious to immortalize the goals they achieved. The visitor today cannot help but agree that who they were, in the end, matters less than what they accomplished.

A rather different impression when one arrives at the Tang tombs. This lavish, cosmopolitan dynasty ruled over a huge, diverse realm. Emperors were giants who grabbed the reins of power and yet wielded the brush of literacy in the cultured manner of Confucian intellectuals. Their tombs are guarded by mythic monsters, lined with fanciful wall paintings of polo-playing courtesans, and crowded with dancing horses, bellowing camels, bemused figurines of alien musicians. The main impression is of swirling lines, robes swept to one side; the calligraphy is in the furtive, playful grass style. Finally, one comes to engravings of the emperors themselves: mustached, individualized heroes of their own age.

The idea of emperor, which was conceived by Qin Shi Huang and imitated over and over again, had, by the Tang era, become something quite different from the idea conveyed by those artfully rigid remains of soldiers at the Qin excavation site. This idea nearly snapped when a woman dared to call herself "emperor," not "empress" or "dowager." Just once in history, during the Tang, Wu Zu Tian (684–710) called herself by the title invented by the visionary barbarian in 221 B.C.

It seemed important to me to visit her tomb. I take a long, long, full-day bus ride to an eastern village. There, in the middle of a mild wave of hills, are the remains of this woman, who, like all other rulers, had made elaborate plans for her own burial. Yet, for all her effort to be just like another emperor—an effort which enraged the world of Chinese officialdom—she was, in the end, different. In the midst of the pomp and the familiar pattern of emperors' tombs, she placed a "no inscription stele." Other emperors had been accustomed to engrave their virtuous deeds in stone, but she chose to erect a blank stele in an audacious gesture of faith. She hoped that future history might commemorate and record her mighty beneficence.

She turned out to be wrong. Soon after her death, the no inscription stele began to be inscribed, mostly by Confucians, who chastised her for her transgression. No other woman ever tried that again. Many others, ambitious, skilled, and conniving, arose in later Chinese history, but they wielded power from "behind the screen." Thus, the Tang tombs at once mark and enforce the uniformity of the idea of the Son of Heaven.

A different kind of heroism is codified in the Xian museum dedicated to the Eighth Route Army—the Communist military force that brought Mao Zedong and his comrades to power in 1949. On a side street the visitor who bothers to look can find the headquarters of this army, which was housed in Xian for nine years, between 1936 and 1945. The Communists' headquarters were separated by a thin wall from that of their supposed allies but actual enemies, the Guomindang (the Nationalist regime). Unassuming in appearance, this is an impressive place indeed. I walk through the simple buildings with a young woman guide. We chat about the history of the revolution in Chinese.

Passing through the tiny cubicles where Mao, Zhou Enlai, Dr. Norman Bethune, and others lived and worked, I begin to see that perhaps these leaders achieved something as unprecedented as First Emperor Qin Shi Huang. Time will tell whether the Communist regime will fare better than the first imperial dynasty. The Communist leaders, who chose to identify with and mobilize the dispossessed, lived simple lives, close to essentials. The barbershop gives testimony to the ordinary orderliness of these soldiers. "In hot days, one comrade fanned while the others shaved," explained my guide, with a sense of the fun that must have gone along with the hard work of making a revolution. In these barren circumstances Communist leaders were able to imagine and plan for a new socialist society. Now they are remembered for giving a sense of full humanity to those who had been mere "grains of sand" in the days of emperors. The photos in the museum show gaunt, intense visionaries—so unlike the soldiers of the Qin or the chubby polo players of the Tang. The opulent tombs where emperors immortalized their own past provide a good contrast to this plain compound where Communist guerrillas crafted a visionary future. Their headquarters are abuzz today with primary-school children, on a tour to learn about the "relevant past."

Qin Shi Huang actually buried Confucian scholars because they threatened his notions of the present through their remembrance of the past. The Communists, too, achieved power through enforced forgetfulness. That forgetfulness is still going on in Xian. During this visit, I become obsessed with the forgetting, the destruction of Buddhism in Xian. I had read and heard about it before I came. Xian had been a center of China's mass faith for many centuries. It was once filled with pagodas, shrines, monasteries.

A few still exist today, mostly as tourist spots for foreigners. On the first morning I go with a group of Americans to Da Yan Tang, the Big Goose Pagoda, from the Tang period. It is a stunning building. We are taken into a temple full of ninth-century Buddhas and monks and other enlightened beings. Two days later I return alone on a bicycle ride. I want to contemplate the sculptures more leisurely. I find the room with the statues boarded up. No foreigners visiting today. It's a pity.

More pathetic still to look for the "Temple of Great Beneficence," which a guidebook from the early 1970s describes as housing a community of lamas and possessing a fine collection of Tibetan paintings. I find the back-road entrance with difficulty. It turns out to be a huge public park. The temple area is locked. An aged Tibetan man is planting a tree. "Those minding this place are off at a meeting," he tells me in Chinese. "Yes, only foreign guests may see the tankas [sacred paintings], and only with previous permission." More of the same when I go looking for what the guidebook describes as the largest Lama temple outside of Tibet. I find nothing but a small machine-tool factory. An old gatekeeper answers my questions in an irritated tone: "They tore that down a long time ago."

I leave wondering why Communism destroyed Buddhism with such vengeance here. What was so threatening about this faith? Its millenarianism, after all, had served peasant uprisings well enough in the past. I wonder whether the masses of peasants might not have been impoverished aesthetically with the destruction of Buddhism. I am beginning to understand slowly why it hurts my American friend back home who studies Tibetan Buddhism even to think about what has been ravaged here.

APRIL 18   *Beginning of a friendship: a worker-peasant-soldier student*   Often, I hear the word "friendship" squandered in current Chinese and American propaganda. A new, shyer meaning is emerging now. I am getting to know a fellow student at the university, Shen Zhaoyan. Just back from Xian, feeling at home in classes again. I shove for a seat in my Wednesday morning lecture class with a practiced push of the elbow. I am also bemoaning to myself the lack of intimacy with the two hundred students who are my classmates. In the middle of these thoughts, Zhaoyan comes up to me. She is a small girl, barely five feet tall, a worker.

I had met her on the first day of classes at the university, when she accompanied me to my first lecture. I felt then that she was different from the beehive of examination students buzzing on my floor each morning, looking for a chance to practice English. Shen Zhaoyan is poor, humble, at the end of her schooling just when the new group of students has unprecedented opportunities for academic advancement. I have been meaning to get together with her. But the frenzy that I fell into during last week's lecture preparation, and the crisis of confidence in my language ability which it provoked, made me shy, too awkward to initiate conversation. I rationalize my reticence. It is probably risky for her, at this time of political rethinking in China, if I seek her out. I am not only a foreigner, after all, but an American to boot.

Still, at the end of class today when Zhaoyan sees me sitting at the end of the row, she comes up readily, shakes my hand warmly. I ask her to come by tonight if she is free. In my room, later, we're off quickly into a conversation about how to study, how to write critical book reports, how not to get sick over exams, and how to savor the pleasures of thought in the privileged interval which a college education provides. It is as if I were talking to one of my student-friends at Wesleyan. Zhaoyan responds with eagerness, with more than polite deprecation of her own academic skills. She tells me in an unassuming way about her fierce struggle for a chance to study.

"I came to the University with an equivalent of a fifth-grade education. I never went to high school, you see. After I finished junior high, the Cultural Revolution began. All schools were closed for two years between 1966 and 1968. When they reopened, students were encouraged—forced—to go out to work. So I went to a factory for seven years. In 1976, I was recommended by my workplace to come and be a student at Peking University. I was so thrilled at the opportunity. We arrived at school only to find that the leadership here was still muddy in its political thinking. Administrators insisted that we go to the countryside and study part-time there while we labored and built grass-hut dorms. We fought with them. We told them that we had plenty of labor experiences, that we needed to study now, that the places we were being sent to had no peasants for miles around. That it was pointless to be sequestered in our own enclave of rusticated youths, with only a few rural vagrants to steal our belongings regularly. Still, they insisted. So we were shipped off for more than half a year."

"In those months," she tells me, "we would have one or two lectures a week by tired, reluctant teachers. They were either forced to labor alongside us, or else shuttled back and forth from Peking. Worn out between their city teaching and our classes in the country, they taught us nothing. We had no proper classrooms. We took notes in a crowded shed while the rain leaked in and we held umbrellas over our heads. After seven months or so we started to organize. Some teachers spurred us on, reminding us to 'Remember the rebellious, glorious spirit of Peking University, with its tradition of student activism from 1919 onward.' We planned a strike, and the teachers collaborated by going back to their city teaching. The Literature Department students were then seen as rowdy crazies by other majors. Our leaders eventually decided that we would confront the authorities by packing up our bags and going back to the University to be regular students."

"The next morning"—here her voice quickens with pride—"about a hundred or so of us were ready. Local officials refused to give us transportation money, so we walked miles to the railroad and paid the expensive fare out of our own pockets. In

Peking, the University officials were outraged. They berated us as anarchists, troublemakers. We told them that they were haughty, blind, no better than the Gang of Four. Many of us slept on the floor, often twelve to a room, in abandoned buildings. Our leaders kept negotiating with the University officials. The officials were obsessed with losing face. We had come from afar and wanted to do the reasonable thing: to study. Finally we won. But to save their face we had to pay our return fare to the countryside. We stayed there one day and then returned 'when called' two days later. All that was in September 1977."

I look at her and wonder aloud how so much could change so fast. Perhaps this round of changes in higher education was won because it was fought for rather than granted in "enlightened" fashion from the top down. Those who fought and risked, in the end, benefited very little from the changes they made possible. As she leaves, Shen Zhaoyan tells me her only wish: "to prolong my study here for one more year." She is a member of the last class of the worker-peasant-soldier group at Beida.

Her dream is impossible. Only the examination candidates will now have the luxury of a four-year undergraduate education. When they, the new elite, graduate, they will earn 50 or 60 yuan per month compared to the 30 or 40 earned by Shen Zhaoyan and her classmates. I hadn't known about these upcoming distinctions.

Neither could I have imagined how little they mattered in comparison to the thirst for learning that dominates the consciousness of this politicized, work-tested graduating class. Shen Zhaoyan just wants another year, to read more literature, to learn more about critical theory, perhaps to undertake a senior thesis, to conquer her own terror of writing. Not possible. Without conscious intention, she left me tonight with an appreciation of her victory, of her seasoned struggle. The qualities that make her strong and focused are unmatched by the chatty cadres' daughters who brush their teeth alongside me in the second-floor bathroom each morning.

I walk out to get hot water, grateful, again, to be in China, glad to know enough Chinese to ask some questions and enough to hear answers that would be unthinkable back home. My ears are tuned to Chinese more alertly nowadays. I hear a voice behind me. A Chinese man is walking along to get water. In a low, husky tone, he says something personal, direct, something like, "You sure look nice." I'm taken aback. This has never happened to me before in China. In over a month here, no male has imposed himself on me verbally, or in any other way. We get to the hot water shed, at the same time. No one else is around. At the sink, as we fill our thermoses, he starts again, in a low voice: "You are very, very pretty." I am surprised, and I let the hot water splash on him a bit maliciously. Still, he is only teasing in a mild, mild way, probably testing his "come-on" powers. Many things previously forbidden in the Mao era are being tried on for size in China these days.

For the first time in two months, Mao Zedong comes to mind explicitly. I wonder if it is my perceptions that are changing, or is Chinese reality changing too? What makes him so distant a figure? He seems nearly absent from ordinary, daily reflections. And yet it was he, and his vision of a socialist, non-elitist China, who made Shen Zhaoyan's education possible in the first place. I will, no doubt, come back to Mao again. China as a whole is reappraising its relationship to him, his thought, and his policies.

APRIL 22   *Putting on the brakes: hardened politics, soft watercolors*   Spring in Peking: soft, slow, dusty, muted, sensuous. Trees are small, branches scrawny and twisted. I have to look hard outside my window to notice the budding leaves. Walking outside in the drizzle so characteristic of North China at this time of the year, I nearly brush into the blooming pink and white lilacs. This weekend, the bushes spilled forth their colors as unobtrusively as the tiny fruit trees released their blossoms a couple of weeks ago. A casual swish of air brings their sweetness toward one's senses. So unlike the insistent sexuality of spring in New England: that dramatic abandonment of modesty as people shed bulky parkas and trees pierce the crisp air with the loud green-yellow of their leaves.

John and Wilma Fairbank were in town last week, august presences with modest insights. John's aura as the founder of American China studies, as the man whose name will grace the Harvard East Asian Center in perpetuity after his retirement, radiates through our group of foreign students in Peking. On Friday afternoon, we gather at the Canadian Embassy to meet and talk with the Fairbanks. Wilma begins with a slide show of the watercolors she painted while they lived just inside the city walls in the 1930s. Walls that no longer exist. She tells us of horseback rides to temples now mostly forgotten, of how they savored friendships with literati who are now either extinct or kept away from our generation of foreign students. We are victims of the rituals of "sino-foreign solidarity."

Forty years after the experience, Wilma emerges as a talented, reflective, playful observer of scenes which have been analyzed in John's more famous scholarship. Now, as possibly then, she seems freer in her response to China. Some contrasting images from her watercolors: John, in their courtyard, studying, propped on pillows amidst antique furniture, poring over flash cards full of Chinese characters. A self-portrait, on top of a mountain cliff, at a Daoist temple to which she climbed for two days to sketch a wispy-bearded priest. She returned home to finish a haunting portrait of the sage, no longer Chinese except for a priestly cap which caught her fancy because of its "Egyptian echoes." She captured in China, almost inadvertently, much of what was significant: the poor scavenging in rubbish, women students, nuns, architects, shy children, behind a mother's skirt or exposed in babypants or strangely familiar with their lotus-shaped "Halloween" lanterns.

John begins his talk self-consciously, purposefully historical. He's asking us to think about our genealogy as foreigners in Chinese society, to own up to our cultural in-betweenness, to reckon with the inevitable projection of ourselves onto all of our perceptions of Chinese life. Although I had read his ruminations about Marco Polo and the Jesuits in standard texts before, I hear him afresh this afternoon. I hear him grappling in new ways with the presence of the West in a culture whose history we have touched with our ideas, desecrated with imperialism, and now are called upon to rebuild with modern technology. This is a culture that has a long past prior to us and is determined to create a future not of our design.

I am moved, respond strongly to this vein of thought. I also find myself envying John and Wilma's nearness to those alley walls in the 1930s, walls which marked their apartness from as well as their commonality with other Peking residents. In the discussion period, I raise the precedent of May Fourth—that previous moment of flushed excitement and openness to the West in 1919. I remark how then, as now, we are part of a synthesis, a mixture of elements we cannot control yet so often mistake as tending our way.

Later, when I say goodbye to the Fairbanks, I feel a combination of warmth and uncertainty. I have started to know the two of them a bit over the past few years. With the ideological squabbles of the 1960s behind us, and the formal respect and fear of my graduate student days receding, I find myself caring for them as friends. Yet I'm far away from them, they are aging, and possibilities for leisurely talks become fewer and fewer. They leave me more open, more aware of myself in China. Also tense, shaken. I know that my perceptions count. They will have some historical weight back home. John and Wilma left few hints about how to experience China in a way broad enough to be at once comprehensible and convincing back home. So, I am floundering. How reliable are my perceptions here after all?

A recent snag in foreigners' perceptions of Chinese realities. Perhaps this is the source of my current worries. Back from Xian, all week I have been talking about my newly discovered freedom and liberation in China, about the safety and peace of mind of traveling alone as a woman. Yesterday, an English student who has many Chinese friends came by with an "internal document": a set of materials collected from current legal cases used for political education in the Philosophy Department. One document is called "Chen Jingshan and Twenty-six Other Criminal Elements— Reference Materials on Their Crimes." It begins with: "Chen Jingshan, twenty-three years old, male, Peking resident, teacher at No. 3 Middle School of ———— district. Earlier, given a one-year punishment for intention to rape. From 1978, was in charge of the class. Raped several girl students, telling them to keep this secret; beat boys brutally. September 28, 1978, was made to discontinue teaching, asked to consider his actions. Wanted to hide his crimes from the public, threatened girl students. October 1, 1978, tricked five girls (four aged fourteen, one aged thirteen) into coming to the bank of the Yong Ding River, tried to force them to jump into the river and drown themselves but failed. October 2, 1978, midnight, brought them to the south bank of the Yong Ding River canal, threatened them saying—'Today you leave your home never to return. You must drown in the water.' One of the five refused, was pushed by him into the canal first. He then pushed the other four into the canal; all drowned. He then attempted suicide but failed. Arrested October 4, 1978."

This document concludes with another item—Item 4: "Liu Fengying, thirty-seven years old, female, Hebei province. Ji Zongpai, thirty-four years old, male citizen of Peking. This couple had been having sex since 1975. Wanted to marry but Liu was married already, her husband would not agree to a divorce. September 12, 1978, Ji raped Liu and urged her to leave her husband. September 13, 1978, at 8 P.M. Liu put poison into rice and gave it to her husband. Husband died of poisoning."

Sexual violence exists in China. I never intended the record of my experience to be evidence against that possible fact. I simply dwelled on my trip to Xian and the group of older men on the train, who, though drunk, were yet scrupulous in their respect toward a young woman. But then, I saw the scene with my foreigner's eye; too hungry for evidence of something better than what I knew at home. It seems I ignored other facts. I have to learn to look harder. One young woman spared sexual advances on the Xian train does not mean that another older one, like the one mentioned in Item 4, is not publicly excoriated for her sexual behavior. A strange twist in China's sexist ideology here. A murderer must be portrayed as at once lustful adulteress and rape victim. How else can she appear so extraordinary in her rather ordinary passions? This is a question I keep turning over in my mind now. Does the "Twenty-six Other Criminal Elements" document render void views I gathered on the trip to Xian? I feel a bit foolish, vulnerable now.

I have been getting letters from friends back home asking about recent changes of the tide in China. My answer emphasizes the political reanchoring of Chinese youth after half a year of drifting under general slogans of modernization. In the last few days, more and more Westerners in China are using the phrase "crackdown." There is something more going on, not just disappointment that modernization did not, in the end, bring about the Westernization hoped for.

Evidence is mounting these days of arrests among intellectuals affiliated with the Democracy Wall movement. Chinese roommates of Western students at Beida are having more and more frequent meetings on a topic broadly defined as "discipline." It is getting harder to find out what that means. Roommates are more covert about the time and content of these meetings. A French woman here is particularly worried: Her Chinese roommate told her casually that she was going to a meeting with her department when another Chinese girl revealed this was a school-wide meeting, the third one in two weeks. Half-truths are beginning to creep into our relations with Chinese friends.

I, too, am aware of a deepening depression among my Chinese friends over the past two weeks. This depression is sparked not so much by the public prohibition against demonstrations and wall posters as by an official distortion of public memory. Two weeks ago, official publications commemorated the 1976 movement as "Party-led." For the hundreds of thousands who participated in this bit of history, this is a bold lie. Those who now read about the Party-led movement have no place to file away the certainty that they had participated in a sudden outbreak against Party autocracy. They know that their courage to speak out against arbitrary authority in 1976 did not come out of their Party membership, but was expressed in spite of it. Now, the new regime is distorting the past by official mummification. With their own history stolen, these youths have little to rely on to counter or to defy prohibitions against gathering in the Tian An Men Square on April fifth each year. Still, the government fears that such gatherings might spark the flame of critical thinking anew.

It might be right. Chinese youths are despondent but not forgetful. The word used by foreign journalists to describe this mood is "turning of the tide." Chinese students themselves use another term—*shache*, "putting on the brakes." This expression hints at something covert and painful. *Shache*, an idiom used publicly for "checking an unhealthy tendency," is now being used privately to bemoan and explain the "cutting off of power" experienced by many young people.

Something has changed, both objectively and subjectively. The democracy movement is being curtailed as "counterproductive," it "hinders" the drive for modernization. Fewer and fewer wall posters, in spaces that are more and more limited, speak in increasingly tame and innocuous voices. At the same time, many of the people who never put up posters in the first place, but enjoyed reading them—who appreciated the promise of intellec-

One of the last cartoons posted on Democracy Wall. It depicts a confused intellectual, unable to keep up with the changing ideological winds.

tual emancipation which began last year—are finding out that "democracy" was something "given" to them. A conditional, tentative indulgence from above, it is now being taken back. Youthful supporters of democracy find themselves to be actors stranded on a stage. For a brief moment, they had believed they were "natural" spokesmen of a governmentally sanctioned, world-wide trend toward fuller human rights.

Sadly, what is hitting them hard now, as it did their May Fourth predecessors in the early 1920s, is the realization that intellectual radicals are beneficiaries of a privileged status they do not control. They are not architects of a new social reality. Like the May Fourth radicals sixty years ago, the current generation will have to choose between the despondency of powerless—*shache'*d—ideas and the gritty effort of making themselves understood and believed by the masses. On April 5, 1976, something did happen. But it was too little to create an enduring mass movement. Participants in that happening chose to interpret themselves as spokesmen for all of Chinese society. For two years now they have been permitted that illusion by officials who needed the legitimating mantle of Zhou Enlai.

I can't tell yet whether young Chinese intellectuals today have the resiliency of the May Fourth generation, the drive to make their own history count. Most of the students I know at Beida seem too eager for individual success, for a chance to learn to speak English well, for a crack at good, travel-related jobs. These are goals which the "democracy tide" made it possible to express. But they probably can be delivered without democracy as well.

Some students, on the other hand, are tougher, less skilled in talk about "mental emancipation," and more steeled in resistance against the official line—people like Shen Zhaoyan, who, with a few hardy others, fought her way into this institution in 1976, the year of the April Fifth movement.

So I am forced, again, to confront my own murky perceptions of China, my own even murkier projections onto China. I find myself still hoping that the revolution will go on. I take some consolation from John Fairbank's informed conviction that the revolution is far from over. We probably mean different things by *revolution*, but it doesn't much matter. He and I share a doubt about the current sighs of relief in the West—relief that the social turmoil in China is over, that China's era of prosperous, enlightened, mutually enriching collaboration with capitalist nations has begun.

I also take some heart in what I see and hear around me daily. A conversation with the taxi driver last night, a twenty-four-year-old ex-soldier from Nanjing, now lonely, overworked, and underpaid in Peking. He laughs hard as he tells how he became so thin and lost his innocence. He describes the good life he had in the People's Liberation Army working as personal chauffeur to some high cadre. Now, he wants to join other cab drivers in a "strike" (really a slowdown) for better food, right in front of the foreigners' eyes at the Peking Hotel: "We cannot call it a strike, you know, since we are forbidden to strike by law in our country. But we workers do it nonetheless. Just like what we saw on TV three or four months ago about workers and the unemployed in the United States. All that, of course, was before we were swamped with more recent programs about your so-called fine, advanced technology and modernized industry."

I remain unimpressed about the Chinese roots of the "democracy movement." Still, I am optimistic about the transformation of consciousness begun by Mao and his generation of May Fourth intellectuals. The changes championed by Mao have less to do with freedom to think, and more with participation in mass rebellion. Something about his concern with how to be the subject of one's own social existence, rather than the object of naturalized social relations, lingers on in China today.

APRIL 28 *No longer horseback: frogs in spring rice paddies* There is an apt Chinese expression about fleeting perspectives: "ride a horse to look at flowers."
This has been the hallmark of the American perspective since the opening of China in the early 1970s. We used to come to China for two or three weeks, rush through major cities, take as many pictures as we could. We used to scavenge each encounter with a cab driver, vendor, child, or passing woman, to glimpse the "real China." Back home, eager audiences spurred us on to talk, write, pontificate. So, we slipped into the role of "new China hands" without ever summing up critically what the old ones had learned. We didn't stop long enough to realize that in the new

China foreign hands were to be more like appendages, reflecting views from a confident yet elusive center.

My own trip in 1977 was like all the rest. The only difference: my muteness upon return. Unlike others who had traveled with me, I could not quite grasp my impressions in a way that felt publicly reliable. I did give one slide show at Wesleyan, and a joint talk and slide show in Hartford with a woman from our trip. Unlike me, she was quite unembarrassed by the fleeting quality of our time in China, unencumbered by ignorance of Chinese names, Chinese history. That fall of 1977, I taught my best course yet on traditional Chinese history, perhaps obliquely inspired by fleeting views of a counter-history I had glimpsed on our tour. Peasant uprisings in ancient dynasties were documented so pervasively then in China's public places. My impossible dream in 1977, as I entered Hong Kong, tearful about leaving China behind: "If only I could ever have two months there."

I have been in China eight weeks now. Long enough to still feel the thrill of being one of the first Americans to live here since the Cold War. But the thrill has become milder. I am finally able to catch my breath. The weight of responsibility to see everything, to talk to as many Chinese people as possible, is less crushing. I have ten more months here and will have plenty of time to rethink back home. So, I am slowly starting to dismount: a couple of days ago, walking to get boiled water from the shed two buildings away, I had time to see tiny wild violets beneath the thick and drooping white lilacs. Also, I had time to pick some of each, in defiance of school regulations against using public adornments in private dwellings.

Today, riding my bike back to school, in a foul mood despite the spring warmth (and in spite of the by-now-familiar stares which quickly enough change into smiles) I huff along a rice paddy outside the university side gate. My sullenness is confronted by the green-yellow of the sprouting shoots. My grumpy silence suddenly pierced by a cacophony of frogs calling to each other in the filmy wetness.

Before coming to live here, I had read so much about the unique color of young rice, about how it was used as a signal for fertility rites in ancient China, about couples copulating in the fields. When I lived in Taiwan, in 1973–74, I saw rice seedlings transplanted twice. Still, I had never heard how alive rice paddies can be. Now, here, I am finally dismounting. Off the horse, I am learning to stop the race for quick impressions.

This afternoon, running with Christine, a Dutch economist friend, I decide to share with her the noise of the paddy. We jog to the east gate, walk along the mud ridge into the paddy, squat peasant-style, and listen for a long, long time. Long enough to feel that our newly stretched muscles are no match for the habitual suppleness of market-town idlers in China, long enough to see and smell the film of human refuse that floats on the paddy water. So that's what makes those frogs ever so comfortable and riotous! Long enough to imagine what it must be like to step in that mud, among those croaking creatures, to transplant rice seedlings. Chinese peasants have no galoshes for spring labor. Nothing much stands between them and the parasites that burrow underneath their skin.

Very little here to screen us Westerners from the obstacles and disappointments which are part of dismounting. My own mild whiff of "horse droppings" this week: Two months ago, I requested permission to attend the National Conference on the Sixtieth Anniversary of the May Fourth Movement, sponsored by the Academy of Social Sciences in Peking. Zhou Peiyuan, head of the Chinese Science Academy, seemed full of generous hints when I met him at the ceremonial reception the night after we arrived in China. There in front of the cameras, in the high mood of ritualized beginning, I had been introduced all around as the "May Fourth scholar from America," who would benefit from the conference and report back on the renaissance of scholarship in China today. For the past two months I have been riding on this mood of openness and intellectual intimacy. I expected some kind of fruition at the national conference.

I wrote two letters to confirm the informal invitation I received that ceremonial evening. An oblique response comes from the Foreign Students' Office at Peking University: "It doesn't look too possible." Reading this, I have no idea what is being denied to me or why. All these words are oblique. Further conversations don't clear matters any further: "Well, you see, there are so many other foreign scholars in China that we cannot afford this precedent."

"But no one else here is focusing research on May Fourth." I respond by explaining how my past work and this current opportunity will enable me to report in a well-informed, effective fashion to the scholarly community outside of China.

"Well, you see, we would like to help you, but really we have no authority."

I feel myself swimming in a sea of words. I decide to go through the American Embassy directly to the Ministry of Education—a lot of highhandedness for what I am convinced is beneficial for China's scholarly reputation abroad. (Amazing how fast, how subtly we identify our interest with China's benefit. Not much difference here between us and our nineteenth-century predecessors who were damned for their imperialist habits by the Chinese.)

No news for the past few days. I remain hopeful, reluctant to back down from my public position and my personal conviction that China is really "open" to scholarly communication. I decide to stay in town over the week of May 1 to May 4, when the university goes on vacation. I expect, still hope, for that invitation to the national conference. There is much joking among the foreign students about the missing feather in my cap, about all those buses we see gathering in front of the Academy of Social Sciences building. I am beginning to feel silly, not just frustrated and impatient. I went to the Foreign Students' Office yesterday to ask again. The answer, even after an Embassy letter, turns out to be "not possible." The refusal is still oblique, but unbudgeable.

I leave fuming about the shortsightedness of the Chinese authorities, angry at myself for having been caught up in this cycle of promises and disappointments, furious at being in a passive situation, at the mercy of a bureaucratic structure staffed by cautious officials who have no stake in rocking the boat. All this I knew before, as I knew about seedlings and flowers, from horseback. My own impotent rage yesterday is an intimation, perhaps, of what it means to live with rather than theorize about Chinese bureaucracy. I wonder if Max Weber, who wrote about the rationalization of charisma in the celestial empire, really understood the inertia that lies beneath the striking edifice of Chinese organization. I am not sure I do. Having dismounted from horseback, I smell something. Whatever I smell tells me I'm not quite prepared for China.

And yet. Dismounting from horseback doesn't change the scene, only our perception of it. Living in China means simply (simply?)

that I will have to relearn much of what I knew before. Here, after hankering for an official opening into my area of specialized knowledge, I keep finding that I learn the most when I go the Chinese way—the way that is circuitous but efficient.

For example, by enrolling in the Literature Department I am able to carry on research in intellectual history, something that would be impossible in the History Department, which is still thwarted by the requirements of political ideology.

Another instance, the visit to the "February Seventh" locomotive factory last Thursday, where we hear two old workers retell the story, the history of the 1923 strike which marked the proletarian beginnings of the Chinese revolution. One of the workers, now eighty-one, spoke for about an hour.

Some bits of what I took down, as close to verbatim as I could: "Please understand that we workers still lack culture [*wenhua*], so our contribution to politics is necessarily limited. But let me first talk to you about the economic and social background of China at the turn of the century." This old worker then goes on to give an informed analysis of the demise of the last dynasty and the shortcomings of the revolution of 1911, which toppled the last emperor and inaugurated the period of internal chaos and outward floundering known as the Warlord Era.

"I remember well," he claims, "the decade of 1910 to 1920, all those changes of rulers in Peking." He goes on to name all the warlords whose names I have never been able to keep straight either for my doctoral orals or in my modern Chinese history lectures.

"The first Marxists in China, you see, were intellectuals, mostly students from Peking University," the old man tells us. "They knew little about the working class, and nothing of the power of unity or organization. In 1919–20, both the Marxist students and the central government set up schools for the 'common people.'" Then he describes at length how these schools competed for the workers' attention, how the first local strike succeeded in meeting a few of the workers' demands, how one of their leaders was bought off by the boss. He gets especially excited as he recalls how workers found the turncoat and beat him. Then he describes what it was like to scrounge for bits of food around the frying pan of the labor boss who then deducted half a day's pay for the scraps, how the nascent union chased out the already jittery French

Firsthand history at last:
the two retired locomotive
factory workers who
talked to us about their
experiences before and after
the 1923 strike.

and Belgian managers of the factory. Railroad workers, he insists,
were and still are in the best position to coordinate labor organizing in China, to transport propaganda and organizational mes-
sages among the other progressive, politicized unions. "The
seamen's union and the miners' union, after all, took part in the
revolution only later on." The story that emerges is one of many
struggles, of intermediate victories, of a tenuous but continuously
revitalized connection between the labor movement and the Communist Party, which eventually came to power through peasant
support.

I listen closely to the thin old man and go up to talk with him
some more during the break. His eyes are nearly closed with
exhaustion, and yellow mucus drips from their corners. But his

mind is sharp as he describes to me his struggle during the Anti-Japanese War, how he joined the Party after Liberation, how he finally got down to studying Marxism after his retirement, fifteen years ago. I marvel at his clear thinking, wondering again, as so often already in these past weeks, "Where else?"

Where else would a man who has labored hard and harshly for much of his life be given a chance to acquire knowledge which enhances rather than denigrates his own life experience? There is something very political about this octogenarian's lack of senility. It is not that opportunities for oral history or adult education are absent in Appalachia or on the Lower East Side of New York. Just that in China, workers are not inadvertent sources for an awkward tale of woe, but esteemed witnesses of a victory they helped to create. They hardly know the theoretical reasons why "the working class must inherit the future." But they know enough to want to tell their story and to make it compelling for the rest of society. In their old age, these workers have learned more about the meaning of their own past. The Party did not school them out of their experience, rather it gave them a chance to become smarter as they grew older. So unlike the pitiful aging that is portrayed in boarding-house interviews in the movie *Union Maids* back home.

My last view as we leave the factory: the old man being led by the factory manager to the bathroom to relieve himself. The cadre's arm is touching the old man gingerly, as one might handle a treasure. Where else indeed.

Last night I went for a walk in the Forbidden City with a foreign friend whom I knew from Taiwan. Five years ago he was an ex-Green Beret squirming out of nightmares, and I was blundering along with theories about intellectuals and revolutions. We shared some love, some travel, some silliness in learning Mandarin among the Taibei mandarins. Then we lost touch for three years. Neither of us expected to meet again. Certainly not in Peking. And yet a combination of will and circumstance (which China both invites and facilitates) brought us together during his tour from Hong Kong. We caught up on our pasts quickly. All that made much easier for having so much to rethink together about China. After my factory visit and his trip to the Great Wall and the Ming Tombs, we meet for dinner and go for a walk.

I suggest the Forbidden City. I had read in a recent novel, *The*

Song of Youth, that it used to be the hiding place for Communist students in the 1930s. Laughing, high on our re-found comradeship and good Peking wine, we approached the Tian An Men entrance to the Forbidden City. This "Gate of Heavenly Peace" has become the symbol of social change in the half century from the May Fourth demonstration of 1919 to the Red Guard rallies of the Cultural Revolution in the 1960s. I remember that during my 1977 slide show, I talked of how the Forbidden City had been built to intimidate. The pictures I took then were meant to convey an architecture which had made barbarians shiver with awe and Chinese ministers tremble with fear as they approached the Son of Heaven. Imperial audiences were most often held at dawn— that eerie hour when a rider set out in the dark to arrive at the gates of the imperial palace with the first sun rays. The golden roof shimmered with a shade of gold reserved for the Forbidden City only. The visitor, then, would dismount in the haze and walk through hall after hall filled with soldiers, eunuchs, to the inner courtyard. There the Emperor sat, still-distant, ceremonious, forbidding.

I remember telling my audience in 1977 as I flashed slides of the Forbidden City: "Imagine it is dark and you are walking miles toward your dawn audience with the Son of Heaven." Well, all that imagining turned out to be a highly abstract intimation of the fear and awe I feel as we walk through Tian An Men Gate on Thursday night. Bicyclists are few, pedestrians absent. We giggle during the long minutes it takes us to walk through the courtyard, past the stables and slave quarters to yet another gate.

Then, we find ourselves at the red-walled courtyard that was— and is—the main entrance to the Forbidden City. In this huge open plaza, two parapets jut out, crowned by sentry towers from the Ming dynasty. These towers pull one deep into the darkness, toward the two golden characters marking this as the "Central Gate." About fifteen stories high, the structure encloses within its painted darkness an iron-studded wooden gate that is ten times our height. Its golden handles are well above anyone not elevated on a chariot or on human backs.

It is 10.30 at night, total silence. Terrified, I hold on to my friend's hand. I joke nervously about the evil ghosts of dead emperors. No puns in Chinese about the well-deserved demise of "ruling classes" insulate me now from a bodily understanding of the psychology of terror enshrined in stone here.

So I am slowly, at times fearfully, unlearning and relearning the Chinese history I had studied and taught from books. The same is required with respect to present-day China. My notions, not unlike those of journalists from the West, have been overly colored by the recent opening of China and by the loudly proclaimed modernization movement. Everyone seems to be bemoaning the "turning of the tide of Westernization." Perhaps this is something that never was.

I read today *Newsweek*'s special "Peking Clamps Down" by James Pringle. In January, when he first came to China, Pringle dwelt on the "relaxed mood." He focused on the phenomenon of dissent, on the call for human rights, and the "praise of the capitalist West" which he thought he saw there. Now, back in China after three months, he confesses: "a Westerner cannot help but feel depressed about China's political and economic rollback." He concludes: "Given China's traditions, perhaps this is the best that one can hope for." Pringle, like so many of us Americans here, can't help being thrilled about "new romantic movies" in China, about "the new legal framework to curb arbitrary arrests and detention." Yet, he is worried, a touch hysterical in fact, about restrictions on dancing parties. Rumors about increased punishments for "selling secrets to foreigners" proliferate. Pringle's fears are based on premonitions that the Peking Police Bureau is "discouraging informal contacts between Chinese and foreigners." These rumors, not surprisingly, hit hardest journalists riveted by Democracy Wall posters, the only "news" not far from their isolation in the Peking Hotel. Pringle concludes: "the government seems to be encouraging the traditional xenophobia of the Chinese. . . . Officials have revived a play called 'The Teahouse' with a message that everything bad in China always stemmed from foreigners. The show plays to full houses."

Pringle, a "horserider" by force of circumstance, misses some of the most fragrant "flowers." *The Teahouse* is, according to my Chinese friends, a concrete sign of the "intellectual emancipation" begun by the Deng Xiaoping regime about a year and a half ago. It is a play written by Lao She, one of China's most talented modern authors, an intellectual who committed suicide during the Cultural Revolution. The fact that it is being performed again is a tribute to its talented, rebellious author, now begrudgingly recognized as a martyr of the Gang of Four. The play itself is rich in details of life at the turn of the twentieth century. Its complex, skilled use of Pekinese dialect, a verbal delight even for us foreign speakers of Chinese, is finally sanctioned once again.

Strange how Pringle uses this play to raise the specter of Chinese tradition. Such reports spare us confrontation with our own preconceptions about China and its "built-in limits on freedom." Is the xenophobia which Pringle reports, after all, just a sign that China is not going the way of the West?

And yet. Antiforeignism is hardly absent in China today. Rumors of an assault on black students in Nanjing turn out to be true enough. A wave of wall posters preceded the incident attacking the Chinese government for excessively high fellowships to foreign students. At a time of material scarcity for China's own college candidates, this is an explosive issue indeed.

Here in Peking, a personal, very material experience of antiforeignism. Riding my bike through the campus on Saturday, I come upon workers spraying the trees with white bug-killing chemicals. One of them quickly, purposefully turns the hose on me as I ride by. With face, clothes, bicycle covered with the white stuff, I arrive at the dorm a bit stunned. I tell the story to the Chinese house-matrons and to my Dutch friend, Christine.

I am more amazed by my lack of response than by the man's action. At that moment, something in me acquiesced, guiltily, to Chinese xenophobia. I ask myself what prevented me from yelling back, "Hey, what the hell is wrong with you?" Instead, I rode on, filled with a vague terror that all Chinese hate all Westerners beneath it all. The strange legacy of imperialism?

The point is that if and when we dismount as horseriders in China, we are bound to step through some shit. The unsightly things that await us include not only Chinese prejudices, but our own as well.

CHAPTER 3

MAY 1979 *Official History and Beyond*

MAY 1 *Setback: May Fourth Conference debacle*

I am more rankled by the Academy of Social Sciences' refusal to let me attend the national conference on the May Fourth movement than I can admit, even to myself. In the morning I wake up imageless, but a line keeps recurring from a dream: "You don't have to answer my very important question." Perhaps I have been trying too hard to prove my ability to report on the conference. Am I being driven by anything more than the pride of being the only foreign observer there?

The conference, like my studies of the May Fourth movement itself, is too laden with subjective concerns. My questions about the relationship of intellectuals and revolution have yet to become truly historical. What I would like to understand through research now is how intellectuals revolutionize culture. How does revolutionary politics affect intellectuals? This dialectic between history and consciousness has been the subject of my work for over a decade already. But that work has been burdened by a quarrel with the paradigm of "the tragedy of intellectuals" which has characterized so much Western scholarship on modern Chinese history. I want, and need, to move beyond criticism to actual scholarship. But in this, China frustrates me.

The "nail hit" (*peng dingzi*, a Chinese expression for running into unforeseen obstacles) is that my question doesn't matter to Chinese authorities in quite the way that it matters to me. I have tried to use my scholarly prestige, I have sent my credentials to the U.S. Embassy to be forwarded to the Chinese Ministry of

74

Education. I have argued with Peking University authorities about the public benefit that would result from my attendance at the national conference on May Fourth: "I might be able to persuade doubting Western academics about the renaissance of Chinese scholarship after the Gang of Four, you know."

Still, the authorities are not persuaded. From reports in the official media I gather that the conference has not been "purely scholarly." The name of the Academy of Social Sciences seems to have been attached to an essentially Communist Party affair. Old May Fourth luminaries have been invited to inspire and to admonish Chinese youth about modernization. The speeches reported in the daily papers are dull, predictable in their orthodox watering-down of the May Fourth cultural rebellion. All that is being commemorated is scientific study.

Nonetheless, the photos that accompany these articles interest and excite me. I feel cheated out of a chance to witness the mood of commemoration. I wonder to myself: How much could I learn about generational differences if only I could see and hear octogenarians like Xu Deheng sing songs and share anecdotes with young Communist activists?* I catch myself wanting to be part of a history that is not mine. I remember how I used to berate my own students for seeking refuge from our Western present in China's past. I remember, too, that refuge is different from learning. So I try not to narrow my quest to unanswerable questions.

Strange that Western journalists should dwell so much on "the cutting down of formal contacts with Chinese." Perhaps they are spending too much time in dance halls. Mingling between foreigners and local people is, indeed, nearly forbidden. But other avenues of intimacy persist. Last Saturday night I was alone in my room. For the first time in five weeks, there is no dinner, no dance, no party to go to with one or another of my American friends. I try to rouse up some company but find others already have plans. So I hole up for the evening to write in this journal. At 7:30, halfway through the first page, Gao Yangming comes in. He is an instructor in the Economics Department. We had one previous conversation during a school trip to see a foreign movie.

*Four years later, in the spring of 1983, I did get to meet Xu Deheng. Our conversation about the historical significance of the May Fourth movement was reported in the *People's Daily* of May 27, 1983.

On the bus back I mentioned the Fairbanks' recent visit to Peking. Gao told me that there are three elderly professors in the Economics Department who have Harvard Ph.D.'s and who knew Fairbank in Cambridge. I was enthusiastic, but casual in letting him know how much I would like to meet Chinese intellectuals of this generation. They hold the key to a history I have studied from books too long. "I'll see what I can do for you," he said. I assumed this was a polite way of saying no.

On Saturday night, the last person I expect to see is Gao. He comes in, clearly wanting to chat (I whip the page of my journal out of my typewriter since he reads English well). "I talked to all three old professors. Two are in poor health, but one, Chen Zhenhan, really the most interesting, is well and has agreed to see you. How about next Monday at 3:00 in the afternoon?"

We go on to talk about how useful it would be for me if I could get inside the Peking Municipal Library. Yangming reads Western periodicals there once a month. But, not surprisingly, I cannot. It is still closed to foreign scholars, and to most Chinese researchers as well. (Gao himself got a card only after a highly placed friend of his, another young Communist cadre, left him his card when he was moved out of the Peking area.) Reading books in China these days is more a matter of reward for political reliability than a recognition of scholarly necessity.

Gao complains at length about China's backwardness. What bothers him is not only that his homeland is economically underdeveloped—the way any Communist might think—but also that it is so far behind in the intellectual emancipation proclaimed publicly. Most Chinese, he tells me, are still afraid to think for themselves; "Consequently, they fear foreigners rather than want to learn from them." I listen to his "underside" version of the recent wave of "learning from the West." In my room, tonight, this young, not very worldly Communist cadre is struggling to define some livable, implementable criteria of critical thought. "You would have to include more openness to Westerners as individuals, a more varied, refined sense of the West—the once all bad now all good version won't do." He asks me for more critical sources about the American economy and the theory of marketplace competition.

"If critical thought is really to thrive in China," he argues, "scholars like you would have to be able to move about more freely. Certainly, you should be able to use the Municipal Library." He shares openly in my disappointment about the Academy of Social Sciences' refusal (I tell him of my anger because it is too difficult to hide it tonight). He goes on to express his hope that I have other chances to meet with open-minded Chinese intellectuals. I am just about to tell him of my fine, open relationship with the Literature Department when there is another knock at my door. Since it's 8:30 on a Saturday night, I am surprised. A bit worried, too, about being found and interrupted in this "informal contact" when informal contacts are supposedly being cut back by "order of official leaders." I open my door and find Wang Tiansheng, a history professor, and his wife—another spontaneous visit.

They live in a dorm two blocks away. Still, I never really expected a sudden visit, much less a family one. At first I am nervous, but Gao and Wang seem to know each other well. The older intellectual had taught the younger one in 1975–76. It seems they have become closer since then. They recall sitting next to one another on a bench and "sharing frank thoughts" during a mass meeting at Peking University called to denounce the Gang of Four.

It soon becomes clear that Gao Yangming respects and admires Wang Tiansheng. He knows himself to be both less knowledgeable about Marxism and less courageous than Wang about speaking his mind. Both are Communist cadres. Wang, in turn, is open and nurturing toward Gao, much the way he treats other worker-peasant-soldier students in his large lecture classes. Wang's wife is a fine-looking, intense, quiet women. She is not quite comfortable during this, her first visit to an American's room. Yet she is not too worried or scared about "consequences."

I rush around, offer tea, coffee, bits of old cake, and some chewing gum—courtesy of my parents in Miami. I am delighted that my solitary Saturday night is turning out to be an occasion to meet with and make Chinese friends.

Wang brought me copies of an article I am planning to translate about a literary controversy. Like the author of the article, he has doubts about whether an intellectual who comes from a petit bourgeois background can ever become fully and completely a Marxist-Leninist. His doubts run counter to the certainties of more ahistorical party ideologues. The more we talk, the more I realize that Wang delights in his own doubts. He quotes Lenin to support his own tampering with the Party's more dogmatic "sacred truths."

Gao Yangming, the younger colleague, grasps only part of this high-flown discussion. Still, he wonders aloud: "Isn't China's problem exactly that Mao Zedong's thought was once considered all too infallible, too immutable?"

Wang and Gao start a fast-paced conversation. They tell each other about inner doubts during the Gang of Four era. I learn that they both went down to Tian An Men Square on the night of April 4, 1976, on the eve of the mass demonstration. Forbidden to attend by the University Party Committee, they went nonetheless, furtively. They returned home, Mrs. Wang adds, to share doubts and hopes "behind closed doors." They talked about how good it is to be justified by subsequent history.

I miss some of what they are saying. The conversation is moving too fast. Still, I can tell that there is something novel in this political sharing among three Chinese guests in a foreign student's dormitory room. All three have lived through much, and thought deeply, repeatedly about events that happened around and to them. That thinking, perhaps more than any of their activities, enables them now to recover from a demoralizing decade of twists and turns.

I ask them how they survived. How were they able to maintain their critical faculties as Marxists, their faith as Communist Party members? They tell me, in turn, about "repeated relapses," about wavering beliefs that now strengthen critical reflection.

I am not sure I understand them fully, either their words or ideas. I tell them how disillusioned Westerners doubt that there are any Marxists left in China, if there ever were any.

We talk about Togliatti and Gramsci, the Italian Communist theoreticians (a British student had recently bet that no Chinese had heard anything about Togliatti or Gramsci). I tell my guests about the concern and sympathy of Western liberals for Chinese intellectuals during the Cultural Revolution. They answer, "We need understanding, not sympathy."

They leave around 11. Some optimistic last words about "Western friends" who might be able to contribute to that understanding. I promise to try. I know I owe it to myself as much as to them.

Monday morning in the library. I have been putting off the

"opportunity" to read old newspapers and magazines, part of the archives now officially opened to me. Both the History and the Literature departments have been urging me to go on with my research project on May Fourth intellectuals. The Literature Department forwarded to library authorities a list of rare periodicals which I drew up for the 1920s. The History Department presented the same authorities with five pages of sources that they believe essential for my studies. Today I decide to look up a 1918 treatise, "On Ibsenism." I find it and try to get it duplicated. I want to lessen my time away from the daily learning about China that waits outside the library door.

This Monday there is a small breakthrough. I will be able to use the off-limits faculty reading room on the fourth floor. Materials will no longer be brought down to me through the crowded, stuffy student reading rooms. The fourth floor sanctuary turns out to be precious not only because of its proximity to the stacks of old journals. It has many windows. It is also the room which houses current Western-language periodicals.

I am ushered upstairs. I run into Li Renjiang, an elderly history professor who seems to have been looking for me. We have talked a few times before. Always he tries to be very helpful. At the same time, he is unable to control some huge fear that comes through in discomfort and awkwardness. He seems both drawn to me and trapped by his contact with me. This morning, he wants to introduce me to library authorities, to be sure I get all the help I need. I mention to him that my adviser from Stanford, Lyman Van Slyke, is coming to Peking at the end of May, that he might be a good person to talk with the department faculty. (They had asked me to lecture on contemporary American approaches to Chinese history. I turned them down for now.)

Professor Li is visibly upset, as if I had wounded him: "It would have to be arranged; it is all very difficult, you know. I'll try to raise the matter with the others . . ." Something so anguished in his manner. He looks, acts terrified. His lips tremble, his hands scratch at the zipper of his bookbag.

I say goodbye quickly, wanting to end his discomfort, also to remove myself from a fear that is nameless, yet something I can almost smell. I don't like my response. Something uncomfortably familiar here, something an American friend recently called the "bourgeois intellectual's hatred of weakness."

I mention these feelings to Christine, my Dutch friend. She suggests that I voice my discomfort explicitly to Professor Li before too long. She suggests I ask him outright why he is so afraid. A tale of persecution may be buried there that could either be spilled out or buried deeper. She warns me that all this is worthwhile only if I can take the risk, if I am prepared for the overwhelming openness or absolute retreat that might follow. I am not. Yet.

I am ashamed to realize how much I have fled from this man's story, how I "reasoned" it was unsayable. I used to believe I came to China to learn more about intellectuals and revolution. In fact, I find I act not unlike my predecessors—the missionaries, the businessmen, the educators, and the revolutionaries. All wanted to see what they already knew.

I resolve to talk to Professor Li soon, when the time and the occasion is appropriate. Just now, I am glad that this afternoon I will meet the Harvard-trained economist Chen Zhenhan, an intellectual whose tale I gather is also full of hardship. But I also hear that he carries himself with remarkable composure despite twenty years of public harassment as a "rightist element."

Professor Chen is in his early seventies, spry, and well dressed. He has a strong, skilled, analytical mind. It is a privileged occasion. I hoped to be relaxed during our first meeting. So, I try to dwell on anecdotes about his experiences as a student at Harvard. To be sure, the anecdotes reveal something about how Western know-how applies or does not apply to China.

Details about Chen Zhenhan's educational career come out swiftly, as he keeps asking me about mine: born in Zhejiang, home of many Confucian scholars as wall as Jiang Jieshi (Chiang Kai-shek) and Lu Xun. He studied as an undergraduate at Nankai University, a prestigious center for modern social science in Tianjin. His professors there in the 1930s had Ph.D.'s from the United States. He was in the third group of nationally selected examination candidates. With a three-year fellowship, he went off to study at Harvard in 1936. Actually, it took him four years to pass the oral exams and to finish his dissertation on the development of the cotton industry from New England to the South.

As we talk, it becomes clear to me that he knows America well. At the same time, he seems remarkably free of the vanity and the vague longings of other elderly American-educated Chinese intellectuals I have met. He speaks of the "few friends I had there.

I had to work and study all the time. You know, Fairbank was one of my friends. In those years he was just an instructor." He tells me how he traveled around the country, how he watched closely the end of the depression, the coming of the war. This quest for personal impressions probably set him apart from other Chinese students in the United States at that time. "So many others stuck to Chinese circles or got lost in the temptations of American modernity."

Professor Chen's insight and dignity today, in the end, have little to do with his Harvard Ph.D. (he turned in his Harvard diploma in the early 1950s as a sign of his dedication to the new, Communist regime). His strength comes from history. It is not a history he has contributed to actively. Not long after he returned to war-ravaged China in the late 1940s, he was labeled a "rightist element" in 1957. Rather, it is the history he has endured that has made him so tough. For two decades, Chen Zhenhan lived in more or less public disgrace. He was rehabilitated a few months ago.

What is most striking today is how much he has learned from that history, the evenhanded way in which he recounts it now. Clearly, he has tried to give his best to the New China (although I guess he never joined the Communist Party). During the years when he went from being chairman of the department to persona non grata, he edited the economics documents of the last dynasty: "They are not published yet, of course."

After an hour or so, our conversation drifts rather naturally toward the Cultural Revolution. He becomes visibly tense. His knees shake but his voice remains firm and direct. With his eyes on mine, unflinching, in a manner so direct, so rare in China, he tells me: "I was sent to the countryside to work in a farm labor camp from autumn 1969 to the summer of 1971. I was in my late sixties, but by no means the oldest in our group. My wife was sent down as well, to another part of the country with her institute. It was a bitter, bitter experience, but an experience nonetheless."

He goes on to talk about the situation in China during those years. His own predicament fades into the background as he speaks about his concern for the social disorder that had spread everywhere: "Most factories had no bookkeeping for nearly a decade. The entire staff of the Central Board of Statistics was sent down to the countryside. How can you possibly have planning under these conditions?"

He uses the English expression "mob rule" to describe what happened in China during the Cultural Revolution. He tells me that socialism is better for China than capitalism, and that the material base necessary for building communism has not yet been achieved in China.

He believes that Mao's policy toward intellectuals was "right" in the early 1950s. It was correct to try to change one's consciousness, one's "world view," then. He had been attacked at that time as well. What seems to him very different, very "wrong," is the "reckless use of class struggle" that wrecked Chinese society during the Cultural Revolution.

I listen hard to his focused reasoning. I wish my Chinese language skills were better, that I knew more so that I could draw him out on issues of his academic specialty. We say goodbye after two hours. His handshake is strong, his eyes warm. He tells me that he hopes we will meet again, and I believe he means it.

The one concept that kept coming back to my mind over and over again during our conversation was academic freedom. Is it something peculiar, limited to Western societies? The more I think about it the less clear the problem becomes. I guess this is what China does: It shakes our certainties, especially those least examined. Over dinner with an English student I ask: "What do we mean back home about 'freedom of academic discussion'?" We agree that it is something to do with freedom to persuade others of our version of the facts.

Few Chinese intellectuals understand the double connotation of the English expression "academic freedom." Sometimes, it is "merely academic" freedom, circumscribed to ideas only. My British friend tells me of the quiet exasperation with Party interference in academic life which he hears from Chinese friends. I, too, sense an unspoken but absolute conviction among younger students that the Party, with its blatant, politicized utilitarian notions, is all that stands between intellectuals and Truth.

I am left wondering when, if ever, these students will realize that there is not one single Truth—or at least not one that can be considered permanently true. I wonder whether my friends here would even want to hear about the mutability of truth which is at the core of recent Western science (like Gödel's theory in mathematics). Maybe they want, need, an older "modernity."

MAY 2　*Brecht in China: a need* More than the freedom to think,
for absolute truth Chinese intellectuals long for the freedom to believe that truth exists. No wonder, then, that they find inspiration and solace in Galileo. No wonder, too, that they use and misread Bertolt Brecht, the German playwright.

A week ago I found out that Brecht's play *Galileo* had opened in Peking. According to one Westerner it was "a stunning production." It is impossible to get tickets at the public booths. The same afternoon that I hear the news, I march into the Foreign Students' Office at the university and tell the "responsible person" (by now nearly a friend after all our hassles over the Academy of Social Sciences conference) that I must get a ticket to this play. I tell him that I have written an article comparing Lu Xun and Brecht—a partial truth. I try to persuade this official of my premonition that contemporary China has much to learn from someone like Brecht. In the end, as always, he hedges: "Well, it is hard to get tickets, you know. Surely impossible to get them for all the students." "I'll see what I can do for you. By the way, did you see the newspaper essay introducing Brecht to Chinese audiences?"

"No. I would like to read it."

"Fine, I'll find it and clip it for you."

Today, as the possibility of an invitation to the May Fourth conference begins to recede even more, I push harder to get the Brecht ticket. I get my way. Another marginal victory. This one, however, is germane to my concerns about intellectuals and social change. Perhaps I have become too fixated on the May Fourth conference. This afternoon I get the ticket, and two articles: one from the official Chinese intelligentsia newspaper *Guangming ribao* and one from *China Youth*.

As I see Brecht performed in Peking and read those two articles, I am finally able to disentangle my own questions about Chinese intellectual history and the concerns of Chinese intellectuals around me. The way they approach Brecht today is not unlike the way their precursors approached Ibsen and Marx during the May Fourth movement. Emblematic ideas were repeatedly adapted to Chinese needs at a certain time and a certain place. Brecht is now used to mirror dilemmas inherent in a Chinese situation. Thus I am being forced to learn through Brecht about China and through China about the West. This, I am coming to see, is a circuitous but effective path.

The *Galileo* production was truly fine. There is a striking effort to be faithful to Western culture in the play. Chinese actors wear blonde and brunette wigs. They are covered with white face makeup. Eyeliner is used to create the illusion of blueish eyes. Sumptuous costumes approximate the papal court, the renaissance nobility, and Italian artisans. The music for the evening is entirely original yet evokes the style of post-renaissance madrigals and minuets. The ballads are faithful to the spirit of Brecht, the stage props stark, colorful abstracts. More impressive than the reproduction of a Western mood, however, is its innovative fidelity to Brecht's view of the rich and the poor. A ball in Rome, with its courtly robes and measured dance steps, is set off against a raucous peasant festival full of flirtation, masks, and racy jokes. The Chinese director of the play seems to have grasped the problem of class quickly, smartly. Maybe she is able to do justice to this aspect of Brecht's theater better than a Westerner because China's history and current social values allow and facilitate the portrayal of class differences, of class antagonisms.

And yet, this production does not do justice to the overall spirit of Brecht's *Galileo*. It is a morality play about Brecht's message of no morals. In the entrance to the theater, there is an exhibition about the play. A wall poster essay entitled "Is Galileo to Be Admired or Not?" is followed by a quote from Brecht: *"Galileo is not a tragedy."* On stage, however, as in the wall poster, we are presented with a tragedy: The noble scientist discovers truth and then betrays it, under political pressure. The acting is melodramatic. The climax comes during Galileo's interrogation by Church authorities: his disciples pray fervently to God that their master would not cave in under pressure from Rome. For a few minutes, they affirm their faith that "truth is the supreme virtue" in a joyful dance. In the next scene, the bell announces Galileo's recantation. The disciples sob despondently. The finest of Galileo's disciples, Anatole, the one described in the Chinese press as "proletarian and brilliant," collapses in agony. We, the audience, are meant to be shattered as well.

This Chinese *Galileo,* I am convinced, lacks Brecht's materialist, relativist approach to thought. Brecht tried to illustrate the mundane, physical *pleasure* of reason. This point is lost in the morality play staged in Peking. The handbill extracts the main message of the play: "Thought provides the loftiest happiness for mankind." Galileo's rowdy sensuality becomes ethereal here. This Chinese *Galileo* instructs not about the material basis of truth, but about brave defiance of authority.

In a society where for decades intellectuals have been thwarted in their quest for knowledge, it is no wonder that they turn for inspiration to the defiant Galileo. They are missing, however, Brecht's message that all truth is temporal, changeable, according to the needs and circumstances of its proponents and its opponents. The articles in *China Youth* and the *Guangming ribao* review Brecht in light of the current slogan "Search truth from facts." Their purpose seems to be to persuade China's political authorities to be more understanding toward truth and more forgiving toward those who seek and generate it.

The longing for "truth without fear and dread" is not Brecht's. It is the hope of contemporary Chinese intellectuals. They want and need some absolute, inviolable certainties after the bruising of the past two decades. Galileo thus attracts them while he remains incomprehensible, even repulsive in his betrayal. They salvaged the scientist's faith in absolute reason by damning the society in which he lived. The *Guangming* article concludes: "Galileo's weakness is an innocent one, a product of social circumstances. Society cheated Galileo and distorted his individual character. It was society that dealt with this genius scientist in a cool and heartless fashion. We, the audience, should not criticize him excessively. The people who would hate Galileo's shameless betrayal must first hate the inhumane society which produced him."

In these lines, as on the stage, part of an ongoing self-apology of Chinese intellectuals. They want forgiveness for being meek during the Cultural Revolution. So, now they crave the possibility of permanent truth.

I leave the theater a bit more aware of their complex predicament. Saddened, too, that their need for absolutes prevents them from hearing Brecht's consolation that truth is always social, always artificial, and therefore changeable. As I take the bus back to the university, I wonder how my Chinese friends would interpret the play. I doubt they can get tickets.

Tonight is the day after International Workers' Day. There is a cool breeze through the Peking streets, still festive with silk flags. A row of red flags alternates with yellows, greens, pinks, and blues. Yesterday I spent the morning translating the articles on Brecht, then riding my bike in the afternoon flow of Peking residents. I, too, luxuriate in this rare day off. There were no parades. They are considered expensive leftovers from the Gang of Four period. So, people are really free. Nowhere in particular where one must go, no powerful attraction that cannot be missed.

The holiday is happening all around, softly. Lovers linger a bit longer than on a Sunday afternoon outing, fathers take a bit more time to laugh with their children as they ride them on the handlebars of their bicycles. Nothing unusual except that the ordinary day is bedecked and more slow-paced. Nothing stops, all stores are open. More buses are put on the lines.

The city looks festive. Official buildings, party headquarters, the Peking Hotel, our own university gates, all are draped in silk and hung with ceremonial red lanterns—a traditional Chinese display for auspicious events. At night, the dark fluttering of flags sounds scary to me, like an approaching yet invisible windstorm. My fear is momentary. What lingers is a delight in the public sensuality of commemoration. I look forward to May fourth. Official history now moves closer to my concerns. I feel expectant, touched, even though this history is not "mine," except through study, of course.

MAY 7   *The sixtieth anniversary of May Fourth*   "The May Fourth Movement is rapidly approaching the venerable Confucian age of sixty. As this iconoclastic event settles into historical tradition, future scholars will be able to study it more dispassionately, underscore more continuities and reconnect it with a past it sought to overthrow. When I began research on this theme seven years ago, however, May Fourth did not seem so safely past."

Today I reread this preface of my 1977 doctoral thesis, *From Renaissance to Revolution.*

Back home, when I finished my dissertation and when the idea of living in China seemed improbable, I felt it important to explain (really to apologize for) explicitly the passion I had invested in my studies of the May Fourth movement. Now I am settled at Peking University, where it all began. To be sure, the physical location of the university has changed. The downtown campus moved into the suburbs in the 1950s, to the old site of Yanjing University. But the tradition of May Fourth lingers on at this new Beida. An opportunity here to rein in my earlier emotions. As May fourth nears, all of China, and most obviously the university here, readies for anniversary ceremonies. I try to stay calm, to center my energies. I want to pay attention to the changing, evolving significance of May Fourth through commemoration (this was the theme of the last chapter of my dissertation). I also ask myself once more, more sharply than before, why does May Fourth matter to me?

On the night of the third, by chance I get a ticket to a movie shown on campus for Chinese students, *The Song of Youth.* This film, based on a novel by the woman writer Yang Mo, describes the student movement at Peking University in the mid-1930s. Lush in color and drenched with high ideals, the movie, like the book, conveys the message that the tradition of May Fourth lives on. It is alive in the hearts and minds of young intellectuals who gather at this university, no matter at what time and no matter around what causes. This message echoes ahead in time. It reminds the audience that both the Hundred Flowers movement of 1957 and the Cultural Revolution of 1966 began with student activism at Peking University.

At the end of the movie I leave my balcony seat, one among eight hundred or so students in the place. I am surprised to find tears in my eyes as in theirs. I am surprised how moved I was by the last shot: the beautiful heroine walking arm and arm with Communist comrades to defy the forces of darkness and oppression—in this particular case, the Japanese invaders. I catch myself asking again: "Why am I getting so weepy about the Chinese past, its mythologies? Shouldn't I be immune by now to a movie which presents such a maudlin view of May Fourth?"

I decide to ride my bike around the lake after the film, slowly in the late, crisp spring night. I try to locate myself more concretely in this place, try to face the next morning's ceremonies more attentively. Less subjectively perhaps. In the cool shadows of the water tower, I force myself to hand over the occasion to Chinese intellectuals. This May fourth, as the one in 1919, I tell myself over and over again, is theirs. Here, as in my studies, I have to stand to the side. I have to learn to become an observer.

I try to recall what pulled me toward the event of 1919 as early as my first Chinese history course at Vassar. A quote from Nietzsche may explain the source of that attraction: "Believe me, friend hellish noise: the greatest events—they're not our loudest but our stillest hours. Not around the inventors of new noises, but around the inventors of new values does the world revolve; it revolves inaudibly." In Zarathustra's words, my own long-buried interest in the dichotomy between loud, outer events and important, silent, inner ones. The loud student demonstration of 1919 was, after all, a culmination of a more subterranean new cultural movement. The connection between new politics and new culture still eludes me. But I do share Nietzsche's conviction (prejudice?) that the world does indeed revolve around "inventors of new values." What was and remains to me inspiring about the May Fourth "inventors" is that they managed to make the world revolve a little bit more around their new values.

Anti-Confucian and patriotic, the young intellectuals of 1919 had refused to keep quiet. They tried to break with the ceremonious and cautious tradition of their literati predecessors. Wearing long gowns, arrogant, and still class-unconscious, they declared traditional Confucian values and contemporary warlord politics to be "hellish." They inserted themselves and Peking University into China's revolutionary history. They made 1919 into a dramatic, eventful moment. While their demonstration emphasized national salvation, they also dared to say, in public, that China was weak because of its inner, cultural rottenness.

The slogans of the May Fourth movement—"We must learn from the West. We must create and venerate the spirit of Science and Democracy"—were deemed dangerous and subversive in 1919. These same words spoken today by aging Communist officials sound much tamer, of course. Their words, however, cannot erase the fact that the hopes of May Fourth remain unfulfilled. China still needs the values of Science and Democracy. The context of the problems has changed, to be sure. But May Fourth cannot yet be safely enshrined as just the "revolutionary heritage" of the past.

Not so long ago, in 1976, the May Fourth legacy was revived in a new, contentious spirit. During the April Fifth movement (the mass action in Tian An Men Square commemorating the death of Zhou Enlai), young workers and students claimed that the event of 1919 justified their own rebellious politics.

Today, the event of 1976 has been worn rather thin. Official commemorations have domesticated it, as they are now taming the iconoclasm of May Fourth on its sixtieth anniversary. And yet, ripples of unorthodox remembrance remain and are felt sometimes. In a poem from Democracy Wall, a young man seeks to shore up his revolutionary faith by "Strolling on May Fourth Avenue." Although the poem is not particularly good, it helps me look afresh at May Fourth.

I ask fellow students at the university if there is, in fact, a May Fourth Avenue in Peking. "No" is the repeated answer. Today I take a bus downtown looking for a park with a Tibetan temple and a bank at which to exchange my fellowship stipend into Chinese money. By mistake, I get off a stop too early. The street sign reads "May Fourth Avenue." Across the street, a large placard with a quotation from Mao Zedong—one of the very few still left in a city that is beautifying itself these days with traditional-style paintings and consumer advertising. The placard declares: "Do not cease from furthering political work in the realm of thought."

Another recent discovery: the anniversary of May Fourth used to be "academic scholarship month" in the early days of the People's Republic. That tradition was stopped during the Cultural Revolution. This year, for the sixtieth anniversary, it is being revived again. The news comes out in a rather casual remark from an official in the Foreign Students' Office. He shows me a booklet of seminar topics for this week: "Faculty have been preparing research papers on all sorts of topics, you know. It has been a tradition since the 1950s. Unfortunately, all this was interrupted by the Gang of Four." Now that I have heard the news, I am becoming aware that the campus is abuzz with academic activities. Scientists are reporting on nuclear energy research, linguists are talking about Shakespeare, philosophers are returning for another look at Hegel.

Friday night, another "accident." I am brushing my teeth alongside a Chinese student from the Literature Department. I ask her about the lectures going on. "You absolutely have to go to tomorrow's talk on May Fourth poetry since Liberation. The lecturer is one of our smartest, most daring critics." At 8:30 the next morning, I splash over to the lecture hall in the rain. I am somewhat doubtful because the announced title, "Composing Poetry along with New China," sounds conventional, laudatory, and official. It turns out to be nothing of the sort.

In a large, crowded auditorium, for two hours, Xia Yan, a short, thin man with a high-pitched voice, chronicles the steady betrayal of the spirit of May Fourth in China since 1957. At one time, he was an editor of the national poetry magazine. Now this Peking University professor is an impassioned and undaunted admonisher of young poets. He urges them to think hard and independently about politics. He wants them to hold up a mirror to society, to stand alongside the common people rather than heed the latest official directives from above. He bemoans all those who in the 1960s sold their voices to praise each new wave of the "so-called political movement" and the "so-called class struggle."

Xia Yan concludes with a plea addressed to young people. He chastises their generation for its uncritical, "nearly religious enthusiasm" during the Cultural Revolution and even in 1976. He insists that they "must not forget to hate as well as to love, to notice that the ugly exists alongside the beautiful, to curse as well as to praise." His voice rises in pitch, almost out of control. He is trying to name the unmentionable in public. He bears witness at once to the spirit of May Fourth and to its unfulfilled challenge.

Perhaps, the "political work" mentioned in the Mao placard on May Fourth Avenue is most alive in literature today. But then, this literature is calling into question not just Mao's ends but also his means.

An official, more serene occasion culminates the day of May Fourth itself. In the municipal stadium, where Seiji Ozawa had conducted the Boston Symphony, thousands of school children and university students gather for a celebration sponsored by Peking University. The huge hall is ringed with slogans, "Warmly

Hail the Sixtieth Anniversary of May Fourth and the Eighty-first Anniversary of the Great Peking University."

Our bus full of foreign students arrives a few minutes late, in the middle of a speech by the seventy-six-year-old president of the university, Zhou Peiyuan. His strong voice defies his age. I wonder: How much of his aura comes from a practiced willingness to lend his voice as a renowned physicist and May Fourth luminary to the changing directives of party officials? Zhou, in the middle of floodlights, stands flanked by high officials and foreign dignitaries. He strikes a monumental pose.

His demeanor is strikingly different from that of the thirty or so old professors sitting in a guest booth behind him. They, too, are living monuments to the event of 1919. Looking at that booth, I think to myself that there must surely be among them some whom I have been studying as student rebels of the new culture movement. For the rest of the morning, my attention remains riveted on the faces of those old men. One has a long beard. A sign, maybe, of lingering iconoclasm in a society which frowns on all and any idiosyncratic appearance? Two others are holding their canes with restless hands. They sit through an hour of speeches about the movement they created more than half a century ago. I am struck by their drooping, clenched lips. In their tired, worn bodies I sense an effort to stay awake, and also not to show any feelings. To me, they look bitter about the public misreading of history by officials who need to legitimate the present line.

Here are intellectuals at the mercy of the times they helped to bring about. As cultural radicals, they had a hand in establishing the Communist regime. They helped to tear down the credibility of traditional culture, they exposed the cruelties of the KMT. After 1949, many became victims of a younger, rural-based generation of political revolutionaries. There is more to the suffering of these intellectuals than the pain of forced labor or the agony of wasted scholarship. What seems harshest is that they have been forced to relinquish their connections with the history they made. If the present regime were less gleeful about the "glories" of the May Fourth tradition, would May Fourth intellectuals be more indignant? Would they reclaim their role in an event described by Mao as the "proletarian May Fourth"? Instead, they sit sullenly, bedraggled mementos of an earlier cultural revolution.

After the speeches, there is a ten-minute intermission, followed by two hours of musical extravaganza in honor of May Fourth: singers, dancers, acrobats. The old men are fully awake now. Hearing aids turned up, they smile broadly. Not quite soothed or pacified, they can still relish this celebration of their event. The melodious voices of school children belting out revolutionary songs delights them more than the speeches of all the officials. I notice Chen Zhenhan, the economics professor with a Harvard Ph.D., smiles in a half-critical, half-amused way as a famous Chinese singer thrills the audience with "Doe, a Deer, A Female Deer" in English.

On the way home from the athletic stadium, I think back to our visit to the locomotive factory a month ago. A sharp contrast comes to mind between old workers retelling the story of their 1923 strike and aged intellectuals sitting through a loudspeaker version of the student movement of 1919.

The workers have been allowed and encouraged to become more knowledgeable about the history in which they have participated. Their belated schooling was about their own history, not against it. They also have something more precious than the schooling: the right to speak for their own event. They embody rather than merely symbolize a myth which the Communist regime needs.

The old intellectuals, on the other hand, have been asked, urged, forced to rewrite their history many, many times, always in accord with the changing needs of the present. Their schooling since Liberation is meant to train them out of habits of mind acquired earlier. In public, they are merely a backdrop for an updated version of May Fourth.

An item of news the week before this sixtieth anniversary: "Eighty-nine-year-old Joins the Communist Party." Xu Deheng, a Peking University student in 1919, was one of the organizers of the May Fourth demonstration. He became one of the most prominent non-Communist intellectuals in the period after 1949. He served, for a while, as vice chairman of the Standing Committee of the National People's Congress. Why, I ask myself, would Xu Deheng want to become a Commmunist before he dies? Clearly not for more security or privilege. He has plenty of both right now.

The newspaper story focuses on "his determination to serve

the Four Modernizations, his new hopes since the Gang of Four." I sense something else. Close to ninety, Xu Deheng wants to confirm a logic of history which he has come to believe in. He needs to prove, perhaps to himself most of all, that May Fourth was leading all along to a Communist future. The *Peking Review* article quotes part of his party application essay: "I realized the truth that only the Communist Party can save China." Here is a belated recognition of the inevitable. This recognition makes Xu Deheng a collaborator in the past and in the future.

Does consciousness really transform or merely rationalize necessity? Xu Deheng's choice hints at both. His action is a counterpoint to the solemn pomposity of official commemorations of May Fourth.

MAY 10   *Beyond official history: reflections on tragedy in a socialist society*   Public celebrations of the event of 1919 ended more than a week ago. The red lanterns that had decorated the university gate were taken down last Friday night. The officially sponsored event is over. Now the eventfulness of history has moved from the stadium to the seminar rooms. Here at Beida, lectures and discussions are still going on. The return to the pre-Cultural Revolution tradition of an academic scholarship month is vigorous. Revived in 1978, the tradition seems to be relished more than ever before. After deliberations with "authorities," my adviser wins for me an invitation to a faculty seminar (not open to the public). The topic, explicitly forbidden for the past decade, is "Marxist Views of Tragedy."

So, on Wednesday, the ninth, I rushed to the 2 P.M. opening of the seminar. In a regular classroom, the small individual student's desks are pushed together to form a central table. Around it gather about forty people. My adviser and I are forcefully pushed to sit closer to the table. Most others prefer seats further away, toward the back. I had read the paper to be discussed beforehand. It is a rather well informed discussion of Marx and Engels's critique of nineteenth-century historical drama. The author of the paper, following up hints in Marx and Engels, defines "tragedy" as a conflict between historical means and ends.

The paper concludes with some impassioned but vaguely

phrased questions: "Can there be a tragedy under socialism? Might tragedy be the result of socialism? How can tragedy be talked about in the new China?" I hear two people whispering behind me: "This paper is daring, for sure. Even with the new propaganda about emancipation of thought, you know . . ." "Yes, we have kept quiet about these questions for too long. I only hope the discussion can match the author's courage."

It did. From the chairman's opening remarks welcoming visiting scholars from other provinces and other countries (meaning myself) to his concluding remarks three hours later, I am intensely aware of how novel and how awkward the theme of tragedy is for these intellectuals. The form of a seminar discussion is equally disconcerting. For more than ten years they had not been allowed to mention the dark side of life. They have been forbidden to gather together to voice questions. After this decade of sloganeering, affirmation of bright truths, and shouts of mutual accusation, groups such as this are finally allowed to settle down, to share ideas, to raise some doubts.

Two speakers open the seminar. The author of the paper I had read is an inward man who talks briefly about the background of his work: "my personal point of view and the evolution of my questions." He reads a few thoughts from a tiny plastic notebook with pink flowers on the cover, which he holds in his hands. From its schoolgirlish pages pour forth some very tough questions about the tragedy of revolution in general, the painful tension between the aims of those who would usher in a new age and the limited ability, of leaders and followers alike, to translate vision into reality. He doesn't stop with these general ruminations. He goes on to talk about the tragedies generated by socialism in China. He refuses to let the Gang of Four era pass off as historical accident.

He asks over and over again, "How come?" He calls the April Fifth movement of 1976 a "revolutionary tragedy." This forces his listeners to remember that the events of three years ago, now enshrined as "progressive," were at that time bitterly crushed. How come? He concludes, "I have no answers but I must share my questions. They are pressing for us all."

The second speaker is a young man, maybe still a student. I realize from other seminars I attended this week that this is a pattern: to pair up presentations by older, "less safe" scholars with remarks by younger, more dogmatic students. Less well-read, more unseasoned, the students serve as a counterbalance to the critical views of their teachers. Also, I gather this is an opportunity to give youth practice in public discussion of scholarship.

The young man is tense, his voice too loud. He flounders a bit around theoretical materials from Marx and Engels as he tries to outline three types of tragedy that existed in the "old China." He dwells on victories, on Lu Xun's militant portrayal of the dark side of life in the 1920s. He concludes with a shrill declaration that the concept of tragedy is meaningful only for bourgeois revolutions like the one that China went through in 1911. He insists that all of this is not applicable to the situation under socialism.

The chairman tries to get the discussion going. It is very awkward for a few long minutes. He looks around the room, his eyes inviting as he pleads with those present to express their opinion: "Just say anything, it doesn't have to be related to these particular papers." I fidget uncomfortably, wondering how much of the reticence and tension in the room might be the result of my presence. A participant-observer, I am keenly aware of the disturbance caused by my supposed "objectivity"—that is, my distance from events which concern all others here so directly.

In the end, I force myself to calm down. I am, after all, not so important in this setting. It is not my presence, but ten years of recent history, that is thwarting discussion in this room. These intellectuals have their own reasons for cautiousness. I don't. Eventually, a gray-haired philosopher of aesthetics starts to speak. I am beginning to realize how much traditional politeness and a conventional pecking order are at work here.

This concern with decorum makes discussion stilted at first. The speaker seems to be eminent and safely orthodox. He expresses judgment, not reason. He declares that the young man is "right." At the same time, he knows Marx and Engels well, and so is able to flesh out his judgments. He is long-winded. In the end he concludes with an interesting warning: "We must distinguish between the tragedy of revolutionaries and the tragedy of the revolution itself."

There is something here about men being smaller than their times which catches my interest. I sense a backhanded sympathy for dreamers caught in a trivializing reality. After the philosopher has expressed this expected, and acceptable, point of view, other speakers raise questions for the next two hours. The discussion deepens as the problem of tragedy becomes linked with ethical choice of means and ends. The probing here of this old theme strikes me as deeper than similar discussions I have heard back home. Words count here for those who speak them. They have a certain weight, an urgency that comes from a shared, suppressed history. A subtle pressure to confess is at work, even in this moment of relatively calm reflection.

These intellectuals are thinking about means and ends *after* being forced to grab whatever means the revolution offered. They are talking about choice *after* having lost their say over ends in general.

Some hopeful, tough words from a chain-smoking man in his late thirties. He shakes his long hair: "We must rethink the tragedy of intellectuals caught between classes. In a moment of historical transition, they wanted to serve the cause of the new, rising masses. Yet, they discovered that their attachment to old values and to their own class was stronger than the pull of new, abstract ideas."

Another man, in his late forties, very tense yet calmly articulate: "Engels and Marx are not too helpful anymore to our discussion of tragedy in present-day China. They were right to point out the disparity between necessity and consciousness in revolutionary times. Since ours is a socialist, not a bourgeois, revolution, we can and should expect our contradictions to be more acute than anything imagined by Marx and Engels. Our tragedies are deeper, more complex."

One of the last speakers is an artist, a painter in her fifties. She's thin and has work-worn hands. Her voice is strong, perhaps from practiced leadership. She speaks in images, feelings. She asks us to think of some of the universal dimensions of tragedy, encourages us to take emotions evoked by portrayals of despair seriously. She talks about two paintings by her students dealing with the events of 1976. One, she calls "effective" because it conveys an understated view of tragedy: a girl student, beaten by the security police in the Tian An Men Square demonstration, is being taken care of by a few worried friends. The other she calls "bombastic, dull"—a hackneyed portrayal of surging masses on the day of April 5, 1976. She concludes with a bitter, pointed criticism of the Gang of Four era. At that time, she says, all depictions of the tragedy were forbidden because they were deemed "too pessimistic."

Through her simple comments, this artist crystallized for me the point of the whole discussion. Her message is simply that tragedy is not a matter of attitude (as in bourgeois aesthetic theory) but a matter of historical reality. To depict what is tragic is not to aid and abet gloominess, but to fight it in the most effective way. She argues that whatever is problematic or painful will not go away by being ignored or covered up with the veneer of social optimism.

I am moved by her awkward, gutsy effort to dip down and touch the darkness of this otherwise exuberantly depicted society. I want to say something. I also feel I should, in keeping with recent Chinese convention. Unlike back home, guests here are expected to acknowledge publicly the opportunity to share in the novelty of scholarly discourse. Being too tense, too self-conscious, I just say simply thank you. I leave inwardly furious and outwardly embarrassed. More so, because my one clumsy line was greeted by formal applause.

MAY 13 *New variations on the official history of May Fourth* Yesterday, I attended a History Department seminar on Chen Duxiu, a leading May Fourth intellectual and a founder of the Communist Party. He was expelled as a "renegade" in 1927 and then damned as a "traitor" in 1938. The setting at this seminar is rather official, a lecture-style classroom. The chairman introduces visiting scholars from other institutions and welcomes me by name, adding "Assistant Professor from Stanford University," a well-intentioned falsehood based on the only fact they know about me, that I finished my degree in California. Minor falsehoods based on scanty facts are familiar to these historians. They have been generating them and acquiescing to them for years. More than literary critics, Chinese historians are subjected to the repeated demands and accusations of political leaders. History in China, especially modern history, is too closely tied with the legitimacy of Mao and of the Party to be left to "mere scholars." So many historians have become scared, hollow sounding boards for the changing requirements of the party line.

After the opening talks, the chairman tries to spark discussion, to evoke some expression of opinion after a decade of enforced uniformity. After listening for two hours of "responses" to this demand, I remain unconvinced that a "discussion" is really taking place. What I hear sounds like a trial run for yet another change in the official line. Still, whether orchestrated or not, the discussion testifies to the awkward beginnings of critical thought in the field of history.

Again, there were two papers: the first, by an older, well-read man, raises public doubts about the simplistic condemnation of Chen Duxiu during the last decade of Chinese historiography. His younger colleague is more nervous, more doctrinaire. He argues that Chen Duxiu had "traitorous, bourgeois" qualities all along. After their presentations, again that long, tense silence which I fear could smother the seeds of genuine debate.

I raise my hand to ask the first question. Having been so ceremoniously introduced, I feel as if I will be interfering less than in the literature seminar. I ask about the differences in the Marxist views of Chen Duxiu and Li Dazhao, the other, more approved founder of the Communist Party. Li, too, had been a cultural rebel during the May Fourth movement. An intellectual, he had read far less of Marxism than Chen Duxiu. What makes one incorrect and the other not? The room sinks around me in worried surprise. It looks as though I assumed too much when I implied that Chen Duxiu was a Marxist after all. After what seems to me endless minutes, finally the chairman rises to answer me. He is brief, emphasizing the criteria which make an intellectual a Marxist: "These are very complex, you know. They ought to be a matter of historical evidence drawn from the historical context."

He concludes, "We cannot rest with Mao's declaration that a Communist intellectual is only a person who unites with the masses of workers, peasants, and soldiers. What does it mean to unite, after all? Does it mean every day? All the time? Through labor only? Was Marx uniting with masses as he went off every day to the British Museum Library to work on *Kapital?*"

These are troublesome questions for an audience trained to hear acceptable answers. Those who had been staying within the confines of the party lines are visibly upset by this public invitation to go beyond Mao, to plunge into more "dangerous" historical reasoning.

Next, a rather sad sight, a short talk by an older scholar. His is a rambling, nervous presentation about a less-well-known May Fourth intellectual, a "true proletarian"contemporary of Mao who also became one of the founders of the Communist Party. Yet even this "correct" historical figure was criticized later and retrospectively damned for bourgeois errors. The older scholar's effort to resuscitate him is halting, unconvincing. He seems out of his element, out of his area of expertise, merely dutiful. Watching his recitation of the current historiographical line—that the intellectuals' contribution must be weighed in an appropriate context—I wonder again how much of all this is staged. Is this a "scholarly" rehearsal for the prospective rehabilitation of Cultural Revolution victims? This might well be the Party's way to try out a new, more lenient line toward "renegades" like Liu Shaoqi.

After this talk, other historians get up to raise deeper and deeper questions about Chen Duxiu. They are beginning to acknowledge his complexity as a revolutionary thinker, to warn each other not to judge this early Communist by the criteria of later times. I am struck again by how novel and how explosive an undertaking historical analysis really is in China. How hard it is to find, and to dare to use, historical documentation. How great are the risks in proving anything about the past. The same risks plague China's tentative effort to define rules and regulations for a new legal system. Those who are currently drafting criminal laws are in the same position as those who are trying to write genuinely documentary history. Once assertions have to be proved, a whole can of worms about past decrees and past certainties opens up.

One of the last speakers at the History Department seminar is a young instructor, whom I have talked with often and I believed to be a political hack. He is far more complex, more questioning than I imagined. He stands up to raise a question, "not merely about the problems of historical evidence but the whole theory of historical materialism." With a shaky cigarette in hand, he searches the faces of his colleagues: "If we are not to use later criteria to judge earlier times, if we cannot use Mao's subsequent 'correct' line to damn Chen Duxiu's errors in the 1920s and 1930s, then what made Chen wrong? Why was he labeled an opportunist, a so-called traitor, in the first place? And if he cannot be judged to have been evil in the ways in which we thought he was before, then what about the whole changing party line since the 1930s?"

His last words: "I am feeling very, very confused at the present." Then he sits down, the cigarette still shaking. Soon after, the meeting ends. With applause, as always.

The tension lingers as we disperse. I go up to the young instructor to shake his hand, then leave talking with a German student. His impressions: "It's so sad. These Chinese seem to me trapped in a windowless room. Such arbitrary limits on their discussion! You know, nobody here dares go far at all. So what if they raise trivial questions about the timing of Marxism in China. None of them ever asks, the way we Marxists in Europe do all the time, what is the point of Marxism anyhow." I listen and realize once again how it is next to impossible to see beyond our own assumptions, to perceive the internal problems of the Chinese intellectuals around us. Yet I sense (perhaps I am still too conceited?) that I am a little beyond blaming the Chinese for not being like us.

I answer my German friend: "But just imagine how much hangs here on the questions of these historians. Western Marxists have never had to assume such weighty political responsibility for their theoretical musings. No matter how narrow the confines of this debate seem to us, its depths are certain. Everything has consequences here. Just because these historians' discussions are halting and circular, we cannot assume that their tasks are superficial. Faster than we can imagine, their discussion can call into question Mao, even the party."

MAY 31   *Back from the south of China*   I got in this morning at 6 A.M. after six days in Nanjing (Nanking). The excuse for the trip was an academic conference on the Taiping Rebellion of 1850–64. A month ago, when my disappointment about the May Fourth conference was most bitter, I heard some rumors about another international conference of historians at Nanjing University. I decide to press for permission to attend, mostly because I want to get out of the capital, to see another part of China, to get some new impressions, to force myself to ask another range of questions. I am surprised how swiftly arrangements are made for me by the Peking University Foreign Students' Office. Again, matters far away from my specialization are easier to arrange than those closer by.

The lonely train ride to and from Nanjing is as instructive as the scholarly opportunities I quest for so breathlessly. Like on my April trip to Xian, I travel south on a hard-class sleeper. The train schedule, with departures (both ways) at 3 P.M., gives me just enough time to nap, wake up for dinner, read, look around for a couple of hours, sleep a long restful night, and arrive at the destination around 6 A.M. (The Beijing-Nanjing schedule might be China's most humane, civilized timetable, rather fitting for the distance between the two traditional capitals, Beijing, "Northern Peace," and Nanjing, "Southern Peace.")

On the train down, I have the middle bunk. Foreigners who are "foolish enough" to prefer hard-class over first-class sleepers tend to be given this space, the most airy yet private part of the six-person area. The lower bunk is just too open, almost a public seating area, and the top bunk is tiny, stuffy. Below me, an older man in his sixties, gray cropped hair, fine simple gray shirt, matching gray socks, brown pants. I guess he is an intellectual. He takes out the *Literary Supplement* magazine as soon as the train starts and spends the next sixteen hours either reading or sleeping. This encourages me to take out my *Nanjing University Bulletin*, a recent issue with some articles about the Taiping Rebellion. I end up reading little but feel more comfortable than before on a Chinese train. I imagine myself as just another person making sense of characters on a page. My acute self-consciousness about being a foreigner is slowly wearing off.

Across from me, a PLA (People's Liberation Army) officer in his mid-forties. He is very handsome, restrained, serious, quietly engrossed in a book of memoirs about the defense of Ya'nan (Mao's stronghold during the Anti-Japanese War). I can't help looking at him for much of the trip. He's almost too perfect an approximation of a movie character: the simple, virtuous Communist soldier of pre-Liberation days. Yet, the man who faces me is more real, a contemporary even if a rare sight these days. More and more officers, although still shunning the outward signs of rank, travel first-class now. They are served extra-fine dinners and look chubby, complacent in their finely tailored woolen "common soldier" uniforms. This officer, on the other hand, wears simple cotton fatigues over a student's blue athletic jersey. The only clue to his status is an expensive looking, many-zippered, key-locked briefcase.

After dinner, the officer starts a conversation with an older, yet obviously lower-ranking, army man. They talk of their home-towns, prices, their bits of shared history from the land reform movement of the early 1950s. I listen closely, finding that I learn more from comments between Chinese travelers than from con-versations in which I'm a participant. Too often, comments ad-dressed to me are prefaced by "Oh, your Chinese is so good! You are really from America? Are you used to our surroundings yet? What's the weather like in the place you come from?" All this makes me too much the subject of a situation I want and need simply to observe.

I am asked to eat in the dining room. Seated across from a traveling railway supervisor, I enjoy a good beef and onion dish. On my table, fresh potted plants. These luxuries are characteristics of the better Chinese trains. On my way back to the hard-class sleeper, I stop to smoke a cigarette in the first-class section. I feel awkward these days whenever I light up a cigarette among Chinese people. Women generally don't smoke here, especially not in the cities, and certainly not among the educated youth.

Not smoking in public places is just one of the adjustments I have made to try to slip into Chinese society more easily. By being less offensive to local sensibilities, I try to draw less attention to myself. Most of these adjustments, I make initially for "them." In the end, like the pure cotton, baggy pants and shirt I bought for this trip to the South, they increase my own comfort and well-being as well. Puffing contentedly in the sunset, I overhear Ro-manian spoken from behind the half-shut door of the paneled, cushioned cabin. It turns out to be a group of high government officials from Bucharest.

They look rather capitalistic with their gold cufflinks and pin-stripe suits. I speak to them in their language, my own. We all delight in this chance encounter. Our meeting on a Chinese train makes the world feel small, familiar. The Romanians ask about my background. When did I leave the home country? What brings me to China? Why don't I come for a visit to their Peking embassy? I go back to my cubicle a touch smug about being an American who is fluent in Chinese. Although my clothes are simple, local, "poor" in their eyes, I know myself to be better off than the fancy

Romanians off to dinner with their translator. (I don't quite know why I need to keep on winning these retrospective victories against my native land in my mind.)

On this train ride, I feel at ease with China. During my stay in Nanjing, however, I have to wear the cloak of darkness to cover my foreignness. I had heard that it is a "more Chinese" city than Peking. After I arrive, I realize this means it is less covert about its backwardness. In the late dusk, I walk through the neighborhood next to the University. The windows are open, and life spills out into the streets. Families gather for dinner. Passing alley after alley of small dwellings, one- or two-room shacks, I can see into front rooms lit by one electric bulb. Tired men around small tables, served by women going back and forth from an adjacent, unlit cooking hole.

Outside these tiny dwellings, some people are washing clothes, some are smoking pipes on the low wicker recliners characteristic of the South. Grandmothers with bound feet are put out to be aired. In the semidarkness, they look like antique furniture, cherished but useless. Then, I recall that I passed such women during the day carrying baskets and babies.

The mood of Nanjing in the dusk is one of exhaustion, not desolation. After a day's hard work, so much left to be done for the basic subsistence of home life. There is little time or energy for higher leisures. I pass an all-night market with long lines of workers waiting for wilted vegetables. I notice that there are very few tomatoes. I had heard they were plentiful these days.

In Nanjing I also experience some moments of privilege and unexpected graciousness. One of the reasons I asked to come here was to meet an Episcopalian bishop, K. H. Ting, a friend of friends back home. Once head of the Nanjing Theological Seminary, he is still a believer, I gather. Now he is on the faculty of the Religion Department of Nanjing University. I have lunch at his house: a fine two-storied building set in a courtyard of rose bushes. I meet his ailing but beautiful wife and their two handsome, shy sons. One will soon be off to Berkeley for two years of study. The other is a freshman at the university here, as well as the inventor of a duplicating machine. Both sons are strengthened by skills acquired during years of factory work.

We lunch on sea delicacies served by a live-in lady. The dessert is delicious ice cream with homegrown strawberries. Our conversation is mostly in English. K. H. and his wife are more urbane in their use of English than I could ever hope to be. We talk of their days in New York in 1950. K. H. shares with me his interpretation of the Jonestown Massacre. I am struck by the informed, analytical, reasoned morality of my Christian hosts.

Something familiar yet new as well here. K. H. and his wife are sophisticated but not Western or bourgeois in their ways. They have simple, historically tested political concerns. I don't know how China can tolerate or use such people. But I sense that they are necessary to what China is trying to accomplish. They seem to me to foreshadow a broad kind of humanism. Perhaps, in the distant future, when other Chinese people also have more leisure, more living space, better news of the world, this humanism will flourish. I don't think the Chinese government wants to, can, or should keep the masses from becoming more like the Tings.

The conference on the Taiping Rebellion is more lively, more open than I expected. It is a difficult task to discuss the topic objectively. This event was canonized by Mao as a forerunner of the Communist Revolution. In fact, the Taiping Rebellion was led by Hong Xiuquan, a failed Confucian scholar, who dreamed he was the younger brother of Jesus Christ. Hong then developed a new faith and an organization which led the rebellion of 1850–64. The rebels occupied Nanjing, came close to toppling the Qing dynasty. For a while, they were supported by the missionaries. Eventually the rebellion was put down with the help of British mercenaries.

Some memorable encounters at the conference: Professor Wang Yumin, on the Nanjing University faculty, presents a paper on the corruption of Christian thought during the peasant rebellion. Over the next few days, I spend quite a bit of time talking with Professor Wang about his criteria for "true Christianity," about the state of Chinese scholarship on the history of religion, about the recent, skilled use by Taiping historians of the Bible as a primary document. Wang, I find out later, is a fundamentalist Christian himself.

Professor Wang Qingcheng, from the Academy of Social Sciences in Peking presents a brilliant paper on the sociology of ideas in the early Taiping period. A short and intense man in his mid-fifties, he is a dominant presence in our small discussion group (the conference of more than three hundred participants was di-

vided into eight small groups). He seems to be one of the nationally known advocates of the "emancipation of thought" in
the field of historical research. During his presentation, he calls
for the end of the praise-blame paradigm characteristic of both
Confucian and Communist historiography. Wang goes on to outline the responsibilities of a true Marxist historian. I grasp only
parts of his complex argument. Maybe we will be able to meet in
Peking and talk some more.

Another chance encounter. During the first morning in our
small group discussion, I sit toward the back of the room. I strike
up a conversation with a young Chinese woman. She turns out
to be a graduate student in intellectual history at People's University in Peking. We exchange names. For the next three days,
we debate issues of historiography. I find that I am not prepared
(my prejudiced mind always surprises me) for meeting such a
talented, young, inquisitive historian. I am repeatedly taken aback
by her daring insights. She seems at once fearless and competent.
During a large gathering in which foreign experts present papers,
she takes the microphone and asks some tough questions about
the assumptions and implications of Chinese studies in the U.S.
I offer to give her materials about the critique of American sinology
developed in the 1960s by the Committee of Concerned Asian
Scholars. I hope that we will be allowed to meet and talk with
each other in Peking.

A flirtatious Japanese student, enrolled at Nanjing University,
takes me for a morning walk up a mountain to the tomb of Sun
Yat-sen. We both wonder why China's revolutionaries still venerate so highly such a mediocre "founding father." Our conversation during the four-hour outing is all in Chinese, a new
experience for me. On the way back to the university he hires a
pedicab. My stomach churns with discomfort. I am wracked by
images of imperialism as our thin, tanned driver puffs along the
streets of Nanjing. I see myself as I might be seen. A Western
woman out for a ride with a Japanese bureaucrat (he does work
for the Japanese Foreign Office). Later, I calm down. How much
of my political righteousness, I ask myself, is academic? My virtuous views perhaps shielded by my ignorance of Chinese history.
Too often, I am upset about appearances, like the appearance of
Japanese imperialism, more than I understand them. My emo-

tions about China have, for too long, been rooted in a lack of understanding.

I leave Nanjing determined to become a more conscious, more conscientious observer. In this setting I cannot, perhaps should not even try to, be objective. All I can do is to strive for a more highly polished subjectivity. As with a gem, all I can hope is to develop more facets in myself so that I may reflect more of what comes my way. In Chinese, the opposite of "subjectivity" (literally one-sidedness), is "many-sidedness." No haughty ambition here to get at essences out there. Just a painstaking, slow effort to see more aspects of what may never be known in itself.

All I can hope for is to see more than the official one-sided face which China turns toward me.

On the train ride from Nanjing to Beijing, I sleep a lot. I finish a short story about a Czech farmer, "Neighbor Rosicky," by Willa Cather. I find myself crying, awkward about my tears in this crowded Chinese space. My tears keep falling from behind my sunglasses as I watch a young woman (no more than twenty-six), a PLA soldier who is breastfeeding her daughter in the dusk over the first set of hills as the train crosses the Yellow River. The lilting string music coming over the loudspeaker is so typical of the South. It does little to help my struggle against my own sentimentality.

Eventually I pull myself together, focusing my attention on the hard labor going on in the fields outside the train window. The first crop of rice is being harvested just now. The dry yellow fields of the South are dotted in the early evening with groups of bent backs. Brigades are out cutting the stalks or busy in thrashing courtyards where mounds of grain bespeak hard-earned but tenuous prosperity.

On this train ride, I refuse the invitation to the dining car. I buy instead a box dinner along with other "hard-sleepers." For less than 15 cents, I eat a large helping of low-grade rice (very much coarser than what is served in the dining car), topped with about a cup of greens and about two tablespoons of fatty pork stew. Filling, cheap nourishment.

On this train ride, more than ever before, I feel comfortable in cramped Chinese spaces. Not going more than ten feet in either direction of my cubicle for seventeen hours, I gain new understanding of the circumstances of ordinary Chinese people. To be sure, the hard-class sleeper space is probably luxurious for most of these travelers. In their own homes, they have to share beds with parents, children, spouses.

We are many and close, and yet don't impose on each other. Everyone can see everybody else. I wake up along with the others around 5 A.M., an hour outside of Peking. All the passengers are busy stripping pillowcases and bedding, folding up blankets and sheets. This is to help the railway personnel prepare the train for its next ride. Following their quiet yet mandatory example, I struggle in the middle bunk to do the same. Now the space feels cramped. By the time the train pulls into Peking Station, the used linen has been stacked away, new bedding has been put in. It is impressive to witness this feat of training and discipline. Everyone cooperates under the watchful eyes of everyone else. Could China get by without this overwhelming conformity? Probably not. To maintain conformity, however, will be harder and harder if more prosperous times increase the material base for individual differences.

CHAPTER 4

JUNE 7 *Bits of an almost familiar China*

We are, I am, you are
By cowardice or courage
The one who finds our way
Back to the scene
Carrying a knife, a camera
A book of myths
In which
Our names do not appear.
(Adrienne Rich, "Diving into the Wreck")

A week ago the possibility of finally knowing China seemed real enough. Now, after getting back home to Peking, I feel shaken. Away, traveling, I was feeling at ease, especially on the train to and from Nanjing. Back here, I find I am rubbed raw by the enduring strangeness of all that I expect to be familiar by now. For someone like me who has shifted cultures so often, each time the old comes up against the new it hurts. Each time my name is called in yet another language (these days it is in Chinese, over the dormitory intercom), I dread that I will forget who I am. But then Adrienne Rich's poem helps me probe further: Why have I come so far? Would I swim out so deep if I had not meant to challenge my fear of drowning?

A week ago my adviser from Stanford, Lyman Van Slyke, and his wife Barbara arrived in Peking. I rushed back from the South to greet them. Down there in the soft warmth of an afternoon's sightseeing, I saw young Chinese scholars walking hand in hand with their old teachers in the palace of Ming emperors, which had been the Taiping rebel headquarters. In that setting, I glimpsed a patient, delicate rebirth of affection between generations of Chinese intellectuals who had been shouting political accusations at each other for over a decade now. I came back eager to meet my own teacher of Chinese history in China. I try to be both Chinese and American, both filial and friendly. It is harder than I expected. Our time together in Peking is filled with gestures in which I "treat": a lunch, a beer, a snack, a cotton jacket. All these givings are awkward repayment for years of receiving. Such debilitating, un-Chinese calculations. Yet, they go on endlessly inside my head. Also, I didn't expect that I wouldn't be able to answer their simplest questions about life in China today: How much does it cost for a Chinese university student to eat each month in the canteen? Since then, I found out—eighteen dollars. Such questions thrust me back to my pre–oral examination terror. I feel that I am a pretender, who claims to know but in fact knows nothing.

I meet Van and Barbara in the hallway of the Peking Hotel. Our three-way hug is sweet, rooted in eight years of friendship, in their loyalty to me during my marriage and divorce, in their willingness to show and to share their own difficult changes as they grow into middle age. Our first talk is breathless, crowded by news of my months in China. They tell me about their group of powerful and wealthy Los Angeles tourists interested in foreign affairs. Later, a quiet, late night walk by the Forbidden City walls.

The next day, Barbara comes out to the university with a gift: Adrienne Rich's *Selected New Poems, 1950–1974*. I had given Rich's *Dream of a Common Language* to her and Van for their twentieth wedding anniversary last summer. Now, I listen to how their lives are changing. She speaks to me intensely, in the familiar voice of those years in California. Her unburdening is friendly, loving. Yet I find it wears me down. After months of prolonged solitude in the midst of Chinese reticence about the self, my ears ache. I am running out of breath as I listen. In the end, I'm left frantic and embarrassed. I ask Barbara if she would mind taking a bike ride in silence for a while.

The following day, Van comes to class with me at the university. We sit among a hundred and fifty Chinese undergraduates, listening to Yuan Liangjun lecture about Mao's literary theories and the cultural innovations of the Ya'nan period. A precious moment: to see my American teacher in the presence of my Chinese one. It is, however, marred by a gnawing sense of inadequacy: Why don't I understand more of the jokes in Chinese? Why can't I measure up to both of my teachers' hopes?

After a few days, this sense of being a fraud recedes a bit. I finally feel free to ask Van some questions. I become his student again. During a bike ride in the late afternoon, I ask him: How is Peking different from Taibei? How do we incorporate the horror stories of the Cultural Revolution into our previous understanding of modern China? What happened in the "Battle of the Hundred Regiments" in 1940? Whenever I stop feeling that I have to know all the answers, I start to think again. Van's visit makes me realize that thinking about China is hard, almost impossible, to do alone.

This week another privileged opening: I have been accepted into a study group of China-based Westerners. Many have been here for decades. Some were here during the Cultural Revolution, all were wounded by it. One woman's eyes tell the whole story. Still alert and hopeful, they wander off frequently in some remembered pain, especially when she speaks, with a shaky voice, of her thwarted desire to teach literature. In our group, too, a new Canadian friend and her son. I ride over to the meeting with them in the first downpour of the Peking summer. Drenched, muddy, I feel like a puppy, so glad to be off for an evening of good, substantive conversation with other longtime residents of Peking.

The discussion topic for tonight: What constitutes a crime in China? We follow up news about an "open trial" of a twenty-four-year-old factory worker who allegedly crippled the girl who rejected his love by hitting her with a hammer. Some of the foreign experts in our group (those working as employees of the Chinese government) had been invited as spectators to the trial. We keep coming back to the question: Why is there such a lack of interest in China in the psychological dimension of criminality? Could the Chinese legal system be strengthened by a more effective diagnosis of mental illness and more options for reform outside the prison? Work? We are well aware of the rationalizations which are part of the "temporary insanity" plea in the West.

We discuss questions that would be hard to ask our Chinese hosts directly: What is a political crime? Can one be considered a political criminal within the framework of the present Chinese constitution? How can people be arrested for the contents of their wall posters at the same time that the government is claiming to uphold the constitutional right to write big character posters? How can torture be forbidden as long as confessions remain a prerequisite to rehabilitation? Our questions touch some raw, exposed nerves. A young man declares: "It is impossible for legal officials to know if a person is lying." An older man, drawing upon years of imprisonment and confession writing during the Cultural Revolution, cautions: "It is harder still for the accused himself to know."

I hear far more than I can understand tonight. The conversation has the integrity of a lived experience that I will never share. I am glad I have the rest of the year to listen and to learn. I wonder when, if ever, I will be able to make sense of the revelations I hear in China today. The myths I brought from the outside, myths about the China of the 1960s, still color my perceptions. Again, Adrienne Rich proves helpful. Although my own name does not appear in "the book of myths" her poem alludes to, I am plunging into the "wreck" of the Cultural Revolution. There is much to reckon with here. I feel as though I too collaborated in the ravage of that event by negating the rumors of violence that were coming out of Chi ' at that time. That feeling of being an accomplice, however neg. tive, is my only concrete connection to China's recent history.

Most of this week I try to make sense of what is really going on in China but can't. I am aware of something, something not quite obvious: the sexual frustrations of youth, the murderous criticism against old leaders. I grasp at these bits. The more frenzied my need to know China, however, the less I talk, the less I go out, the less I engage my Chinese friends in conversation. Nothing seems sharp these days except my desire to fling myself against some edge of real truth. If I only knew where it could be found.

Then, another accidental occurrence. Today after lunch, I stop to chat a minute longer with a Swiss student whom I have found delightfully witty before. He asks to ride on the back of my bike. I like the idea of trying something I have never done before. I don't even get too crushed when he criticizes my riding in fluent Chinese. His practiced body knows how to balance better than I can ride: "You shake too much. What's the matter with you? Did you just learn to ride a bike this year?" He asks me up to his room for coffee. There, as his Chinese roommate sleeps, he shows me his photographs. Some that I liked the most: a palace roof, a girl in contemplation, a father's nose brushing the cheek of his baby daughter.

We talk about art. He hopes his pictures are more than beautiful, that they serve something more deeply human. He tells me at length about the agony he went through to choose the most accurate Swiss lens ever made. I look more than I listen. My eyes, hungry, rove over the clear images. His way of seeing seems so much sharper, so much more effective, than mine. I wonder how much of his skill in photography depends on his knowledge of Chinese architecture. His image of two roofs in stark contrast is so fine.

I wonder if it is his foreigner's preconception about China that makes the little girl's relaxed contemplation seem so unique. Her shy inwardness, a momentary gift of trust to the Swiss photographer. I am particularly taken with the photograph of the father with his baby daughter. In this culture that once viewed women as useless, in which baby girls were often killed, this father's tenderness seems a concrete sign of the new social order.

For many years, I used to oppose art and meaning. I used to believe that everything moral was on the side of the latter. Truth, too, used to be firmly, conveniently, on the side of meaning. Now, in China, my categories are being scrambled. With a wedge driven between what I see and what I know, the only way left to be truthful has something to do with art. In Nanjing, the image I came up with for truth-seeking objectivity was a gem. Today I hit upon the idea of a bell: some absolutely clear sound that would echo so deeply inside that it would be heard as compelling on the outside. I realize this might require a vacuum. So I go on trying to create stillness around me.

JUNE 19   *Habits of unseeing:*
China through American eyes
The U.S.A. seems a place so remote in space that at times I am prone to forget my ties to it. Then, some clippings sent by my parents in Miami remind me. The gas crisis has gotten worse in California and Carter is close to losing the election. Also two articles by Jack Anderson: "Red Chinese Turmoil Defies Analysis" and "Inscrutable Man Puzzles Analysts Studying China." The first begins: "Red China is the despair of

Western intelligence experts. If, as Churchill observed, Russia is a riddle wrapped inside an enigma, mainland China is a fortune cookie wrapped in an egg roll inside a bowl of fried rice." The second concludes with the CIA assessment of Hua Guofeng: "He doesn't know where the bodies are buried. He hasn't been around long enough to be the top man."

At first I am filled with an old, futile rage: Why this ceaseless projection of American fears onto Chinese realities? Then, I calm down and acknowledge that I have no more idea of Chinese realities living here in Peking than does Jack Anderson, living far away. Still, why are these old images of an inscrutable China and worn homilies about Chinatown foods used to describe Chinese politics in June 1979? What has made them serviceable, credible again? What makes the asking of these questions so hard is that I have no place yet from which to answer them. But then again, these words from home are not opaque to me.

The voices of the "analysts" quoted by Anderson are not alien to me. I am coming to know them: young men in polyester suits who work in the Embassy's political office. We meet at cocktail parties for visiting dignitaries such as Isaac Stern, we exchange quips about aged compatriots who tend to drop dead on summer tours of this still-forbidden city. I recognize in their faces my fellow graduate students at Yale and Stanford. Having spent a long time in Taiwan, they speak Chinese well. They work hard to cope with the expanding U.S.-China business. They generate and process information. Nothing too pernicious—some photographs of people milling around Democracy Wall, a collection of so-called underground newspapers. They are courteous to the Chinese employees and kind toward their own, not infrequently Chinese, wives. In sum, decent men, with respectable credentials, out to do a good job. So why do they reinforce the shortsightedness back home?

Perhaps their stories of a mysterious, befuddling China are so convincing because the Chinese themselves are so confused about China today. Riding in a cab last week, I pass the Great Hall of the People, center of ceremonial politics in the People's Republic. Fifty or so buses are lined up in front: a sure sign that the National Political Consultative Conference has begun. I ask the driver what he thinks of this occasion. "Yeah, I guess it's pretty important. Big economic decision afoot. Nope, I can't say I know much about the issues. To tell you the truth, I can't get too excited about things so big, so far, so hard to grasp." I recall a peasant saying in traditional China: "Heaven is high, the Emperor is far away. What has it got to do with us?"

Plenty, of course. In the past, exorbitant taxes used to be set according to false estimates of local harvest conditions. Today, a new legal code is about to be promulgated based on a hurried repudiation of Cultural Revolution "crimes." The current meeting in the capital is a gathering of more than two hundred representatives from various organizations, professional associations, so-called democratic parties. Something like a congress, this *renda,* "Great mass meeting," meets irregularly and approves policies already decided by the Party Central Committee. Still, the fact that it is being convened at all right now suggests that policies are shifting. There is likely to be considerable debate about the "readjustment" of the overly ambitious 1978 modernization plan.

Officials are concerned that these disputes remain secret. Peking is shrouding itself in bureaucratic reserve. There are rumors, again, of cutbacks in relations with foreigners. While I sense a general tightening in the city, my own contacts are more or less open. Perhaps I feel less closed off because I know two representatives at the congress: old Professor Li Tiezheng, the roving expert-adviser on foreign affairs, and K. H. Ting, the Christian representative from Nanjing. They are optimistic about a new, creative mood of discussion. Perhaps a new policy toward Taiwan might emerge. Certainly more freedom for religious belief is about to be sanctioned.

These are bits, to be sure. I am left with a general impression that much is going on. But I'm not sure what is at stake here and for whom. Getting out of the cab to take the train to Tianjin (Tientsin), I catch myself missing "democracy" explicitly for the first time since we arrived. The simple fact of regularly scheduled elections back home and the obvious phenomenon of newspapers that print more than Carter's welcoming speeches to foreign dignitaries are stunning now by virtue of their absence in China. I am growing keenly aware of how much power we have back home through free information. Here, there is so little information about power, or about anything else for that matter, that neither the people nor the government realize their growing apartness.

Two days in Tianjin, a grimy industrial center south of Peking, visiting a new English friend. Ravaged in rapid sequence by the political violence of the Cultural Revolution and by the 1976 earthquake, the city endures in great dilapidation with a gritty will. Contrasting impressions: young hoodlums spending a hot afternoon at Kissling's Cafe, a remnant of the imperialist era. The cafe offers cushioned booths and mounds of meat dishes. Its clientele is supposed to have been schooled out of material desires. Hardly.

A dusk walk through earthquake shelter settlements. Now, three years old, they are still tiny, temporary dwellings. They were built from rubbish, spare bricks, tarpaper, park railings. All have newspaper windows. One cottage decorated with a red flag is the neighborhood model for cleanliness. The others, not to be outdone, sprout little gardens, potted vegetables, bicycle sheds, and, of course, grandmothers and babies. Again, I am struck how little it takes to retain dignity, sanitation, and the will to procreate.

JUNE 20 *A morning in the wheat fields*

Yesterday afternoon, by chance I read an announcement on the bulletin board of our dorm: "Foreign students who wish to participate in labor tomorrow can do so along with their department." I ask a fellow Chinese student standing by what this really means. She tells me it is a project to harvest wheat. "We're getting up at 3 A.M. If you want to, you can join, I guess." I'm eager. In the past, whenever we asked school officials to take us to factories and communes for a look at the "open-door schooling" of the Cultural Revolution days, we were put off, repeatedly and forcefully: "You would be too much of a burden on the peasants . . ." Here, now, we have a chance. Probably only out of economic need. It has been raining for a whole week. The wheat must be taken in promptly, or it will rot.

It seems that all university, middle-school, and army units around Peking have been mobilized for a day of labor to help out local communes. After reading the announcement, I rush upstairs to find my friend Zhang Jihong, another member of the group of worker-peasant-soldier students who are being impatiently graduated from Peking University. She has been my contact with the Literature Department since the first day of class. She happens to be in her room, and is delighted by my decision to join in the labor project. Other girls I run into, many of whom were admitted into the University this year by examination rather than political merit, respond with silly laughs when I tell them I'm going to join in the labor. They are full of excuses about illness and study which will get them out of this requirement. Either the spirit of the Cultural Revolution has died out very fast, or perhaps it never touched very deeply these intellectual elites whom Mao had meant to transform.

Zhang Jihong agrees to come get me at 3 A.M. We will eat breakfast and go on together to the field with her *ban*, a small group within each class, within each department. Hers is made up of thirty-five or so worker-peasant-soldier students. All of them entered together in 1977. Together they fought their way back to classes in opposition to the leadership of the university, which had decided that they needed, after five years of labor, some more "practical experience."

The next morning I wake up at 3:00 A.M. after four hours of sleep (our study group went on until 11:00 P.M. talking about the problems of intellectuals since Liberation). I gulp a cup of coffee, put on sneakers, old jeans, and a gray cotton shirt I bought here. My head in a red scarf, I wait for Zhang Jihong. She comes fifteen minutes late (she cannot afford an alarm clock like the cadres' children).

We rush to the Chinese students' cafeteria, excited, chattering in the still night. She pays for a bread roll for me. I manage to turn down the bowl of gruel. This turns out to be just the beginning of a day-long effort to take care of me, with food, water, etc. We walk hand in hand over to the men's dormitories where her *ban* is to assemble. The noisy, sleepy guys tumble down the stairs, too tired to show surprise that a foreign woman is about to join their group. At about 3:40 A.M. we start out, our small group now filled out by fifteen to twenty men whom I had seen in the modern literature class and by some of Zhang Jihong's other women friends. To my left walks a beautiful girl with a huge straw hat called Xiao Xie (Little Shoe); another girl from an Inner Mongolian village joins us. In our group, also a girl with a bright buck-tooth smile names Xiao Xiong (Little Tiger). I also recognize a girl considered the "party spy" by some Westerners. She's the lanky daughter of army parents who, rumor has it, makes more regular and more eager reports about foreigners' activities than any other Chinese student in our dorm. All I know is that she is bold in pursuit of English conversation partners and unabashed about liking to party and to dance with Western men.

We arrive at the wheat fields with the dawn. Commune members are still asleep, except for the handful of "responsible persons" on hand to greet us. They point us toward the dark, wet fields in which lies the wheat cut down by yesterday's volunteers. We set out across mud paths toward the assigned area. Our task: to bundle the wheat and haul it to the thrashing terrace. In our *ban* there are a bunch of young soldiers with ropes around their waists. Experienced "countrysiders," they came prepared for carrying in the harvest. One among them slows down by my side: "Are you not Teacher Shu (my name in Chinese is Shu Hengzhe)? Didn't you give a talk to the Literature Department graduate students a while ago? You know, I was there, and would like to know more about the Western theory of structuralism you mentioned. How could it be used to interpret Chinese literature? Can I come to talk with you next Monday night? Zhang Jihong, will you come along with me to talk with Professor Shu, O.K.?" Excited laughter all around. My friend looks proud but not arrogant. She agrees and explains to others more of who I am and what I teach. There is a general excitement in the air. We all know it is a rare chance indeed for an American teacher and Chinese students to work together in the wheat fields.

I grab three bunches of wheat stacked by the experienced hands of the soldiers in our group. With this wet, heavy, fragrant load (about twenty-five pounds), I walk behind Zhang Jihong to the thrashing area. Those with ropes on their backs can haul more. Their experience in the countryside enables them to be more effective than those of us just getting a taste of harvest labor. Deep in the thin sliver of mud which separates the wheat fields from the rice paddies, I walk with my bunches, turning down compliments about my strength and the ruggedness of Americans in general.

Finally I am doing something in China, not only wondering in my mind about China. Glad, too, to be giving a bit of myself, not just taking. So well nourished in China, not just by the food but by the generosity of my friends, I feel I am paying back a bit. Not in that familiar, guilty way in which I try to wipe out debts of all

Carrying wheat stalks with Zhang Jihong, a friend and classmate at Beida.

sorts at home, but in some sort of simple, more direct currency which has to do with labor and the roll I ate for breakfast this morning.

On the way back to the next bunch of wheat, I see far off the blonde hair of Melanie, a Canadian friend, my running partner these days. She is carrying a large load on her back. She looks a touch solemn in her purposefulness among the duller History Department crowd. Closer by, I notice Patty Wen, an overseas Chinese girl from Radcliffe. Her white sneakers and purple pullover sweater are somewhat cumbersome for the grimy work she is about to begin. Yet she laughs, undeterred, unselfconscious. The Chinese girls giggle with delight at this compatriot. We also pass by Felix, an older Mexican student, with his sombrero and camera. He offers to take a picture of me and Zhang Jihong.

Back in our field, I hear a high-pitched voice. I turn to recognize the face of Xia Yan, the poetry critic who delivered that impassioned talk about thwarted creativity during the May Fourth academic conference. He smiles and greets me. During my next march to the thrashing area, the same smile greets me from the faces of the graduate students in the Literature Department. Many have become good friends in recent months. Later I run into a professor from the Philosophy Department with whom I had talked about Hegel's logic. On top of the rising mound of wheat by the thrashing machine, I look up to recognize other members of the Literature Department faculty, pitchforks in hand. Each time my eyes meet a face, there is an open smile. None of the gawking reserve I face around me daily in my life as a foreigner.

I am still embarrassed by the fact that everyone advises me to carry less, to slow down. Nonetheless, in the general hilarity, I feel free to say, somewhat surprised to hear my own voice: "I will not let down the American people in this friendly competition with Chinese labor." I feel free to laugh along with Chinese friends at the wisecracks about the "Communist spirit." Much jovial, mutual teasing about "You foxy old cadre, you sure know how to get away with giving orders and no work." Even funnier, if a bit more cutting, are lines like, "Hey, you look like the landlord's field mammy." This, I gather, after hilarious explanations, used to be the expression for the wet nurses of the landed gentry in the old society.

As the morning gets lighter, we talk less and laugh more. We skip over frogs, invent better ways to carry more wheat with ropes found for us by men on our team. After three hours or so, the whistle announces a half-hour break. I sit for awhile on the bunches of wheat among the girls. We eat the extra roll brought along from breakfast. The girls talk about their previous experiences in the countryside, about how hard it is to find a boyfriend if you are twenty-five, about how worried they feel about their work assignments after graduation. I answer openly their questions about American romancing, about my divorce, about my memories of labor in Romania.

Later Zhang Jihong shows me where to wash up. Along the way she slips me a boiled egg. It must have come from another student in our group. Probably some hefty guy had decided, or more likely been persuaded, to give away this extra nourishment to the "American friend." I am embarrassed, but there is no way to turn it down. Later there is water, soup, wine, and more bread.

By the end of our rest period the peasants are awake, out and about, busy with their own work. They seem curious and warm toward these educated youths who have been sent down in the all-too-familiar routine of harvest help. Both sides are engaged in a practiced ritual of mutual respect. I sense something a bit hollow here. Still, this ritual is not as empty as it is depicted in the newspaper articles about "the need for more political education among educated youth."

The commune radio station is awake, too, broadcasting morning greetings, urging hard work, playing favorite tunes from a recent Indian movie (a soap-opera plot about a righteous judge and his hoodlum son). The morning's broadcast ends with thanks "to Peking university students who have come to help us out, and for the inspiring efforts of our foreign friends who work alongside them." Our group laughs heartily, out loud, not so covertly gratified.

For the last two hours, by hand, we pick up row after row of wheat strands trampled underfoot during the earlier mass hauling. I kneel along with Zhang Jihong. The girl with the big straw hat, kneeling next to us, turns out to have a beautiful voice. She sings for us folk ballads, tunes about village life. I hum along, for once totally unselfconscious about my voice, which cannot reach the lilting heights of that of the girl bending beside me. I am aware only of the shared measure of our work, the rhythm of hands and words in time with songs about "new bright days in commune life" and "where, oh where, are you, my warrior love."

After an hour or so of singing together, after she has taught me some tunes and some verses, Zhang Jihong asks me if I know any Western songs. I get flustered. She laughs and starts in on a Russian tune. I am delighted when I finally remember the melody to "Moscow Nights." By the end, we gather thirty bunches of hand-tied, sweet-smelling, muddy strands of wheat. I feel relaxed enough to sing to her some American songs. I call over to Patty Wen in another field. Together, we do an awkward rendition of "Swing Low, Sweet Chariot" and "If I Had a Hammer."

The morning's work ends, as I learn how to make a rope out of wheat straws and bundle a few bunches on my own. By this time, I am high, tired. I catch myself singing out loud Israeli tunes

I know well, like "Erev shel shoshanim" (Evening of Roses). It is an outpouring of something inside me that remains nameless, yet not beyond language.

Back in the dorm, I take a two-hour nap. I catch myself dreaming in Chinese for the first time since we arrived.

JUNE 28   *Wheat outside the library, Nietzsche and Einstein inside*   A historiographical debate about the "sprouts of capitalism" has been going on in China for the past two decades. Scholars rushed to gather evidence about commercial activity at the end of the Ming dynasty (sixteenth and seventeenth centuries) to prove that China could have become a modern society on its own. The blame for its delayed modernity was, thus, placed on the disastrous interference of Western imperialism. It was the West, the argument goes, which dampened, and then drowned, the "seeds of native capitalism." The storm of this debate has subsided now that "imperialism" fades into historical memory. Mao, the peasant philosopher who had popularized the metaphor of "sprouts" and who worried about restoration of capitalism in China, is fading into the background of current policy debates about modernization. The idea of sprouts, of something incipient, frail, which can become strong and enduring through human effort, is being diluted in China today.

In the meantime, the campus of our university has been smelling particularly acrid these days. The stench of wet, fermenting wheat is strongest around dusk. For the past week, the cement walkways and the entire plaza in front of the library have been covered with husked wheat. It is being put out to dry here because of the shortage of flat, unmuddy space in nearby communes. Classroom entryways are full of workers from the communes who come to spread out the harvest each morning. They take long, leisurely naps throughout the day and then bundle up the wheat around 6 P.M. It begins all over the next day.

The first time I see this, less than twenty-four hours after our participation in harvest labor, I feel it is sacrilegious. To ride my bike through mounds of the wheat that we had bundled with such effort! My rage mounts as I notice the wind scattering the wheat and mounds of coal refuse freely mingling with the wheat

Peasant woman spreading out wheat to dry in front of the Beida Library. In the background, one of the more popular statues of Chairman Mao dating from the Cultural Revolution.

behind the Post Office. The only check on my fury at this spectacle of inefficiency and waste comes when sheets of rain pound the campus at midday. Once again, droves of students are out with shovels hastily helping peasants to get the semidry wheat into thoroughly wet sacks. These sacks, then, are put into damp hallways until the next day of sunshine. As the days go by, more and more of the harvest is scattered in the bushes. Much of it dry by now. but rotting.

Eventually the campus gets cleaned up. Commune workers recede with their bundles and their trucks. With the walkways cleared, students are freer now to rush to classes and to the library. A pervasive terror about exams takes hold. Everybody, including most of the foreign students, is cramming, memorizing facts, preparing outlines for essays, sharing excited worries. Manual work couldn't be further from these academic concerns. It appears that our day of "labor" was a temporary, minimal nod toward the once-politicized education of the Maoist era. At our study group meeting on Tuesday night, I hear that certain "key" (that is, "best") schools in Peking had explicit directives not to let students go off to labor so as not to interfere with their preparations for exams.

This is the first year in which examinations are fully in use in the People's Republic after their abolition during the Cultural Revolution. Not only are entrance examinations for colleges and graduate schools back, but so are end-of-semester tests, berated by Mao in the 1960s because they increased the "mental anguish of students." Faculty members now don't seem particularly bent on ensnaring students, on increasing their worry or pain. And yet, the mood of tension has escalated dramatically during the past few days. Mostly internalized pressure, but powerful nonetheless.

I also spent the last few days in the library. I'm reading a long article written in 1920 by one of China's greatest modern writers, Mao Dun. A young man at the time (only twenty-three or so), he was just beginning his work on the theory of literary criticism. His topic: Nietzsche, a particularly appealing philosopher to the intellectually hungry youths of the post–May Fourth era. Mao Dun not only introduces Nietzsche's philosophy, but appropriates it.

Interested in how Western ideas were changed and used by Chinese modernizers, I take twenty-six pages of notes. I work at this every bit as feverishly as other students do on their exam preparations. Perhaps I am less embarrassed about this focused activity because of a general mood of forgiveness toward abstract study in China these days. But then I realize that Nietzsche and Mao Dun are not abstract for me. Not here, not now. The task of "transvaluation of values," which Mao Dun found so inspiring and so worrisome in Nietzsche's philosophy, matters to me as well. I am also seeking a way of acknowledging the shaping forces of history and culture. At the same time I search for means to shape these forces in turn.

I read Mao Dun slowly, talking with him as a friend, finally talking back at him—as I am learning to do with all the historical figures I respect. In the end, I try to see through Mao Dun. I use him the same way he used Nietzsche, to get another, fuller perspective on things that matter to me in the present.

Another accidental find in Beida Library while reading Mao Dun: the April 1979 issue of *Pensées* from Paris. In it, an article about Einstein's realism. I translate a passage that brings into focus my thoughts of the past few days: "Einstein is a realist. The realism which he invokes as a lesson in relativity implies a new reality. It requires that we consider reality differently."

This connection between relativity and realism is at the core of my experience in China—an ongoing dialectic between Western perspectives and Chinese realities. Leaving home has put a great distance between things familiar—that is, the West—and things interesting—that is, China. The familiar is becoming more interesting as I take it less complacently. Yet, I am at once challenged and depressed about the task of becoming a realist in China. The fact of cultural relativity is confirmed daily. Slowly, I'm getting to know China better.

Still, it is hard to figure out what's what. The daily papers are baffling with their official, opaque voices. Yesterday, I look up unfamiliar characters and still can't figure out the point of Hua Guofeng's speech on the Middle East, on the Palestinian problem and on the nonrecognition of Israel. I am equally baffled by an outpouring of poetry and essays by and about a woman martyr named Zhang Zhixin. She was condemned as a "reactionary" by the Gang of Four. Now she is being rehabilitated as a model of

Communist morality. I follow, but cannot make any sense of the propaganda about a new legal code.

JULY 5   *Unwittingly ourselves:*   A rumor passed through our
the Bob Hope Show in Peking   study group two weeks ago:
"You can't believe what the
Chinese are doing! They are inviting Bob Hope to China! He is going to make an atrocious movie called *The Road to Peking.*"

Striking how those of us who are sympathetic to China, who are concerned that the policies of the People's Republic be understood abroad, see our role here! We try to protect China from the implications of its own actions. Friendly experts, we'd like to play a larger role in introducing the Chinese masses to progressive Western culture. We remember too well Bob Hope's face on TV during the Vietnam War days. He used his jolly voice to cheer soldiers who mocked the "gooks." So, we can't figure out what he is doing here.

But then, Chinese authorities nowadays are showing similar footage from their own war with Vietnam, body counts and all. So perhaps it is not they who are naive, but we, the friends of China. Still, I leave our study group fretful about how China will be seen abroad. I can't imagine why China would let itself be used as a colorful setting for the Bob Hope show. The double meaning of "Beijing" hits me as I ride my bike late at night. In Chinese it means at once "northern capital" and a plain "backdrop." So, China is to be background for Western fun again.

Two requests which the Chinese authorities supposedly denied Bob Hope while he is making his film: they refused to provide Chinese actors to carry him in a palanquin up Coal Hill behind the Forbidden City. They supposedly said "No," even after Bob Hope had found three Americans and needed just one Chinese to walk along. He was, rumor has it, also denied permission to take his own toilet to the Great Wall.

July third, I find out that I have gotten two tickets to the Bob Hope Independence Day Extravaganza, courtesy of the American Embassy. Having just picked up a ticket for a Chinese play about the Han dynasty, I feel torn. The choice is between learning more about what I don't know, Chinese history, or more about what I know only too well, American popular culture. The choice gets less complicated when I see the tentative program with Baryshnikov. He will perform three times, according to the program. It also features disco music and some country western. I give the other ticket to a Chinese friend.

I am a bit embarrassed when she arrives at seven and finds me dressed in fancy clothes. Lamely but truthfully I confess that I did it in the off chance that my parents might see me in the televised audience. I want to reassure them that I am doing well by looking nice. In the cab down to the theater, we joke about how strange it is to celebrate the Fourth of July in China thirteen hours before the U.S. does. Most people in New York have not even climbed out of bed. They have yet to start to line up for gas so that they can take a holiday ride out of the city. We arrive at a fancy refurbished movie theater. My friend's father used to watch experimental movies here in the 1920s.

The Bob Hope show begins with a "warm-up." The audience is asked by a young technician to laugh, applaud, and give an ovation. All this is taped, to be spliced in later with Bob Hope's jokes in the show yet to come. The Chinese translator tried to find a linguistic equivalent for warm-up. He comes up with "getting hot." My friend asks: Why is the TV crew trying to create something phony and call it "live" theater later? I can't suppress a warning: "Take care that your modernization doesn't lead to this false aliveness!" The technician concludes with an announcement: "And now, ladies and gentlemen, America's gift to the world, Bob Hope!" Since China is a society still recovering from the personality cult of the Mao era, this remark leaves us embarrassed.

Ambassador Leonard Woodcock then takes the stage to make some remarks about the historic significance of this first Independence Day after normalization. He concludes with polite, but not overly enthusiastic, praise for "our ambassador of fun and laughter." Finally, Bob Hope comes out, aged but shiny, like an old crystal ball.

The first part of the program is billed as "comedy monologue with translation." It goes on for thirty minutes. At first awkward, then tiresome, and, finally, plain exasperating. Hope's subjects: the adventures of a clever but naive "I" caught among the weird but friendly "they."

I can't help wondering how culture-bound an activity the monologue is, after all. How much does it draw upon a public berating of a fledgling self? Hope starts with a tirade of made-up Chinese words, "their" kind of funny talk. It makes me wince to hear him mispronounce Chinese words so comfortably. Chinese people around me are laughing less and less. They find no fun at all in Bob Hope's lightly lewd joke about their "ever-ready batteries which charge a population of over 900 million." They appear equally unmoved by jokes featuring Bob Hope's spendthrift wife.

After one long stretch of monologue about the super-quick laundry service at the Peking Hotel in which Bob Hope tells of his troubles of being thrown in the wash along with his pajamas, my friend leans over and asks loudly, "Now what is the point of that?" Part of the problem is just plain cultural differences. I find myself bursting out in laughter yet cannot explain to her Hope's quip: "Crossing the street in Peking is like playing baseball in Los Angeles: you are either a Dodger or an Angel."

The largely Chinese audience (more than eighty percent of those in the hall) is sympathetic with the Chinese translator, who cannot explain the jokes about Colonel Sanders, the Hyatt House, or Hilton Hotels. His inability, unwillingness really, to translate these words into Chinese might signal a covert refusal of the very things America wants to give China more of. Hope's last jokes are about the lack of freedom in China. He winks to the American TV audience at home: "Be glad. You have nothing to complain about. Carter, if you are watching, you owe me one!" I ask myself if things at home are falling apart so fast that China needs to be dragged in as a reassuring contrast.

Highlights from the rest of the show. The name of the disco group, Peaches and Herb, sounds very good in Chinese: "Pao he Cao." Their looks, however, jar Chinese eyes. A young black woman appears in purple sequin net that covers her silk underpants and her see-through top. The sounds coming from the undulating singer and her crooning companion are mild by American standards. And yet, Peaches' hips moving back and forth along Herb's front zipper is too much for my neighbor. She turns her head in shock and disgust. I have been trying to introduce her to good black music from back home. But here, I can't help feeling her shame. Embarrassed, I start to talk quickly about how capitalism has thwarted black people's culture, how sequins on a black woman's body should not be mistaken for well-being among most of America's minorities, about how the words of her last song, "Right Here and Now," are meant to make the poor forget their worries about tomorrow. None of my social theorizing can soothe her injured modesty. She feels sad for, hurt by, that sequined girl.

The parts of the program which my friend liked the best: A pantomime about a man who becomes a monkey after eating a banana. He wanders into a city zoo and ends up choosing the safe captivity of the animal world rather than going back to urban humanity. *Sesame Street*'s Big Bird delights her as well. Baryshnikov performs just once, sharing the stage with a Chinese ballerina, Zhang Runping. Their pas de deux from *Giselle* reveals her effort and her limitations.

Zhang Runping, like other Chinese dancers, lives on a rice diet. Deprived of Russian teachers since the 1950s, her technique is rusty. She has been forbidden to dance ballet for the past fifteen years. It was deemed "too bourgeois" during the Cultural Revolution. Out of consideration for her, Baryshnikov is tame, leaps about very little. He conveys a mere hint of his prowess on this Chinese stage. The audience senses his good will and responds warmly.

The last number on the program is a Chinese magician. She is thirtyish, dressed in a demure, Western-style blue skirt and jacket. She begins with gentle tricks. Flowers and cards pour out of her endless, slim sleeves. Her understated, slow performance is full of smiles and cheerful Chinese music—a strong contrast to the flashy magic more familiar at home.

The last trick she performs involves a glass box in full view of the audience. Simply, with a silent message, "See, I am hiding nothing," the magician twirls the box and suddenly, a young girl pops out from nowhere. She holds a bouquet from which the magician spirits forth a pair of doves, two huge flags—those of China and the U.S.A.—and a giant banner which reads in bold Chinese characters: "Long Live the Friendship between the Chinese and American People." In the upbeat mood of this finale, I find myself wondering if Chinese-American friendship is just magic after all. What about the undisturbed prejudices on both sides, not far beneath this bubbly warmth?

Bob Hope brings the curtain down on the show with a new version of an old song about friendship: "If You're Ever in a Jam,

If You're Ever Put in Jail, If You're Ever up a Tree, Call on Me."
No doubt this is exactly what the TV audience back home wants
to hear. After thirty years of the Cold War, a needy, ready-to-be-
saved China has lost none of its appeal.

Back in my dorm at midnight, I find a line in Trevor-Roper's
book *A Hidden Life:* "Backhouse easily infused the Chinoiserie
which he knew into the China he had discovered." If an English-
man who spent half a century in the Central Kingdom could do
this, can Bob Hope be blamed?

JULY 19   *Panic and self-improvement: Beida during exam week*   It started about two weeks ago:
gatherings, like moths, under the
street lamps at night. At first, it
looked like a natural outpouring of life, a sign of the coming of
summer. It has been getting hot. People linger on stoops after
dinner. As the evening hours shade into one another, women
gather to knit and embroider—activities that had been considered
"too feudal" during the decade of the Cultural Revolution. Usually some six to eight women draw together under a street lamp,
talking and sewing. The men, more and more unabashed about
idleness after work, gather for card playing—another "antisocial
activity" forbidden during the Cultural Revolution. The men prefer to play two or three street lamps away from their chatty wives.

Last night, riding back after midnight from the Language Institute to the university, I was enjoying the sharp sound of frogs
in the rice paddies. I am unprepared for the sight of a squatting
figure in the middle of a well-lit, thoroughly deserted intersection.
A high-school student with a wooden board on his bent knees is
practicing a geometry lesson. By the time I get back to Beida it is
nearly 1 A.M. On campus, under nearly every street lamp, I see
a pacing student holding those by now familiar homemade crib
booklets. Some fifty or so thin, three-inch sheets crammed with
information to be memorized. The students are forced outside
because the lights go off by regulation at 10 P.M. in the Chinese
dormitories.

It is striking how fast the examination frenzy has affected even
the foreign students here. An overseas Chinese woman, nearly
thirty years old and a confident mother of three, has been wracked

for a week by diarrhea. She is trying to memorize the chronology of nineteenth-century imperialist invasions and peasant wars. A cool, efficient Canadian woman has been nauseated for days now, weak and shaky as she readies for a philosophy exam on the question of war in Marxism and Mao Zedong's thought.

The mood is infectious. I find myself studying more, memorizing more characters, practicing a few extra hours of Chinese writing. Still, I know I am "free." Little depends for me, here, on how well I retain book knowledge. Yet I feel a vague, restless pressure to generate new perspectives.

I have been running regularly lately. Up around 6:30 A.M. as the summer morning mists evaporate. I wear a Red Star T-shirt and shorts, considered too bold for women in China. No one notices. Mornings on the track are taken up with memorizing language lessons. Every day, three-quarters of the way down the track, I pass a young man, perched on a metal judge's stand, practicing French essays at the top of his voice. On my left, an older student is practicing elementary English. I run past his loud version of "HOW . . . MUCH . . . DOES . . . THAT . . . COST?" The student of French, legitimately exhilarated by the sound of his own fluency, goes on in a high-pitched, nearly Parisian accent, about the virtues of Chinese socialism. Several days later, the English student has advanced to "WHERE ARE YOU PLANNING TO GO THIS MORNING?" He delights in greeting me. A craze for conversational English seems to be sweeping China these days.

In Shanghai last week, three African students were wounded by Chinese students at the Textile Institute. The spark seems to have been the old complaint about privileged foreign students: Why do they get higher stipends from the Chinese government? Why are they not subject to the same social rules as Chinese students? The violence of the response, this time, is startlingly new. Again, as often before, the quarrel began over loud rock music and the casual attitude of African students toward Chinese women.

I am trying to trace the facts behind the rumors of the Shanghai incident. I talk a little bit longer with my black woman friend from Madagascar. She tells me that Chinese students in Shanghai were upset that their girl friends have been pursued too relentlessly by African students. A furious crowd of Chinese students was ready to start an attack for weeks. Then one night there was disturbing music which distressed Chinese students, frantically studying for their examinations. The African students, it seems, had finished their tests earlier and were partying when someone's Chinese roommate asked to have the music turned down. Told to wait a half hour, the furious Chinese student, already on edge, went off to get his equally anxious Chinese friends. Thirty or so of them roughed up the black students quite badly.

I hear vague rumors that the Ministry of Education is calling meetings at every university. "Something must be done" is their plea. It is unclear whether Chinese authorities will be able to keep black students in line, without facing up to the excessively raw nerves of their own students. Chinese students are coping, all at once, with the unfamiliar pressure of examinations and with the even more alien customs of foreigners, whom they are supposed to respect "for the sake of China's modernization."

The impact of the examinations is hitting students with noticeable disparity. I ran into Xin Ling, a freshman in the History Department. Two months ago, when our friendship began with excited conversations about the Japanese Meiji Restoration and about French views of Napoleon's dictatorship, she appeared tense but open-minded. She was eager to undertake genuine, "scientific," historical research. Two days ago, I run into her. She's standing motionless, distressed, outside the dormitory door: "These exams are killing me." She tells me that she has been doing her best and yet can't shake the panic that she needs to give more, to know more.

This afternoon, Xin Ling tumbles out of her room like a dazed, sullen cat. I ask her how her studying is coming along. (In Chinese, casual conversation always begins with comments upon obvious activity. For example, "Have you eaten?" is the Chinese equivalent of "hello" when we meet on the way to and from the dining room.) Xin Ling's eyes are empty, scared. For a few minutes I'm unable to see in them the spirit of the girl I know. She is from Anhui, a poor, rough province. She had labored strenuously before passing the examinations to get into the university, where she has to pass even more exams. As we talk, I recall a rumor I heard from some French girls that Xin Ling might be kicked out of school. It was discovered that she cheated on the entrance exam.

Another, rather different scene, when I drop by to see my friend

Shen Zhaoyan, the slight, tough, worker-peasant-soldier student. She is in her last year at the university. Part of that holdover class from the Maoist era, she wishes she knew more but doesn't fret. Just now, she is studying for her test on modern Chinese literature. I lend her books and assure her that the teacher will surely keep his promise not to make the exam too difficult. We plan our Sunday night out to celebrate the end of her exams. When I leave her, she is calmly memorizing historical events relevant to the transformation of Lu Xun's world view after 1927.

Two years ago when I passed through China, examinations were just being brought back, stealthily, apologetically. Exams were being explored then, along with other criteria—for example, political recommendations. Now, examinations are broadly acclaimed as a countermeasure to or an insurance against all sorts of "special privilege." The problem of privilege arose out of the corruption, in practice, of the theoretical egalitarianism of the Mao era. Especially during the Cultural Revolution, political consciousness had become the sole criterion for educational opportunities. Youths who could prove their "redness" by political work or bribery were given priority in entrance to the university.

At present, quantifiable learning is back as the basis for college entrance examinations. Children of cadres, from already educated families, are climbing back up the ladder of success, legitimated by their achievement in "objective" tests. There is much praise these days for the fairness of the new (really old) examination systems. Ever since the Song dynasty (960–1127), the Chinese literati have been persuading themselves and the illiterate masses about the fairness of state-sponsored examinations. Those who passed the imperial exams earned status, wealth, and power because of their skill in mastering the Confucian classics. When I hear how much better the examination system is than the "feudal" system of the Gang of Four era, I also hear the pious, self-serving rationalizations of educated elites who, both before and after 1949, benefited from scholastic examinations.

And yet, one cannot be blind to the infectious love of study, to the desire to prove one's worth through learning, that is spreading like wildfire through China. To see only the "having to study" that goes on among the students here is to miss the rampant "wanting to study," which is even more pervasive.

After this morning's run, I walk back along the pathway by the side door of our dormitory. For the second day in a row, I notice a group of four women and one young man talking. I stop to pick some flowers and we begin a conversation. I assume that they are students cramming for tomorrow's schoolwide English test. But they are clerical workers from the library. A self-initiated study group of former school teachers, a sales clerk, and a young library attendant. They get together daily to practice English. All share a vague aspiration to pass the college entrance examinations next fall. Their leader is the young man, who is fluent in English. He is eager, even a touch giddy, to show off his language facility. He tells me about his uncle in Boston, a professor. His stories leave the older women in the group even more wide-eyed. I linger with them. Their energy is hopeful and communal rather than selfish and anxious.

Still, I wonder about the connection between the current frenzy for English study and personal ambition. How does personal drive contribute to the collective goals of "socialist modernization"? In today's paper, an article entitled, "What Does One Do If There Is a Contradiction between Work and Study?" It begins with a letter to the editor from a receptionist who considers himself "too unlucky" because his work area is far removed from the television set in his unit. He complains about being cut off from the televised English lessons. The editor's reply is sanctimonious. He asks the young receptionist to remember that one is not studying for one's self alone but "for China and for the greater glory of modernization. Study-time should not come out of work-time. Study must serve the needs of work, not the other way around."

What remains unanswered is why "study" has become so crucial to self-advancement. Identification with the workplace seems to be depleted by the arbitrary system of job placement. There is little or no hope of change. Just now, the thirst for learning in China is indistinguishable from a drive to make it, to try to get out of being stuck. And yet, I sense a difference between wanting to learn and wanting to get out, a difference consciously nurtured by some teachers who are becoming my friends at the university. They, too, are aching to get down to some research, to explore areas of knowledge that might help them make sense of the political ravage they have recently endured. They try to recreate a comprehensive history of the Cultural Revolution. Currently, it is just reprehensible, to be condemned and forgotten.

CHAPTER 5

SEPTEMBER 1979   *Through Space in Search of Time*

SEPTEMBER 3   *Back home in Peking*

And the end of all our exploring
Will be to arrive where we started
And to know the place for the first time.
(T. S. Eliot, "Four Quartets")

I have been back in my second-floor room in dormitory number 25 at Peking University for almost a week now. It is my home. I had to go away, far away, before I could see how much it has become mine, a part of me. For the past six weeks, I have traveled across five thousand miles, through thirteen provinces: Inner Mongolia, Ningxia, Shanxi, Gansu, Xinjiang, Sichuan, Hubei, Hunan, Jiangxi, Zhejiang, Jiangsu, Shandong, Hebei. I had been preparing for this summer's travel ever since I came to China half a year ago. I knew it would challenge my book knowledge of China and its history. I was hungry for that challenge. Almost ready for it.

As I went deep into China's western region, I read a seventeenth-century Chinese folk novel, *Monkey*. Marvelously, unfaithfully excerpted by Arthur Waley, it tells of the demons, goblins, and monsters that lurk in the rivers, quicksands, marshes, and the harsh gravelly deserts which separate the Han people from other civilizations. I read the book with the eyes of remembered history and with ears tuned to the shifting connotations of present-day policy. One cannot help but be awed by the characters of the story: a fierce agile ape, a gluttonous pig, and a timid monk determined to reach the West (India) to bring back solemn truths (Buddhist sutras). Not unlike today. Their "journey to the West" was forbidding, nearly impossible. Yet our three hereos were

134

helped along the way by beneficent spirits. Then the Boddhisattvas of the Western Paradise, now the local cadres of the China
Travel Service. I read Waley's book during one hundred hours of
train rides from July 23 to August 14. This story of China's reaching outward mirrors my own journey, a reaching deeper into
Chinese society.

For months before the departure of our school-sponsored trip,
I ran every day. I ate extra-healthy food to build up the resistance
my Chinese friends were convinced I would need to survive the
hot, long trek out to the wild west. They were a bit incredulous,
and a touch envious too, that the Beida Liuban (our university's
Foreign Students' Office) was able to get permission for forty
foreign students to go from Inner Mongolia to the western edge
of the Gobi desert for a mere 320 yuan per person (approximately
$200 U.S.). We are to visit Huhehot (Huhhot, capital of Chinese
Mongolia and gateway to the grasslands), Dunhuang (the cave
monastery complex on the silk route, with the finest Buddhist
wall paintings in China spanning over seven thousand years of
Chinese art), and Ürümqi (the capital of Chinese Turkestan). My
Peking friends are taken aback even more by my decision to continue my travels on my own after the group trip to the northwest.
I plan to go into the southwest, down the Yangzi gorges. They
don't quite believe that I will be able to carry through my decision
to visit Shaoxing, the birthplace of Lu Xun, China's foremost
modern writer. Shaoxing has been off limits to individual travelers
up to now.

At the end of this journey, lying thoroughly exhausted and
nearly penniless in a Shanghai hotel, I wondered if I had indeed
taken on too much. By then, however, I had done it all. My
drained body was just a small down payment on the vast precious
learning I could not have gained any other way. Back now at
home as I face the typewriter, I am again wondering if it was too
much. Certainly, too full to tell in a few pages.

Some images from the summer linger into fall. Crowded, tall
yellow petals in the middle of miles and miles of small, bright
purple wild flowers in the Mongolian grasslands. The sharp contrast of color, justly the fame of Mongolian springtime. A similar
tension in the swift shoulders of Mongolian dancers and the skilled
wrists of Mongolian horseriders. Snow-covered mountains rising straight out of the sultry Gobi desert in Xinjiang. A volatile

contrast of hot and cold, passion and fury, I came to treasure as I wander in Ürümqi. The harsh, Moslem flavor of the northwest, in turn so different from the soft, misty dawn as the boat approaches the Yangzi gorges. When I get up at dawn, still alone on the deck, egg-white clouds rise out of the sky-blue waters and float up and around gray pine peaks. There, in the gateway to South China, my face is caressed by the sweetest of breezes.

Beyond these images, some excerpts from the diaries I kept throughout the trip. Can the parts ever add up to the whole? Only the months after this journey can tell whether, as T. S. Eliot promised, I have arrived where I started, whether I have come to know this place, China, for the first time.

TUESDAY, JULY 24, 9:30 P.M.
Mongolia, outside Huhehot in the grasslands
Before we came here, we were told we would spend some time deep in the grasslands. We were promised an evening or two in yurts. We were told we would ride horses. We imagined seeing and learning what nomadic life meant to the Mongolian people themselves.

A Mongolian culture show is being put on for us now. Flowery costumes, butterflies sewn onto blue silk overalls. The string instruments we hear are metal: soft, rhythmic, hushed all at once. The horse show we saw during the afternoon is also remote, staged far away from where we sit in a sky-blue domed grandstand. Our yurts are "made for foreigners." Special electric lights, little wooden tables and dressers inside. Question: What is meaning of "less" (*shao*) in the Chinese expression for minority: *shaoshu minzu* (people who are less in number)? When, how did "few" come to mean "less"?

Still, I could not have imagined the smell of the grasslands, the wind moving softly through the many-colored flowers. The air is sharp, the hills are green, as definite as the gestures of the riders at the grandstand. No harsh edges here. Sharp flowers, not fragile, yet delicately white. The purple ones echo the hills and the stones with their many variations.

We are staying and dining in the courtyard of a Buddhist (actually Lamaist, a Mongolian faith related to Tibetan Buddhism) temple. It was destroyed in 1966, then refurbished for tourism last year. During the Mongolian culture show put on for us, a Canadian friend and I talk softly, critically about the Minorities' Dance Institute in Peking. It is the center for training dancers and musicians like the ones we see tonight. It plucks talented Mongolian children out of their native province for "special training" in the capital. Its mission: to preserve minority cultures and make them more Han. The result: abstract gestures, "perfected" and drained of their expressive, "sloppy" minority spirit. We sense an anti-Han feeling among the minorities here. We search, in vain, for local voices in this sea of Han "introductions" to Mongolian culture.

WEDNESDAY, JULY 25, 10 P.M.
Huhehot

Exhausted, a bit drunk after yet another mutton banquet and singing of foreign songs. Today, on the ride back through the grasslands, we pass truck drivers collecting wild flowers to hang on the windows of their huge machines.

Yesterday, we talked with Yu Beichen, Sichuanese president of Inner Mongolia University. A short, fiery man, he is full of figures about discrimination against the Mongols. He is sober in his response to our purist question: Can a Han official really help further the cause of Mongolian education? We are thinking of blacks back home. He answers: "I have given the last twenty years of my life to this mission." Very outspoken about the fate of intellectuals, the wastefulness of the Gang of Four line, Yu Beichen confesses that it still lingers on in education. He is possessed by an unrelenting yet not incapacitating fury when he talks about how poor China is, how poverty cramps the effort to rehabilitate minds, how hard it is to get back to creative work after the ravages of the last decade. He strikes me as a man in a hurry, purposeful, expansive, tested by more than two decades of hard, punishing life in Mongolia.

We see very few Mongols on this whole trip. Few broad cheeks, an absence of the red, flushed coloring I had seen in propaganda pictures. An old Mongol man passed me in the morning in the grassland village. We tried to chat. He spoke a little Mandarin and had blue eyes, a liquid, soft color much like the hills.

THURSDAY, JULY 26, 4:30 P.M.   Ningxia is changing outside the
On the train passing through   window: wet, green, rainy.
Ningxia province, the marshlands   Young trees and large hills of
sand on the horizon. Looks like a friendly, almost hospitable
desert. By 6:30 Gansu province is in full view. Vastly different:
large chains of red-brown mountains, covered by dense vegeta-
tion. Harsh, old civilization, Zuo Zongtang country here. He was
a great nineteenth-century general, sent by the Qing imperial
court to "pacify" this border area. The Old Qing forts are still
visible: gray stone walls among gray sheep and sullen herders.
Crevices open below the desert surface. Their yellow depths mirror the green-brown heights above. Uneven, vengeful Moslem
land.

Later, the land is covered with burned squares of hay. A poor
people's effort to hold the soil with fire. Clearly an old part of
China. Harsh, not just impoverished. A haven for rebels against
Peking authorities, from the nineteenth-century Moslems to twentieth-century Communists.

FRIDAY, JULY 27, 6:30 P.M.   Getting ready for Shabbat, wine
Lanzhou, Gansu   on the the table. Hills shading
into the evening mist and the
industrial pollution outside our hotel window . . . Spent the
afternoon in a park full of Ming period temples, high on a hill over-
looking the Yellow River.

The people of Lanzhou: poor, scared, sullen in their watchful
gazing at us. Older men in patched, torn clothes, pipes in drawn
lips. Their eyes calm, their forbearance unlike the agitated glances
of undernourished kids. High up in the park, I take many photographs of an old woman against the mountain. She is simple,
stark, like a blackbird. Composed, knees drawn up against her
face, patient. Nothing much these people have not been through.
Even if they have not seen much beyond Lanzhou.

SUNDAY, JULY 29, 7 A.M.   Red, shimmering mountains in
Heading into Gansu Corridor,   pools of marshy water from yes-
toward Gobi desert   terday's rains. The mountains are

not tall. A gray, angular chain about one mile away from the train. The land right before the Gobi desert corridor looks arable, not rich, but then again not impossible to work. I wonder why the poor of this province stayed stuck in the Han region of Lanzhou or moved southeast into further misery rather than choosing to risk farming in this part of the northwest. To live as Chinese (Han) is to remain loyal to the family and the clan. Even when forced to pull up roots, one gravitates toward areas familiar to kin however distant from the family. Those with aspirations of officialdom had even more incentive to stay close to the Han areas. They depended on family ties. But what about the poor?

SUNDAY, JULY 29, 4:15 P.M.   The name of this place was orig-
In Jiuquan (Spring of Wine)   inally "Jinquan," Golden Spring, because of its crystal-clear water source. Han Wudi, the Martial Emperor (141–87 B.C.), sent a general to pacify this area. After his victory, the emperor sent him a gift: the finest wine from the capital, Changan. The wine was not enough for this generous, righteous general to share with all his troops. So he dumped the imperial wine into the spring water and asked all to share. Hence "Jiuquan," or spring of wine.

This and other fine tales about jade wineglasses and Tang poetry are told to us by an articulate guide, a demure Peking woman. She has been here for over ten years with her husband, who works in the oilfields. They are city cadres through and through, but not especially bitter about their isolation here. In fact, they are somewhat aware that material life in Jiuquan—fruits, vegetables, meats freely sold by peasants in the streets!—is more plentiful than in the big cities. We talk of how much more important it is for people working with foreigners to know about China than to be proficient in foreign languages.

MONDAY, JULY 30, 11:30 A.M.   It rained in Jiuquan last night. A summer storm created a flood for this community. Train lines through the Gobi desert washed out. We're stranded. But people of this town are warm, open, hospitable. This morning, waiting for a meeting to begin, I wander outside the hostel. A long chat with an elderly lady outside her flooded yard. She's not too worried, biding her time, coping. Neighbors gather to chat. The flood provides an occasion to slow down, to exchange news, to catch up with gossip. A lady who works in the bank arrives with pants rolled up. She, too, is open, talkative, worldly. They draw me into their daily talk. I delight in simply hanging around like everybody else. News here is all by word of mouth. It requires, invites social contact.

Later, walking out of the north end of the town, I wander into side streets. The flood looks more credible here: kids wading at the end of the alley. I run into two girls, Wang Bing and Wang Li, twenty-three and twenty-two, workers in a bicycle repair factory. They're out of work today because of the power failure, off to investigate the "news" of the flood. They grew up in Jiuquan and say this flood is unprecedented. I ask to join in their search for news. They gladly agree.

The two of them turn out to be old friends. Wang Bing is the more talkative of the two, yet very unassuming. They grew up here together, went to school together, off for two years to the countryside, and now are co-workers. We wander through the canals and back alleys of the flooded area.

An army barracks and hospital are badly hit. About two hundred people with their belongings stand outside, moved out. Not a disaster but an unexpected natural disturbance. Lots of young soldiers, with pants rolled up, wade knee deep in the road, which has become a river. Older people stand watch over family property, not especially worried. Many sturdy-looking things, furniture, beds, stoves, desks, chickens, blankets. Signs of a thriving community.

I am worried that Wang Bing might be noticed too much in my presence. I walk on. She stops, pulls me back, introduces me to her work supervisor, an older woman with a daughter who seems to be eight or so. Other neighbors stop by, talk. Wang Bing is not exactly relaxed in the midst of this laughing crowd. But then again not uncomfortable or show-offish, either. I keep worrying for her, take a look at what is being washed down the river, walk back, say a prompt goodbye. I don't want to cause trouble, future criticism for her. I leave wondering if I acted too worried, rude.

I stop in a store and hear my name: Shu Hengzhe. Wang Bing

is back, asking me over to her house to spend this morning of no work together. Delighted, I go along. We arrive at her courtyard. Flowerpots and bricks at entrance. Her family's house has three rooms, neat, spacious. Photos of the family on the wall: father and brother-in-law in the army, an older sister, and a younger one, a fat old grandmother. We sit, talk for about an hour or so. She tells me it costs 2,000 yuan ($1,500 U.S.) to get married in Jiuquan. Out-of-towners here don't want to marry local people. Her family, too, is from out of town: from Sichuan. She knows they are here to stay, but doesn't see herself as stuck. She's getting on with what is expected of her—work, marriage—but making some autonomous choices, mostly about boyfriends. Getting done what must be done. I leave, taking pictures of the family and receiving a fine red notebook as a present.

Walking away, I am accompanied by little girls. One whose family comes from Shandong, another outsider, asks me to her house. I refuse, and walk back to the hostel, delighted, tired. Up in the bathroom, one of the women who works here has a fine Zhou Enlai button on her blouse. I admire it. She insists I take it as a present.

Simple generosity and curiosity here. Ordinary civilities of Chinese society prevail. Still, I'm constantly worried about the consequences to others for associating with me. After lunch, there is an order: no one can go out. I'm angry!

TUESDAY, JULY 31, 8 A.M.   Last night went for a walk to the bridge again. I wander off the main road, thinking of visiting Wang Bing and Wang Li again. I find myself on the side street which leads to their alley. Suddenly, surrounded by twenty or so local kids. They're laughing harder and harder, screaming, pointing at me. An increasing, and to my ears nearly hysterical, tempo of local dialect. Not understanding, I try to be understood. I speak a few words of *putonghua*, the national language, only to have it ripple through the crowd. My words are repeated with disbelieving echo. Ripples of voices, fast paced. Feeling crowded, village kids all around, I decide to avoid going to my friends' house. I start off toward a path in the fields behind a factory.

I try to stave off mutual hysteria by talking softly with some of the kids. They're shy, very, very local people. Nearly stunned by a foreigner, so curious. Beginnings of a response, some rapport: older boys ask if I am lost, two middle-aged ladies bring a baby girl to say "Hello auntie" to me. I walk back to the hostel with a girl of eight, while her aunt and grandmother chat quietly behind us.

A night which started with a clumsy, draining crowd encounter ends softly. Something so basic about these meetings in this far-away, poor, marginal outpost. I am moved by the generous curiosity of those whose main business is survival in small spaces and accidental bits of time.

WEDNESDAY, AUGUST 1, 11:45 A.M.   *Back in Jiuquan after visiting a commune*

Drove about twenty minutes to a commune not usually shown to foreigners. Stranded, we must be entertained, educated. Our suggestion to visit a commune was approved by school authorities and local officials. Roads are paved but full of potholes. The rainhit hard these mud and grass houses. Watching all the hauling and repair going on, I begin to grasp how thin the margin of survival is in this northwest corner of China. It takes so little rain to topple years of work. But then again, in a few days minimal life is functioning again.

It is a relatively wealthy vegetable commune: 700 acres, 2,100 members, 400 families, most of them in housing built since 1965, one primary school, and one middle school. The formal briefing over, I wander around the back alleys of the commune with an Icelandic fellow student. We pass fields of local marijuana, private crops of older peasants. We are shyly, forcefully invited through the back kitchen door by an old lady in black velvet jacket. She is fifty-four with four kids, poor. She asks us repeatedly to sit. We must because of her heartfelt insistence. The husband comes in. His face is lined, brown; he has a few wispy hairs for a beard and eyes that are deep, watery, contained, yet embracing. He is short, healthy, full of straightforward energy. Sits down fast, with open delight that the day's monotony has been broken by our visit. He takes my hands and holds them tight in his warm, ridged palms. We talk for half an hour or so. He tells me of his life before Liberation: he was sold as a boy by his parents because they were too poor to feed him but too kind to kill him. He worked as a kitchen aide for the armies passing through: Nationalist, Japanese, then Communist. His first wife died in the early 1950s, "her health too rotten by war to benefit from the new life." It took him ten years, "more, really," to get enough money together to marry again. "This is my wife for the past seventeen years only. We're old, worn, but happy, you know." Their children, not yet teen-agers, come back from the field. They ask me about landlords in the States. Then, "Did you see a new movie in Peking which," they heard, "has such fine pictures of our beautiful Great Wall?" No, I haven't.

Back at the hostel, I wonder whether anything new was said during our kitchen visit. Those working people were, after all, within earshot of cadres. Still, those five days in Jiuquan (July 27 to August 2) remain, for me, the most concrete exposure yet to real life in China. I learn much here about the ordinary, difficult business of survival in North China. I see how little it takes for nature to wipe out so much human effort. I also see the flimsy result of China's prolonged reliance on intensive labor. Houses are made of mud and straw; roads and train tracks have been literally flung across the desert without any foundation at all. All wash away, too frail to stand the test of time. Having seen those shaky structures, I now grasp a little bit better the burden of material scarcity. It makes peasant life so vulnerable to the slight-est natural disaster or even the slightest adversity!

In such places as Jiuquan a normal amount of bureaucratic mis-management can easily converge with an inadequate harvest. And life collapses, over and over again. I also see how little material aid it takes to bring back life, to activate the efforts of the people to rebuild, to resettle, to begin again the tasks of cultivation.

As I leave Jiuquan, I keep thinking over some lines from Adrienne Rich's poetry. Chance encounters here have brought me closer, than ever before, to those:

> who age after age, perversely,
> with no extraordinary power
> reconstitute the world.

FRIDAY, AUGUST 3, 9:15 A.M.　　We came into Dunhuang from
Dunhuang　　　　　　　　　　　Anxi. Two and a half hours on a
　　　　　　　　　　　　　　　　bumping bus. The Gobi is grav-
elly, evening out into sand and eventually rounding out into gray,
stony foothills. On both sides of the bus are sand dunes. Brushed
with soft green moss, they ease the eye toward the first, empty
cave, a demure, time-bound beginning of Chinese Buddhism.
Reading a French guide to these desert caves I look out over worn,
hole-ridden hills: twelve hundred years ago! How to fathom this
awesome history?

A thread of time, a quest to verify its passage, runs through all
my ramblings through Chinese space. I'm a historian, true. But
that hasn't been particularly helpful this year. My previous categories are constantly being scrambled by the lived experiences
of the people I've met. Not to mention the huge, increasing gaps
in things I thought I knew about Chinese art, Chinese law, Chinese
economics, Chinese folk traditions. So all I can do is to claim an
interest in China's past. And an unflinching conviction that this
past is the bedrock which both facilitates and stymies the revolutionary modernization of China today.

When I set out on this summer travel, I knew I would encounter
at least three aspects of Chinese history that I already felt I knew
well. China's domestication of Indian Buddhism in the period
between the Han and the Tang (A.D. 210–618); the twentieth-
century attack on traditional Confucian values spearheaded by
Lu Xun, who joined the battle laden with the language and customs of his home town of Shaoxing; and Mao Zedong's peasant
revolution, which erupted in and around Changsha in Hunan
province in the 1920s. All three are engraved as monumental in
Chinese consciousness: Dunhuang, the pinnacle of traditional art;
Lu Xun, the oracle of revolutionary literature; and Mao Zedong,
the revolutionary genius of China's mass movement. All three, I
hoped, would lose a bit of their gripping greatness if I journeyed
to their origins in time and place. All three turned out to be
impressive in ways I was not quite prepared to see.

Before this trip, I knew least about the desert caves on the silk
route between India and China. For years before going to live in
Peking, I had heard graduate students, friends of mine, say that
if only they could get to Dunhuang so many puzzles in the history

of Chinese art and Chinese thought would be resolved. I also remember the summer of 1972, when Audrey Topping (daughter of Canada's foremost China hand and a *New York Times* journalist herself) talked to me about how hard it had been, despite all her fame and China-born connections, to get permission to visit this corner of the Gansu Corridor. Her awe was contagious. To this day I recall her halting, impassioned descriptions of the colors in the caves, colors more than twelve hundred years old, which the Gobi kept and bequeathed to posterity.

Just before I left Peking on this journey, a Chinese friend who is an expert in Buddhism gave me an introduction to what I would see. For three hours one night, he explained the transformation in Indian stone architecture that was effected with wooden beams in Dunhuang. He told me to look for the changing pattern in the geometrical images on the cave ceilings, for differences in the placement of statues from the Indian (Ajanta) wall niches to the Chinese deity set off apart in the center of the cave. He told me to notice the evolution of painted heavens from the other-worldliness of the Northern Wei (A.D. 386–557) to the materialistic sensuality of the Tang. His words sharpened my eyes, but they did not prepare me for the intense aesthetic and spiritual experience of the twelve hours I was able to spend in Dunhuang on Friday, August 3, 1979.

After the flood at Jiuquan, after the repeated efforts of local Gansu officials to fly our group back to Peking on the next available flight, after our teachers snickered, "Why would you want to spend more than one day at Dunhuang anyway; after all, one cave looks just like the next," after a full day's drive on a dreadful bus to the hamlet of Anxi, after yet another two-hour bus ride, we finally neared this edge of the Gobi desert.

A humble sight. Wooden stairs and walkways stretch along three levels. The entire expanse no larger than half of the facade of a 1940s building in lower Manhattan. A young graduate from Peking University's History Department was our guide. I can date her education more readily than I can date the site she shows us. She left the university at a time when the curriculum was—as it still is—impoverished by the Cultural Revolution. She knows and tells only certain approved, memorized stories about the Buddhist past. She holds the keys to the caves we are to see. She tells us we will be shown "representative" works from each period during which Buddhism flourished here. A hint, too, that we might go on to as many caves as our legs can hold out for and for as long as our bare heads can endure this hot, twelve-hour day. By the time we leave at 7:30 that night, I had seen twenty caves. Physically exhausted, eyes overfull.

Without those twelve hours at Dunhuang I might still think of the Period of Disunion—those four hundred years which stretch between the two great dynasties of the Han (202 B.C.–A.D. 220) and the Tang (618–907)—in Confucian terms: as a pitiful cultural desert occupied by "barbarian" rulers and superstitious "masses." Now, the shy, scared imaginings of the Toba Wei (386–534) nobles, those northwestern horseriders who laid the foundation for the faith that unified China, are more real to me. They laid the groundwork for the greatness of the Tang.

SATURDAY, AUGUST 4, 7:30 A.M. Last, lasting impressions of Dun-
Back in Anxi, Gansu huang: a concentrated coming together, in my eyes, at least, of art and history. How empty has the Period of Disunion between the Han and the Tang dynasties seemed to me before! Just tales of barbarians marauding, growing class inequality. The conflicting passions, the fears which riddled the rulers of that time had no place in those tales.

Two caves in which I could have lingered for months: number 285 from the fifth century and number 339 from the ninth. In the first, a story on the wall captures the visions and nightmares of harsh rulers in cruel times: amidst wild, rushing horses, a king sets out on a conquest. He becomes hungry, prepares to slay and eat his wife. The son offers himself in her place. In the middle of the painting (in stunningly skilled brushwork, calligraphic style): the bones of the now sainted youth lying between a fierce dog and a tiger. At the end of the painting, a victorious, repentant ruler is shown building a fine colorful set of temples in memory of his son. He and his wife pay homage to the Buddha.

Below this painting an even more compact image of the faith that animated and made barely tolerable those murderous times. A row of huge, bulging demons at the bottom. Blobs of swirling black ink with chalk-white dots for eyes and mouths. Above, an expanse of lean angels in livid blues and reds. Their circling auras and indistinct faces are of the same mixture of ink and chalk as the demons below. In between, a tightly ordered procession of worldly worshipers. Tiny Confucian gentlemen and ladies, with robes, wispy beards, and coiffed hair painted with swift, soft strokes of yellow and brown ink.

I wonder to myself how the spirituality of the Wei could contain, explain, tame the fears of such primitive believers. The mirroring of heaven and hell offers none of the refuge I remember from Christian art.

I sit for a long, long time in front of the main Buddha sculpture in this cave. Even with its right arm missing, this huge, still reddish wooden image embodies the most serene beauty I have ever seen. Unnatural in its bodily proportions, the towering torso holds up a full face, thoroughly self-contained. A withdrawn yet inviting smile rises out of layers of folded robes. The folds spill over slightly crossed knees. In these folds of the wood I glimpse an ordered fancifulness. Perhaps this is what was so healing for the Northern Wei.

Cave number 339, the confident, cosmopolitan Buddhism of the Tang. On the wall behind a huge sleeping Buddha—the restful image of passing beyond death which so enchanted both elites and masses at that time—there is a large painting of the mourning disciples. In a city-block-long expanse, two rows of faces. Masterful, individual expressions captured in playful colors. The faces of semi-enlightened monks and fully awakened heavenly beings tell the tale of conflicting responses to Buddha's death.

The problem of death, which had been so raw, so dreadful for the Northern Wei, becomes symbolic, intriguing to the satisfied and secure nobles of the mid-Tang. The first row of faces shows the Lohans, the monks. Gaunt men with faces distorted by weeping, their bony shoulders sticking out, their chests collapsed, their fingers clawing. Limbs worn out by sadness. All detail concentrated on the experience of loss and despondency in the wake of the master's death. Above, between these traumatized mortals are the faces of the Phusas, the heavenly beings. Their serene demeanor contradicts the faces of the devoted disciples, who do not yet know that death is emptiness, a temporary weightless flight from one illusion to the next. They have reached nirvana.

The triumph of Tang art and faith: its ability not to imagine

Buddhist cave paintings from the Tang dynasty (618–907), at Dunhuang.

enlightenment complacently. Renowned court painters, brought out to this desert monastery, carried with them a lively remembrance of human forms and human passions. The Phusas are powerful, dominating figures with playfully bulging eyes, engorged throats, their auras nearly bursting with concentrated wisdom.

Among the laughing, mocking faces of these "awakened ones" who have passed beyond illusion are scattered some furious beings, realistic evocations of Inner Asian peoples, whom the Chinese elites of the time must have encountered in the capital of Changan. These foreigners entranced rather than threatened the Chinese world view. Unlike any other period in Chinese history before or after the Tang, foreigners are enshrined along with Chinese-looking mortals in the pantheon of Tang enlightenment.

As we drive out into the desert at dusk that night, I ask myself: What happened to the passionate imaginings of the Wei? Why did China not experience them ever again? Why has she never been frightened into sacredness since? What happened to the unabashed cosmopolitanism of the Tang?

SUNDAY, AUGUST 5, 8:30 A.M.   Well into Xinjiang on the train. Outside, the Gobi lies parched. Mountains with snow rising in the distance.

9:45 P.M.   *Ürümqi, Xinjiang*   Official briefing about minorities by the chief of the local Foreign Affairs Office. A stuffy, middle-aged man who claims he didn't learn how to speak Chinese until 1960. Yet he sounds so fluent in this second language. He tells us about foreigners who helped open up this "wild land." He rambles on about geographical peculiarities of the area, about Heavenly Lake, of "great interest to foreign guests." His Chinese is difficult to understand, clipped, almost without tones. One can still hear a Turkish intonation. He tells us about the thirteen minorities in this area. The Uighurs and the Khazaks are most numerous. The Russians are the fewest. Seven of the minorities are

Islamic. He slips all too easily into English for words like "materialism," "idealism"—a facility with other people's tongues that I noticed in the Israeli desert around Jericho. A quick, pick-up knowledge of foreign words from marketing activity.

Next comes the local cadre, a Khazak, in his forties. He's lean, handsome, worldly, just back from two months in Pakistan. He's quick, alert to our differences as foreigners: American, Canadian, Pakistani, French, New Zealander, etc. Neither curious nor controlling. Just enough command over and confidence in himself to walk tall, talk tough, look important without having to impose. He talks about particular natural calamities in the area, problems with material production. Doesn't blame it all on the Gang of Four.

TUESDAY, AUGUST 7, 4 P.M. *Back in Ürümqi after a tour of yet another scenic mountain* "Colonization" is the word that keeps coming to my mind here, as in Mongolia. Here, too, the undulating shoulders and bellies of the locals have been covered with layers of silk. Tamed, civilized, sinified. "Preservation" of minorities' customs is the Han excuse. We manage to see bits of unpolished, unprocessed local culture in an evening of amateur dancing, in a recently revived Uighur-language opera. Mostly, however, Xinjiang is embarrassingly close to what we know from home. Too many stories about black people echo in my ears as our Han hosts glow on and on about how "minorities are real good at dancing. Really like to dance, you know."

For sure, most Han Chinese cannot, would not dare to, dance as uninhibitedly as the minorities. They are offended by the alien sensuality of minority peoples. Their own inability to "let go," however, does not keep them from feeling superior to the locals here. Their more literate accomplishments empower them to revise minority customs in keeping with some vague notion of "local color."

The evidence we gather about the colonization is mostly negative. We are prevented from gathering positive proof. In Ürümqi, which we reach against the odds of flooding and after an eighteen-hour train ride, we are whisked out of the teeming and tantalizing

Moslem city for yet another five-hour bus ride to a scenic spot. This mountain lake could have been anywhere in Colorado, except for the crowd of Han army men and their dependents out for a picnic.

On the way to this "scenic spot," I notice some "real" yurts. So I take off on foot to take a look. With a Canadian friend, we walk along the river and find a one-plank footbridge across to a Khazak herder's yurt. The herder and his wife invite us in. We share tea and bread. They introduce to us four of their seven children. A neighbor drops in who shows us how one takes off the outer rubber covering of the soft leather native boots.

We sit down around the center of the yurt. Two foreign guests seated deep inside, close to the private quarters of the family. We talk for awhile. We take pictures, glad for this chance to touch some of the genuinely local life. As we get up, my friend and I notice colored photographs taken by other foreigners who also "happened" upon this yurt. We leave wondering about the all too fluent *putonghua* (Mandarin) dialect in which these elderly Khazaks had conversed with us.

Perhaps the quest for the "native" is naive and impossible. We learn most from people living between cultures, like our main guide here, the Khazak cadre, university-educated, married to a woman doctor, recently back from a trip to Pakistan. He is worldly, suave, and yet thoroughly committed to furthering the integrity of his people's culture. Much like Travel Service representatives in other parts of China, with better than average leather shoes, polyester pants, and nylon shirt, he is more temperamental, funnier, more outspoken about topics such as premarital courting and the monthly income of army families than cadres elsewhere.

All that we are able to find in Ürümqi, our responses here, is affected by the local people's dislike of the Han Chinese majority. Out of the Han region, reserve toward and suspicion of foreigners diminishes greatly. Here, in the faraway west, we relish the unabashed openness of the Uighurs. They pinch women's behinds, invite us into their homes, offer to make all sorts of commercial deals in back alleys. Relieved of Chinese civilities and bureaucracy, we become excited (overly so?) about the "liberated" values and customs of the local people.

TUESDAY, AUGUST 7, 11:30 P.M.   In a restaurant tonight, I asked a
Still in Ürümqi   Moslem lady who is serving us
delicious spicy lamb what kind
of son-in-law she would like for her twenty-five-year-old daughter. "I hope she marries a Han. You know, they are the only ones
around here who really help women, who get involved in family
life, who dare to be seen taking care of children."

Walking the streets at dusk tonight, I notice not only the wise,
clever eyes of the bearded old Moslem men whom I saw earlier
during the day congregating around outdoor braziers, Moslem
fashion. I also now notice idle young Uighur men, sitting outside
their houses. Inside, long-haired wives, in colorful rayon dresses,
cook dinner in tiny dark holes, shouting with tired voices at swarms
of kids.

The Chinese government, in a departure from the national birth
control policy, is allowing minorities unlimited births. Not only
a concern with the demographic survival of minorities but also a
concession to Moslem male pride, which seems fierce in its in-
tolerance of unpregnant women. All this not so different from
the Confucian obsession with sons needed for ancestral continuity.

WEDNESDAY, AUGUST 8,   Today we toured an oriental car-
10:00 P.M.   *Ürümqi*   pet-weaving factory. I linger for
a long chat with a young Han
woman, thirty-two years old, drawn to her by her unexemplary,
tired, sweaty face. In this model factory, we're supposed to observe how well minorities are keeping alive their traditional crafts.
She is from a village in Hunan. Married to a Han air-force man
who came to Xinjiang because his uncle told him it was lucrative.
(Wages are much higher in these "hardship" areas.) When the
young soldier went back to his native village, the family had found
him this bride. He brought her out to the wild west.

She commutes to her new home in the suburbs of Ürümqi on
Saturday night for a one-day family visit and to wash clothes and
then returns by bus on Sunday night. She is learning handicrafts
to replace the construction work she used to do in the summer

but cannot continue in the winter months. A warm smile lights up her exhausted face.

"You know, it is easier for these younger, unmarried girls to learn carpet weaving. They can keep their minds in one place more easily. Still, I like it here. I get along pretty well with all these young Moslem girls." Her simple, unapologetic, honest words draw others around us. In this workplace, beneath the aura of "local culture," a complex mixing of cultures. The only commonality: hard work.

FRIDAY, AUGUST 10, NOON
In Turufan, Xinjiang

Lying in bed, with a fierce backache. Can't take another bus trip, no more touring for me. Yesterday, crossing the Gobi in a dust storm. Another six-hour bus ride, because no train tickets were available. All through the storm, I lie on the floor of the bus, the pain of sitting unbearable. I try not to cry. My fury at authorities is strong.

On the floor of the bus, as the desert dust is covering me, burying me, Mary, my New Zealand friend, makes up this song to cheer me up.

Flat on Your Back—Turufan Blues

I've got the Jiuquan, Anxi, Anxi blues
I've got the Anxi, Dunhuang, Dunhuang blues.
Well from Jiuquan to Xinjiang, that was OK
Xinjiang to Turufan the blues are here to stay
The bus keeps going, don't ever stop
The road keeps on going over the top
The desert was wide, and the road it was long
But we keep on going just like this song,
They said it was six hours, but we don't even care
We know we'll all be dead by the time we get there.
Forty-eight *waibin* [foreign guest] graves on the plain
And none of them will ever see Peking again.

I said to the *liuban* [school officials]
Can't you put us on the train
They said: "Oh no baby, you're on the bus again"
I want to go home but I'm frightened to leave

Cause I know that bus, it's gonna make me grieve.
I said to the *liuban*
We can't stand the strain
They said: "Baby better think it over again"
You ain't a *waibin* and you ain't got no dough
And one *meiguo jiaoshou* [one American prof—that's me]
Just ain't no go.

I see you crying and I know the reason why.
You're on this bus till the day that you die
You got the devil for a driver and fire at your wheels
But I ain't gettin on cause I know how it feels.

Much joking on the bus about calling in the U.S. Marines for me and thus saving us all.

This morning, outside the hostel windows, I hear fast clipping donkey hoofs. Little carts driven by little boys under ten. They're carrying gravel back and forth from the back compound. I go out for a little walk after the group leaves for some desert ruins. A flow of donkey carts with minority people of every kind streaming by. Striking common denominator: naked kids. The heat and the dust covering all. Soft gray gets baked by the sun to dusty brown. On many women's heads, white gauze coverings, like the Bedouins I saw in the Sinai.

TUESDAY, AUGUST 14, 9 A.M.
On the train to Sichuan

A relief in some way to leave the "colorful" minority areas and start to wind down into Chinese-Han culture. I left the group last night at Xian.

Dramatic entrance to the lush, southern abundance of Sichuan. Passing through the mountainous northwestern border with Shaanxi. Crossing the Da Ba Shan mountains this morning. Riveted to the window by the swiftly changing landscape. The broad, gray, menacing rivers of the northwest are giving way to winding green streams. Stone-filled gorges are changing into hills full of soft vines and bushes. Yellow mud cave dwellings are rapidly falling behind as the train rushes through bamboo groves. Sensuous leaves discreetly shade white plaster huts. I will spend a week or so in Chengdu, old, cultured capital of China's red-soil basin. Far enough from Peking to be immune to its bureaucratic pomposities, Chengdu was, and remains, a playful center of Chinese civilization.

Good to be on my own again after three weeks with the Beida group. I look forward to wandering aimlessly on a rented bicycle, to eating the good, hot food the province is justly famous for.

TUESDAY, AUGUST 14, 11:45 P.M.   *Chengdu*

My first afternoon, I start to ask about storytellers. The young people I ask deny that they exist at all: "Those pointless, feudal customs are gone by now, you know." People in their forties seem nervous that a foreigner would have heard about, be curious about, such local lore. They suggest I get tickets to a storytelling session staged in the city auditorium.

Around 4 P.M., in the bicycle shop, I happen upon a chattering lady in her sixties. She is delighted that I try, though I mispronounce, the Sichuanese expression for storytelling. I keep asking her about *shuoshu* (book speaking) and she keeps correcting me, "We say *pingshu* (book showing)."

Before I leave the store, she gives me clear instructions: "Go down two streets, turn to the left, then to the right. After the bridge, go to the alley on the left, and there you will find a teahouse which has storytelling every night around eight."

I ride my rented bicycle to the place. A sprawling dark room overfilled with old men. I go back at eight. All the chairs have been moved inside and the room is lit up. Filled with forty or so teenage laborers smoking harsh-smelling cigarettes, middle-aged women in shorts who are also smoking, a few old men with worn faces but strong bodies, perhaps the sewer-sod carriers I passed all day today. They cart human fertilizer from the city to surrounding communes.

In the front of the room four lines of chairs in a circle and a small stand. The table is covered with pink silk. Behind it the storyteller, a man in his early sixties. He has a shimmering voice and an agile face. In his hands he holds a fast-moving fan whose swish alternates with the sound of clappers, "wake-up wood."

A simple, common, black fan. With it the storyteller signals the entrance of officials, kings, generals. The up-and-down shake of the fan shows ministers bowing, kowtowing to higher-ups. The unfurling of the fan with fast-moving wrist signals the naughty, pensive mood of rulers faced with a dilemma of strategy. The storyteller's hands flutter around his face to describe long flowing beards, mythical fairies, sages, martial men who subdue evil, who carry out feats of virtue. At times, he stands up, roars, weeps, makes cutting remarks about *houmen*, back doors.

FRIDAY, AUGUST 17, 11 P.M. *Chengdu* — I go to the teahouse for four nights in a row. I get to know the storyteller well. A cigarette-smoking grandmother tells me about how much she enjoys the Han dynasty story of the "martial duke" Zhu Guoliang.

In the literati version of this story, the *Romance of Three Kingdoms*, this hero was the loyal adviser to the King of Shu, A.D. 220–280. In the storyteller's version, he is a clever schemer who cheats his patron, kills his kinsmen with flying swords, rallies knights-errant to help poison more refined, well-to-do noble enemies. Zhu Guoliang always wins, of course.

In this teahouse, I start to understand why the main character of a recent novel, *Coldest Winter in Peking*, is also called Guoliang. I am beginning to grasp why the rusticated youth who were sent down by Mao to the countryside during the Cultural Revolution and who stealthily sneaked back to Peking in 1976, chose this character to describe their leader. Forbidden to return to the city, Guoliang schemes to survive illegally.

Political irreverence in this city is not limited to folk tales. To-night a fine, funny local opera called "Ensnaring a Son-in-law." In a traditional old theater, with fancy costumes, the story unfolds: three noble families connive to catch a literati groom for their daughters, who are threatened with life captivity in the harem of an emperor in search of concubines. The *xiucai*, a successful candidate of the lowest imperial examination, is the prize commodity of the play.

He appears in a soft, green robe embroidered with pink flowers. A thoroughly ridiculous character, he is bumbling in his ignorance of real life, which he sees through the haze of Confucian sayings. His opposite is a fat, swift old lady, the cunning matchmaker, who runs all three families ragged with her schemes and demands for more money. She is in league with the village trumpeter, a poor peasant who plays at the many fake wedding ceremonies. He can't help spilling the beans, and the play ends with his unmasking the bumbling literati as well as his greedy noble patrons. The righteous officials who hear his confession-indictment are as ridiculous as the "hero."

Today, also, a rainy afternoon. Stranded in a teahouse, next to the temple dedicated to the memory of Zhu Guoliang. Next to my table, a group of old gentlemen. All of them seem to be in their seventies, with fine features, soft hands, neat clothes. A couple of them are sporting long, long bamboo cigarette holders. I watch them for a long time from the corner of my eyes. Then, as I lean back my chair, I see over my shoulders that one of them is reading some English poetry from a neatly written notebook.

We start to talk. He turns out to be an ear-nose-and-throat specialist trained in a Christian medical college in the 1930s. He is retired now. He tells me that he's spent the last decade "writing political poetry against Mao, his wife, and the tyrannical loss of human rights during the Cultural Revolution." Into my ears, not too quietly, he whispers his poems in Chinese. After each recitation, he pauses to repeat the complex classical Chinese verse in impeccable, artful English.

I want to write down his words, but I sense that it is too dangerous. He tells me that he was jailed during the 1960s. As we talk, I notice a severe, middle-aged-looking woman who is leaning close to us, obviously disapproving of this spontaneous conversation between a local and a foreigner. We say goodbye. The doctor's last words to me are a quotation from Shakespeare: "History justifies those who remain true to themselves." I tell him to stay well, healthy. I promise him, and myself, to come back to the teahouse in ten years. We both agree that time then might be more ripe for the "mind-emancipation" proclaimed so loudly in China today.

SATURDAY, AUGUST 18,
10:30 P.M.
In Chongqing (Chunking)

A grim, gray city. Scarred by war. The grime of the bombing during the Anti-Japanese War has not been washed off. Yet the Sichuanese aliveness of the people contradicts the weariness of their city. The fine, strong mobile features and sharp tongue of the southwest prevail. I walk around the streets. Generous curiosity greets me everywhere.

At the bus stop I ask for directions. An old man carrying noodles stops. Helps me to find some way to get across the river. Two young workers take charge of my destination (none really, just want to ride out of the city a bit, to see the countryside and the supposed agricultural miracle worked here by Deng Xiaoping's trusted aide, Zhao Ziyang). Two-hour ride through small, rather poor-looking hamlets (crowded, too) in spite of what I hear as a marked decrease in population growth in this area. The young workers are asking me about the price of everything in the U.S.: meat, rice, bicycles, coal, bread, cars. Things familiar to them, around which their lives revolve. I find myself at a loss, except for the price of cars, of course. I'm most embarrassed when I cannot recall productivity per acre in the U.S. Things to find out when I go home. Only then, I'll have a mental hook to hang China facts on.

Later, walking around the Hall of the People. A huge church, really. A relic of the Cultural Revolution. Now cavernous, empty. Unlit auditoriums, thousands of steps, a hollow, provincial monument. Was it installed by order of national political leaders, or as a brief gesture of faith in participatory democracy?

Off tomorrow, one day ahead of schedule, on the boat down the gorges. I have decided to travel first class. The view from the top is all I want on this trip.

SUNDAY, AUGUST 19, 10:15 P.M. *On the Yangzi, truly "The Long River" (Changjiang) as it is known in Chinese* Misty hills of stark beauty. Chinese poetry and painting more alive now, more real than ever before. A college student from Hong Kong keeps quoting in my ear Li Bo, the great Chinese poet, who built a hut here after being exiled from Changan (modern-day Xian). His poem "The Road to Shu [Sichuan] Is Hard" captures the awe and the fear of one forced by misfortune to brave entry into this region:

Peak upon peak less than a foot from the sky,
Where withered pines hang down from sheer cliffs,

Where brooks and roaring torrents clamor noisily
Dashing upon rocks. A thunderclap from countless valleys.
Such an impenetrable place!
I sigh and ask why anyone should come here from afar.

Li Bo wrote this in the despondent mood of exile. After his death, generation upon generation of leisurely travelers quoted his words, to reexperience his feelings upon their own first sight of the Yangzi gorges.

As I listen to the Hong Kong student, as I take photographs of the layered rocks on both sides of the boat, I am beginning to grasp, for the first time, the intensely Chinese attachment to nature. It is an attachment not only to the raw majesty of the mountains and the river, but to their detailed commemoration in century after century of poetry and painting. I feel my ignorance of the connotations of the Chinese classical language, of history, of art, very keenly. And yet. My eyes, for now, must suffice.

MONDAY, AUGUST 20, 10 P.M. *The night before the end of our boat ride* — Tired from this morning. The gorges, stunning. The first: rough, high, stark cliffs. The second: long, undulating, dream-like. The third: gateway to the open, placid South Chinese landscape, and the highest, most dramatic gorge. It locks up behind it, like a wall, the unruly playfulness of Sichuan.

Long talk after the gorges with a Peking cadre who has a high position in the Agricultural Ministry. An expert, honest man sent to investigate and report on the Yangzi provinces' condition. His no-nonsense attitude clearest when he tells me his suspicions about the current policy of dismantling communes, encouraging free markets, "as if reshuffling the circumstances of production were enough." He insists that the real, enduring problem of the Chinese countryside is the political education of local cadres: "most still act like landlords. Their autocratic tendencies, coupled with an uneducated populace and the area's vulnerability to natural calamity and overpopulation, I am afraid, leave the door wide open for disaster." The most honest assessment of the situation I have heard yet. We exchange addresses. A vague hope of continuing conversations in Peking. Even if we cannot, over these

Down the Yangzi gorges in the early morning light.

meals in this first-class part of the boat we encountered each other as we would never be able to do back home in the bureaucratic capital.

TUESDAY, AUGUST 21, 8 P.M.   What lingers, long after I dis-
Wuhan   mount the boat, is the sensual
                               beauty of the Yangzi and its
gorges. The colors and the breeze so soft, so sweet, unlike any other that brushed past my eyes, my body, before. The gray, rocky ledges that cradle the red soil of Sichuan still sharp in my mind. So, too, the scruffy, blue pines hanging in the rocks. All of it lorded over by The River. Its muddy, yellow depths belie the name once given it by Western travelers (missionaries?), Blue River. It carries the life on its banks with it. Gently. Shimmering over terraced fields and children wading in the water, it doesn't dominate its people. Just inks them in with misty colors.

Back from a walk through Hankou, one part of this industrial conglomeration. Life spilling out into the streets. Bamboo cots on the sidewalk: instant bedrooms for the hot season. Wandered through a neighborhood printshop, where young workers are putting out local newspapers, and do some artistic work in their spare time.

WEDNESDAY, AUGUST 22, NOON   Went out this morning to East
Still in Wuhan   Lake, one of China's natural
                             beauty spots, also engraved in
poetry and painting. It is not as beautiful as its sister, West Lake, in Hangzhou. I take a boat ride to a newly built, rather gaudy pavilion. My boatman, a sixty-seven-year-old woman, from a nearby commune. This is her part-time, retirement work, a way to keep herself fed since her husband's death during the Cultural Revolution. Her children also need her aid, so she comes out here to get some extra money. She worked in a local fishery before Liberation. A hard, hard life. Up to today. Her arms are strong, her eyes weak, her breasts large, droopy. She hums a folk tune as we ride back. Asks me if I'm married. No. "You're lucky, if you don't have to. I did."

I get ready to go on to Changsha, Chairman Mao's hometown.

THURSDAY, AUGUST 23, 1 P.M.   All spring I had been running into
Changsha, Hunan   historical amnesia in Peking. The
capital is in no position to resist
an officially sponsored effort to "get over the Cultural Revolution." This effort to "get over," I am convinced, is subverting any
possibility of a critical analysis either of Mao or of the Cultural
Revolution. So, I decide to come to Changsha to delve beneath
the myth and the forgetfulness. I hope to meet someone to share
questions about Mao's role in history. His role, I thought, could
not be denied in the place which has come to be known as the
Chairman's hometown. Mao spent a formative decade here from
1911–21. Enrolled, then teaching at the local normal school, he
began his radical activities by founding the "New People's Study
Society." Here, too, he wrote his early essays about peasants and
revolution.

In Changsha, which, translated, means Long Sands, I had hoped
to find someone who might be willing to question Mao Zedong's
"greatness." I hoped to find something in between the images of
the unfailing genius and the thundering powermonger—extremes
which still coexist in Chinese and foreign views of Mao. The
museum of modern history which is my destination this morning
turns out to be "closed for repair." Next to it I find a new, fancy
building, dedicated to a funeral robe and a mummified body from
the Western Han dynasty (201–220).

10:30 P.M.   *Back at the hotel,*   Back from a walk in the park be-
Changsha   hind the hotel. I happen upon a
movie, a modern Hunan opera
about commune squabbles. The plot centers on a young tractor
driver who forgets his high principles in these times of "new
freedom." He is neck deep into *yanjiu,* a Chinese pun for "study
a situation" as well as "bribe with cigarettes and liquor." His
girlfriend is a staunch barefoot doctor, his brother is a near-saint
on leave from the army, his would-be sister-in-law is a devoted
brigade leader. The party leader is righteous, his mother anxious.

Only the production team leader is a funny, fallible guy—an ordinary person, a comic not unlike characters in Sichuanese opera.

I enjoy the dusk, the easy mingling with crowds in the park, the hilarious, undisciplined local dialect. Sitting by the lake at sundown, I linger over flowers. Tonight, after a thwarted search for Changsha's revolutionary history, I allow myself to savor the ordinary beauties of the evening among the city's common people.

I can't find any intermediate place here that tells the story of the historical Mao. All over the city loom huge edifices in his honor, built new or refurbished in the 1960s to do justice to the "Great Helmsman," the god of the Cultural Revolution. I did find, this afternoon, the First Normal School, a rambling nineteenth-century structure of white balconies and blue railings. Mao once studied and then taught here. The place is huge, empty, deserted.

FRIDAY, AUGUST 24, 8 P.M.   Today I finally find the city's main
Changsha   exhibit hall, which is dedicated
                               to the early decades of the Chair-
man. A shrine, really, to the "Revolutionary Genius." I walk around for four hours with a young guide who patiently, enthusiastically recites all the labels attached to all the pictures in the exhibit hall. Room after room is filled with small, old things: coins, books, clothes. Also, huge, new statues and paintings which show the Chairman all wise, thoroughly committed, and inevitably successful in his revolutionary strategy.

Nothing here of the early, flawed, awkward beginnings of Mao's social analysis and political organizing. A huge painting "tells it all," according to my guide. It shows the Chairman swearing the first "genuine proletarians" (that is, propertyless peasants) into the Hunan branch of the Communist Party. It shows Mao doing something great, on behalf of the future.

The whole place is a monument dedicated to reading history backward. My guide looks greatly embarrassed when I ask why there are so few visitors. (Two passed through during the whole morning.) "Yes, I gather groups come here less and less. But I wouldn't know why, since I began to work here only last year."

Around the remnants of the Mao cult, Changsha goes about its business. The city is recovering slowly from years of national

Mao Zedong swearing the first "proletarians" into the Hunan branch of the Chinese Communist Party. Oil painting from the Changsha museum.

attention as the Chairman's hometown. It is learning to live with a huge, new, fancy railroad station, built during the Cultural Revolution in anticipation of many, many generations of pilgrims, both foreign and Chinese. It manages to keep daily life buzzing around the edges of this great hotel, intended for the thousands who were expected to come here to hold meetings, to learn the lore of Mao in his native setting.

In the side streets, away from the major boulevards dedicated to Mao's memory, high-school students are busy memorizing English, old ladies are drying red peppers. Here, I am learning something about the strategy of getting by, and getting around, inflated history. When past myths become too big to be grasped, too blubbery to be attacked directly, one learns to stand aside, to carve out tiny spaces for ordinary actions. These actions do not repudiate the myth, yet they foreshadow its end by hidden disbelief.

This afternoon I just walk around the park behind the hotel. I take lots of photographs of the particularly lush tropical garden. After several shots of white and pink blossoms, I sit at the edge of the lake and relish a sweet southern wind. I begin to write a poem. No time to finish. Must catch the train to Shaoxing, the home of the other "Revolutionary genius," Lu Xun. The Chang-sha poem has to wait until I get back to Peking.

SATURDAY, AUGUST 25, 11 P.M.   I came to Shaoxing full of ques-
Shaoxing   tions about a great man, who is
                                                             mythicized as China's greatest
revolutionary writer not unlike Mao, enshrined as the greatest
revolutionary leader. I am hoping that Lu Xun's birthplace can
render him more historical, less awesome. In my ten years of
study and now half a year of living in China, he has remained
the most fruitful, complex companion to my reflections about
Chinese society. Yet by now he overwhelms as much as, if not
more than, he instructs. Critical writers abroad make a point of
tracing their ancestry to his dissecting vision. Simon Leys, author
of *Chinese Shadows;* Chen Jo-hsi, author of *The Execution of Mayor
Yin;* Xia Ziyan, author of *The Coldest Winter in Peking*—all have
claimed inspiration, legitimation from Lu Xun. Inside China, I
have not met a single active or aspiring writer who has not felt
Lu Xun's presence inciting and structuring the words on paper.

The problem for my friends here, as for myself by now, is that
Lu Xun has become a lurking shadow, crowding out the freedom
to imagine, in more halting ways, to be sure, the society of the
present. I am here to learn more about his youth, to see him as
a product of history, of circumstances, of local people and a local
dialect.

I reread Lu Xun's boyhood reminiscence, "Hundred Grasses
Yard," on the train to Shaoxing.

This morning, it is easy to find the Lu Xun Museum, housed
in the nineteenth-century compound he was born in, a typical
gentry household. It is arranged to preserve the "Hundred Grasses
Yard," the mossy dividing wall between the child's sheltered in-ner world and the forbidden, busy, exciting outside world that
Lu Xun recollects so well. Across the alley from the family com-pound, the house of Lu Xun's first Confucian teacher, the master
of the "Three Flavor Study," whom the iconoclastic author re-membered with surprising lack of bitterness.

I am surprised to see that the thick bamboo gate that leads to
the Three Flavor Study is still painted in the intimidating black

that the little boy carrying over the bulky classics for his daily memorization grind found so "awesome."

In the whole museum complex, I'm most struck by the mother's bedroom and by her photograph. A simple, barely literate woman. She kept reading pulp novels and muttering Buddhist prayers long after her son became the most famous revolutionary writer of the day.

I am about to rush through the spacious kitchen, when my guide stops me and says: "It is here that my grandfather first met Lu Xun. They were both young kids. That big straw basket over there was used to cover foods during the summer. My grandfather wove it. He would have starved just farming. So he had to take on winter handicrafts, you know."

My guide's name is Zhang Gui. He is forty-seven years old and is the grandson of Runtu—Lu Xun's boyhood friend who appears as a character in the story *Home Village*.

SUNDAY, AUGUST 26, 10:30 P.M. *Shaoxing*   Today, Zhang Gui told me how he became the curator of the museum. In 1950, Shaoxing-based friends of Lu Xun, who possessed many of his literary and material remains, started to make plans for a commemorative museum. Although they were the obvious guardians of Lu Xun's legacy, they decided to keep themselves out of that task. It was they who found and brought to the museum an illiterate young man who symbolized Lu Xun's political hopes.

With Party encouragement, they followed up hints in the conclusion of the story *Home Village*. There, during a bleak boat ride out of Shaoxing, Lu Xun describes his alienation from his boyhood buddy, the peasant boy whom he calls Runtu. The last lines of the story are: "I hope our descendants won't be like us all over again, with mutual estrangement arising once more. . . . I hope they will not live their lives laboriously tossing about like me, or numbed by toil like Runtu. . . . They must have new lives, lives that we cannot even imagine yet."

With this message in mind, eager to prove that in a Communist society this hope can and must be translated into reality, Lu Xun's intellectual descendants organized a search for the descendants

Lu Xun in 1931—a more intimate glimpse of the man all too often depicted as simply a tireless warrior and revolutionary.

of the real Runtu. In an outlying fishing village they found Zhang Gui. He was seventeen years old then. He told them that Runtu, whose real name was Runshui, had died in the famine of 1936. Runshui's son, Zhang Gui's own father, had been killed during the Anti-Japanese War. His brother and sister were sold before they were ten because the family had nothing to eat.

Asked about his recollection of Lu Xun, Zhang Gui said only that his grandfather had vague warmth toward the gentry family in the faraway city. Four years later, in 1954, this youth, who had not been able to read a word of Lu Xun's stories before 1949, was installed as curator of the commemorative museum in Shaoxing.

For the past twenty-five years, Zhang Gui has been telling Lu Xun's story to thousands of visitors. He was most useful in the periods when Mao was particularly keen on proving Lu Xun's connection to Chinese peasants. In between waves of political mobilization like the Great Leap Forward and the Cultural Revolution, he read and reread the collected works of Lu Xun. He tells me how he has been able to clear up many linguistic problems in Lu Xun's stories. He went to Japan last year, a member of the delegation sent to inaugurate the Lu Xun Museum there.

TUESDAY, AUGUST 28, 5:30 P.M. *On the train from Shaoxing to Shanghai*   I spent four days with Zhang Gui. There were no other foreigners in Shaoxing this week. Few Chinese visitors came to the museum.

Zhang Gui's memory is sharp. He describes well what it was like to be a poor peasant in central China before Liberation. He became, for me, a unique source for the other side of Lu Xun's tales. A voice to flesh out the experiences of the broken-spirited Runtu, the shy and sullen boy who for a short while played with the gentry offspring.

I ask Zhang Gui about his grandfather's and father's experiences in the once-wealthy household, about their relationship with Lu Xun, the "Young Master." "Well, they were more grateful than intimate, of course. Being so poor they would have starved to death just farming and fishing. They had to spend winters in the city, in Shaoxing, doing odd jobs. They were handiworkers. It was the lowliest and harshest kind of work. They repaired bridges [over Shaoxing's many canals] with frozen fingers. They built houses and wove baskets."

Zhang Gui relishes the details as he goes on: "All woodwork had to be done in winter, you see. Bugs could then be shaken out of the wood, which had been lying around during the hot, humid weather. So, my grandfather and father came to the city to find work. They would spend the winter months in the Zhou household for free. In return, they fixed things, made toys for the young masters. They got shelter and food for several months. My grandfather talked about his little son to the Zhou family. He brought his son the next winter. It was the same for each generation. The children had some fun, some playtime before they went back to their separate worlds."

With war and poverty, the peasant family of Runtu lost contact with the literati Zhou household. I find out that Zhang Gui had never seen Shaoxing before Liberation. He tells me that the six-hour boat ride would have required renting a boat from a local landlord, and a good excuse, good enough to risk going to town. One had to have produce to sell or work waiting for the trip to be worthwhile. Zhang Gui had neither.

He describes his first impressions of Shaoxing in 1949. "I was surprised to find that there was really such a thing as an electric bulb. We had heard fantastic rumors in the village that you could pull a string and the whole room would light up. I was amazed to find shops open in the afternoon. In our village they were open only for a few morning hours. I was also stunned, almost embarrassed, by displays in the windows of models wearing clothes. Before, all I had seen was bunches of stuff, in mounds, in the corner of our local store. Most bewildering, perhaps, were the two-way streets and the many, many bicycles. At home, you see, we only had a few mud lanes. Mostly we got by with small boats. Everything moved too fast. There were too many people all around. What did I like the best? A thermos, the first I ever saw."

Less than four years after he bought his first thermos bottle, Zhang Gui came for his second visit to Shaoxing. By that time he had been made one of the curators of the Lu Xun Museum.

Often, during those days of talking with Zhang Gui, I wonder about the accidental transformation of his life. I wonder whether he felt himself to be merely an object of history, a "lesson" for others. All that, just because his grandfather happened to make a boyhood impression on a future great writer. I ask myself whether he felt manipulated by the idealistic intellectuals of the 1950s who wanted to concretize Lu Xun's fictional hopes. Why was he plucked out of his native environment and made to recite the life story of a benefactor whose work he had not even heard of? He was just told that he had some part in it.

And yet, the more we talk, the more I notice Zhang Gui's mischievous smile as he pours out the "correct" history of Lu Xun. I have come to see that he is not merely at the mercy of the events he speaks about. Yes, he has been installed, rather passively in the beginning, in this place of historical commemoration. Yet he has managed to make some sense of it on his own.

Zhang Gui is not a Lu Xun expert or a literary critic. He is a poor, illiterate peasant who can now substantiate his own stake in the new generation of descendants envisioned by Lu Xun. The story would have been no different if Zhang Gui had not been looked for in that out-of-the-way village in 1950. Even if he had not agreed to move into the city, even if he had not been involved in twenty-five years of political controversy about the meaning of Lu Xun's life and work, the big picture would have remained the same.

So, it is the detail that matters. Larger issues come alive, stripped of their ideological requirements. What enabled Zhang Gui to survive history, to perform his role so well, is something called "hope," something that Lu Xun describes so well at the end of his story *Home Village*: "I believe that this thing called hope cannot be said to exist or not. It is just like a road on the ground. Although there might not be a road, in fact, if enough people walk on it, then it becomes a road."

Zhang Gui, like Lu Xun, is a special man, but not unique. At different times, against different odds, they kept on walking. They had faith. They knew, somehow, that others would follow. I leave Shaoxing more hopeful than I arrived.

WEDNESDAY, AUGUST 29, 11:15 P.M. *Shanghai*　　Just spent eight hours with Ren Yishu (E-su Zen), the daughter of a May Fourth intellectual, Chen Hengzhe, whom I have been studying for some years now.

Her sister, a sinologist in the U.S., had given me her address. I had written from Peking to set up a meeting. Called to confirm from Shaoxing.

This afternoon, a tall, thin, shy woman walks in the door of the hotel. Later, much later, I see in her a prim Vassar girl, who graduated in 1951 and came back to China. An ageless, broad, unadorned beauty. Pre-sexual and post-innocent all at once.

We talk about my studies of the May Fourth movement and of her parents' generation of Chinese intellectuals. Her mother was the first female professor at Peking University. She, too, graduated from Vassar in 1919 and returned to China to teach Western history in 1920.

All this past so distant from what concerns me, the daughter. My research provides some common ground. I am moved by her tale, not unlike so many others of my Peking friends. Her husband committed suicide during the Cultural Revolution. Her mother died at a time when health care had been most abused by the Gang of Four. E-su is broken inside by all this. Yet, I sense she was shaken long before the Cultural Revolution.

She lives cherishing long-ago images of her years at Vassar. A girl grown old, torn up by terrible decades that would undo far tougher souls. Her health is still not good. She's childless, alone. I want to shake her ossified sensibilities. But who am I to rock this much-shaken woman?

Later, we watch the ghosts of three-masted junks sail down the Huangpu (Whampoo) River. Close, warm together, she asks me about her old teachers at Vassar, Miss Mercer, Miss Lockwood, about the Shakespeare Garden there. I am not prepared for her melancholy memories. I fight off my own.

I ask about possible psychiatric aid for persons wrecked by the Cultural Revolution. She tells me they prescribe vitamins for relaxation. She feels restored after a pleasant trip to a spa in Hangzhou. She claims, and I sort of believe her, that she is afraid of nothing, has nothing left to lose. She hopes to go for a visit back to the U.S. She's afraid, too. Does not want to lose her past dreams. "I don't want to see my image tarnished by any human fallibility."

THURSDAY, AUGUST 30, 6 A.M. *On the train from Shanghai to Peking* More thoughts about E-su. Before we parted last night, she showed me some of the poems she's been writing over the years. In the language and manner of her Vassar youth, she pours out her feelings about events in China over the past three decades. Some readers at home might glimpse from these poems the complex devotion of E-su and her generation of intellectuals to a revolution that had cost them so much. Perhaps the Vassar alumnae magazine.

How could I presume, how could I dare to urge her to go to the U.S.? To risk shattering that dream of Vassar days? If she went and became robbed of her "love," who, then, could help her? Not me, certainly. So I am left with a messy feeling of stirring up deep waters irresponsibly. E-su's last words: "I am happy now, so very, totally free." Then, the awful contrast of those eyes and thin arms. The truth of her loneliness and her sadness are too painful to acknowledge. It is still too soon to tell the truth, I gather.

SEPTEMBER 20   *Back home in Peking* I finally finished the poem I began in Changsha, a month ago. It helps me get ready for the next event, the thirtieth anniversary of the People's Republic. I am still trying to notice quieter changes, on the sidelines, as it were:

Behind the Hunan Hotel, August 24, 1979

Where the East Wind railed and the Master's brush
  inked in victorious peasants,
The past sulks on
  in suddenly cavernous courtyards.
Long Sands is ruffled by a girlish
  summer breeze,
A mustached youth
  in leather sandals
Oils down a sunny road onto
  a blotched, brown canvas.

CHAPTER 6

OCTOBER–NOVEMBER 1979 *On the Sidelines of Momentous Public Events*

OCTOBER 15 *Yom Kippur, the thirtieth anniversary of the People's Republic and Hou Baolin*

One day I forgot Jerusalem,
and my right arm withered.
My right arm, my moving arm,
my rising and
* falling arm*
* My loving arm*
Is withered . . .
(Grace Paley, "A Warning")

This year the thirtieth anniversary of the founding of the People's Republic fell on the same day as Yom Kippur, the Day of Atonement. October 1, 1949, Mao stood in Tian An Men Square and declared: "China has finally stood up." October 1, 1979, the beginning of the Jewish year 6740.

Two weeks ago, October 1, a gray, drizzly Monday in Peking. The end of the sharp colors and of the soft autumn air. I stay in my room all day, make a list of sins to atone, read Elie Wiesel's *Les Chants des Morts*. His plea on behalf of the dead especially useful to me here. Before China, I had been unable to recall my grandparents killed in the Holocaust without terror and helplessness. Now I can. Wiesel's French takes me back to them indirectly: "Sache d'où tu viens, disaient les sages d'Israël. Seulement, tout dépend de l'attitude intérieure de qui se retourne vers l'origine; si c'est par pure curiosité intellectuelle, sa vision fera de lui une statue de salon." [Know where you come from, said the sages of Israel. It all depends on the inner attitude of the one who turns toward the point of origin. If it is just out of pure intellectual curiosity, the quest turns you into an ornamental statue.]

173

How to avoid this paralysis, the fate of Lot's wife? How to go back into the past or out into the world with something other than pure intellectual curiosity? How to wrest something for the present, something that will make life here and now different, better?

In China, now, I feel I am nurturing in myself the seeds of an understanding. What Lu Xun meant by "appropriation," by *"nalai zhuyi"* (literally take-ism) is not unlike what Wiesel puts in the mouths of the sages of Israel. Lu Xun argued that China's successful, fruitful encounter with the West depends on its daring inwardness, on the class and cultural self-consciousness of its appropriators. Only those willing to discard can be effective "takers." These qualities are as rare in China as anywhere else.

On October 1 I also take time to read some Marx. His definition of religion is more complex than the often-quoted "opium of the people." On this Yom Kippur, I find him helpful in confronting the problem of my own faith: "Religion is the sigh of the oppressed creature, the feeling of a heartless world and the soul of soulless circumstances. It is the opium of the people."

Why am I praying when I am no longer oppressed? Because I want to add my voice to the voices of Jews around the world and throughout history. To remember my people in China helps me make more concrete my solidarity with others who still live in a heartless world, with those who still struggle to wrest their dignity out of soulless circumstances.

To pray as a Jew in China does not feel like "smoking opium." But that implication has to be faced. I wonder to myself if there is a congregation gathering downtown in the Peking Hotel. I know that wealthy businessmen from New York and Los Angeles are housed there. I've heard their complaints about how unwilling the Chinese are to buy American products. But I keep away from them on these High Holidays. I have another agenda for my meditation.

Still, I have to explain, to defend my observance to myself and to others here whom I trust. A week ago I was talking to David Crook, the radical son of orthodox English Jews originally from Poland. He has lived in and worked for China for the past thirty years. He throws his head back in delighted puzzle when I ask him if he has a prayer book for the High Holidays: "You're really going to fast and all that? How can you possibly square your interest in Marxism with religion?" I have few answers. I linger longer than usual at his house that night, drinking vodka. David recalls bits of Shabbat melodies. We share tales of bringing non-Jewish spouses into the homes of our parents. We confess our "anthropological curiosity" about Jews back then. Perhaps this is the withering forgetfulness Grace Paley writes about . . . I don't know how many Jews fasted in Peking on Monday. Maybe none.

And yet, it is really not that difficult to remember Jerusalem on this thirtieth anniversary of the People's Republic. Not much is going on in Peking. Officially, public demonstrations have been forbidden by the Party Central Committee. The reason given: "economic scarcity." China believes itself too poor these days to afford a flashy display of its military or industrial might. All resources must be channeled into catching up with the modern world. Nonetheless, the leaders must have been glad that it was such a drizzly, gray Monday. It kept down the number of poor, unemployed, disgruntled out-of-towners who had been congregating in Tian An Men Square to demand redress of grievances conveniently forgotten.

I stay in my room that day. But I make sure that I have some trusted eyes outside. My friend Helen, with whom I began political activism eight years ago at Stanford, has come up from Nanjing. She rides my bike into the city and reports that all is quiet. Only a few good books are on sale, despite promises about new releases for this commemorative occasion. She reports that foreigners, looking for "action," felt bored, the rain had forced them toward the Coffee Bar at the Peking Hotel.

A Chinese friend shares tales about anniversary festivities at the Great Hall of the People on Sunday night. Three kinds of tickets were handed out to worthy model workers: green and red tickets entitle one to watch a variety of shows and exhibits on the ground floor. The third kind, the yellow tickets, enable the holder to go upstairs to a dancing party for high officials and their sons and daughters. He sneaked upstairs, even though his ticket was green. "Would you believe it was a disco party?" Yes. He describes in detail a high cadre's daughter of eighteen or so, with fine makeup, tight white pants, red silk shirt, and a glittering metallic belt. Her companion was a young actor, "one of those performing artists who are allowed to express individuality with the width of their pants and the length of their hair. This is a modern privilege which echoes an old feudal belief, you know. Actors are still viewed as pimps or whores." My friend dwells on the striking sensuality of the dancing couple. I have heard since then that dancing parties for high officials are held every Saturday night at the Great Hall of the People.

The day after National Day and Yom Kippur is sunny and bright again. I ride out with some other people from our study group to the Red Star Commune. Along a village wall next to the paddies, we meet twenty or so Americans here on a study tour. They are to live and work for one month in the country and one month at a factory. They ask searching questions about China turning capitalist. We have few answers. What we try to do is share with them some of the context of our own doubts. We leave them unsettled, anxious about the lack of a clear line in the current revolutionary struggle. A black woman from Chicago speaks up at the end of the meeting: "I am upset because all you've told us makes it seem like my father, who has worked all his life in a factory, might have been right when he warned me that Communism doesn't do much for common folks. It just puts new bosses in the old places. My father used to say that poor people would always be kept down." I leave regretting that we have no time or any way to reassure her. I am not sure we could have. At least we might have toned down her lofty vision of socialism as well as her all-too-American worries about totalitarianism. Instead, we have to head back on our long bike ride to Peking.

It is becoming sensible, not merely easy, to stand to the side of dramatic occurrences in China. There are plenty of other foreigners, mostly reporters who are chasing down daily the ever-elusive center of the "Chinese storm." So I feel free to appreciate the view from the sidelines. Since the summer trip, more and more opportunities have opened up for accidental encounters.

Recently I spent two mornings at the house of Hou Baolin, China's most famous comedian. I get there by a curious twist of conversation. While talking to the chairman of the Literature Department about my Sichuan travels, about my delight in storytelling, I hear about a course on folk art offered this semester. Although I have no time to attend, the instructor seeks me out. He invites me to Hou Baolin's house since Hou heard I can get books from the West. He seems to want a new American book, something on *Laughing Is Good for Your Health*.

I go along out of sheer curiosity. Hou Baolin invites me back to give him "a lecture on the theory and practice of American humor." So I scramble to get information from the Embassy on something rather far from my own work. I find five books on American humor and take two days of notes in preparation for the talk. I am becoming more and more interested in the distinction between healthy and sick humor, in the history of the transition from the comic type of the "ordinary man" of the nineteenth century frontier with his cracker-barrel wisdom to the "little man" of the mid-twentieth century with his anxieties and self-laceration about wife, gadgets, and the boss. Putting all this into Chinese takes several days. I wonder if all this effort is worth it.

Hou Baolin's house is behind the Northern Sea, the huge imperial garden beyond the Forbidden City. The university car which takes us there can barely turn into the tiny alley leading to his courtyard. As he greets us, more casually this second time, Hou apologizes for his "terrible living conditions," his outdoor toilet. He is proud of his own unwillingness to go "the back door" to get a new apartment in one of the fancy buildings being put up now for famous cultural dignitaries such as himself. The gate to the courtyard opens onto an orderly clutter of antique pottery, literally spilling over from the sitting room toward which we are led. This collection of Ming and Qing ware would be the envy of many museums.

We are greeted by Hou's wife: a petite, striking woman with jet-black hair hanging down in a long permanent. She holds a cigarette comfortably in her slender fingers. She was a famous singer in the Peking opera in the 1940s before Hou became famous. I gather she has an overseas Chinese background. Hou Baolin is sixty-three, robust, with a big, rather plain face which can change in an instant into the face of a befuddled dandy, a squeamish maiden, a pompous party cadre, a pained beggar. He has played or mocked all these roles in his more than four decades of stage life.

He is a dignitary who wears that image consciously, yet lightly. A big Japanese tape recorder dominates the living room. It allows him to hear his own voice on tapes sent in from Hong Kong as well as record his conversations with the many foreigners who come, obviously with official permission, to visit his home. As he tapes our talk on American humor this morning, I am very nervous about the awkward, highfalutin, incomprehensible Chinese that I use. He laughs a lot, easily, generously. By the time he interrupts my ramblings about American humor with a joke about foreigners' pronunciation, I can simply sit back and enjoy his sharp tongue.

I prepared rather hard for this conversation for several reasons. First because Hou had met Bob Hope in June and seemed taken with his fame. I wanted to counteract Hope's aura, and I wanted to learn for myself if Hou really was "China's Bob Hope," as he likes to call himself for quick recognition among foreigners. Second, I wanted to provide him with something substantial for his new interest, research. I had been moved during my first visit to his house, and during a subsequent talk he gave at Beida, by the obvious, sincere effort he is making to retire from performance and turn to something "less silly for a tired old man."

These are his words. He is making a great effort "to make a contribution to the compilation of the cultural activities of the Chinese people." I don't heed his words about tiredness, but I respect his will to do something new, something substantial for a history of traditional comedy. He knows himself to be one of the last classically trained practitioners.

I try to explain to Hou Baolin, in Chinese, the meaning of "black humor," the difference between Bob Hope and Lenny Bruce. He stops me with a question: "Why would a comic want to insult rather than heal his audience? What is the moral purpose of your underground humor anyway?" We both get a good laugh out of the prohibition in "healthy" American humor against the "private" topics of money and religion, as opposed to the Chinese taboos against sex and politics.

Our conversation becomes considerably less funny when, after a couple of hours of relaxed conversation, I ask: "So, what happened to you during the Cultural Revolution years?" Hou falls silent. Without intending to, I had transgressed the limits of polite talk. Then he leans back, looks me straight in the eye, and says, "There are some things I have not even told my wife yet."

Later, when we both have caught our breath again, he cracks some jokes about how bad it is for one's health to have to crawl in front of a portrait of the Chairman held up by whip-wielding Red Guards. Then for a minute he turns serious again, searches my face to be sure I understand his meaning: "No, not even during the most awful moments did I fear for my life. I knew they were not going to, they could not shoot me. I kept telling myself: 'How could the party of the proletariat ever let them do that to me? A beggar's son who had gone hungry so often before Liberation and who learned to write only after 1949?' I held on to my faith in what Mao had done for the people."

As I left Hou Baolin's house that morning, I felt I was beginning to glimpse the difference between intellectuals and proletarians, in China and at home. I know that among my friends who teach at Peking University the certainty that they would not be shot was terrifyingly lacking. That murderous possibility has been eating away at their faith in the Communist Party, and in Mao as well.

The night after the visit with Hou Baolin is the night of the Mid-Autumn Festival. With my closest Chinese friends, I watch the full moon rise over the lake at the Summer Palace. I have brought the tape recorder and we are listening to Bach, which they love, and to Keith Jarrett, whom I am trying to introduce to them: "It sounds somewhat like classical Chinese melody," is my friends' response to the first part of the Köln Concert. The rest, they did not like at all.

We eat a fabulous array of vegetarian dishes. My friends had to take a lot of time out of their long-delayed writing projects to prepare these for me. They know I like these "Buddhist delicacies." Husband and wife take turns reciting classical Chinese poetry about the moon, about the waters, about the fluid, slippery links between hearts far apart. All three of us are preparing for parting not long from now. The mood is sharpened further, in keeping with the traditional festival, by eating moon cakes and sharing ghost stories.

One I like a lot is about a Nanjing professor in the 1940s, who was up late at night, writing and longing for his deceased wife. The cup she used to bring him tea stands empty. Then, lo and behold, the cup becomes full. Another story they tell, again as "absolute truth," is about a friend of a friend who spent the night in a haunted house in Peking. Hearing noises in the attic he goes upstairs and finds some card players. He joins the game and has great fun until the card partners suggest a break. Then, casually, the players deposit their heads on the table for a rest. . . . I laugh, acting appropriately frightened.

If I hadn't laughed, I probably would be crying. Enveloped by the fullness of the night, surrounded by friends I have come to love, my eyes drink in the moon, frozen over an eighteenth-century pagoda. Here, suddenly a foretaste of how painful it will be to leave China soon.

OCTOBER 16   *Rewriting history:* The Central Committee of the *revolution without Mao?* Chinese Communist Party commemorated the thirtieth anniversary of the founding of the People's Republic in a speech given by the aged general Ye Jianying. It is being hailed, in the words of the *Peking Review*, as a "historic document of great importance . . . meant to guide the work of the whole party, the whole army and the country for a long period." The twenty-five-page document has become required reading matter for the weekly political study sessions still held throughout China.

At Beida, the first Thursday afternoon after Ye's speech, when departmental groups customarily meet for political study, the response was less than enthusiastic. A student friend of mine reports that "many people dozed, some girls took out their knitting needles, others managed to memorize quite a bit of their next day's English lesson while I was assigned to read the speech out loud to the study group." He is angry but not surprised. Attendance at political meetings has been becoming more and more a matter of duty these days: "You know, the mood is so different from the heated, early morning discussion we used to have every day at my factory during the 1960s."

To me, the Ye speech seems a tedious way of talking around the issues which concern people I know here. The special privileges of high cadres, the rising food prices, and the lack of a detailed evaluation of the Cultural Revolution are what matter to my friends now.

Back in the U.S., I gather, the speech is also hailed for its historic importance. *Newsweek* features it in an issue entitled "Eroding Mao's Legacy." Far away from home, I can nonetheless imagine the sigh of relief at this "end of ideological concerns" in China. The periodic mass movements engineered by Mao, like the Great Leap Forward and the Cultural Revolution, have baffled outside observers. At the core of these upheavals was Mao's obsession with the possibility of creating a new society, a new consciousness of social relations. These events had dredged up popular American images of the madness of totalitarianism, had justified the government's cold shoulder to the People's Republic in the decades after 1949. Now that we are eager to be friends again, we explain (excuse, that is) China's new trustworthiness as a commercial and political ally in terms of its "eroding Maoism."

It is curious how both in China and abroad public attention has focused upon the brief, veiled condemnation of the Cultural Revolution in Ye Jianying's speech. Here is the one sentence which has been proclaimed as "historic" in the media and which is deemed puny by many people I've talked to here: "At the time when the Cultural Revolution was launched, the estimate of the situation within the Party and the country ran counter to reality, no accurate definition was given of revisionism, and an erroneous policy and method of struggle was adopted, deviating from the principles of democratric centralism." Exit Mao? The perennially correct Helmsman? Yes. The improvisor of Revolution? No.

What seems to me to be swept under the carpet in the welcome for the Ye speech in China and abroad is the unresolved dispute over Mao and the Cultural Revolution. After several drafts of the speech, each successively watering down any clear analysis of China's recent history, Ye was picked to deliver the final version simply because he is neither Deng Xiaoping nor Hua Guofeng. We know too little about the process of the struggle that took place between September 25 and 29 when the Central Committee met in Peking. We don't know how the themes of the speech were decided, which words were changed, what accusations were hurled, or how the compromise text was produced.

I have heard that the tension was strong. Despite the moderate tone of the speech, I gather that the hatchet between Mao's modernizing foes and his antirevisionist supporters has hardly been buried. Both sides ended up agreeing to fudge the past because they believe the future will prove them right. The current leadership hopes to produce material benefits that might quiet others' angry warnings about elitism and class struggle. Whether China becomes another Soviet Union, with its powerful, privileged bosses and disillusioned masses, remains to be seen. I have little doubt, however, that Mao Zedong will continue to inspire those who want to make China into a more socialist society.

The issue of China's socialist future was neatly dispensed with in the Ye Jianying speech. It states simply that exploitation has been abolished and, therefore, China is socialist. What already is, thus, need not be cause for worry. These words, meant to pacify, provoke more irksome questions: Has exploitation really been abolished in China? Who is being rewarded according to ability and work? The idle cadres in the office above the assembly line where a friend of mine worked for 30 yuan per month, while they got 80? "You know it was not just that they read newspapers and drank tea all day long which bugged the hell out of me. It was that one of them sat there petting her cat all day long while we worked like crazy to fulfill the bicycle production quotas below."

Among my friends at the university, the event of October 1 also evokes conflicting emotions. For students, the Cultural Revolution still looms, unanalyzed. This anniversary has deepened their cynicism about revolutionary ideals. Their personal experiences over the past decade have taught them to be suspicious of words like "Dictatorship of the Proletariat." They had been used as tools in power struggles of the 1960s. Now, by glossing over the concrete history of the Cultural Revolution, the Central Committee's speech deprives them of hope even further.

A very different emotion in a poem by an older intellectual in his late fifties. He joined the revolutionary underground in the 1940s, had worked for land reform in the early 1950s, and then was declared a "rightist" in 1957. He still aches with love for the nation that has pained him so deeply. He writes out the poem as a gift to me. I translate it as a gift to him.

For My Wounded Homeland
In Celebration of Its 30th Anniversary (October 1979)

Ah! homeland, my homeland!
  You are in turmoil, yet calm
  You ache yet celebrate.
  You have suffered insults, have groaned in pain
  Yet are resplendent and reborn again.

How many shame-filled tears
  How many forgiving hearts

How many are those who sank into the darkness?
How many awake with the dawn?
How many still ride the black, monstrous nightmare?
How many already reborn after being stifled?

Ah! homeland,
　You have reached, again, this gloomy recurrent
　Moment when seasons change.

Let greedy fools
　drift on in tides of power and seas of profit.
Let those who would desert you
　pass into oblivion.
Let home-bound sparrows
　go off to build their nests.
Let those who would despair
　dream on their empty dreams.

Ah! homeland,
　Though you are riddled with gaping wounds
　your face unseemly!

Do not grieve, do not worry,
　Close to your breast
　Kissing every inch of your wounded body

Are we!
　arousing mighty waves
　to wash away all shame and filth,

Are we!
　devoting strength, wisdom, sweat, blood,
　to bring you back to youth.

Are we!

Are we!

Since we, generation after generation,
　Live, struggle and die here.

Since every inch of this land
　is mingled with the blood of our ancestors.

Every instant of time
  contains the spirit of our people.

Since we are destined to inherit the fruit of a thousand years
  Let history extend itself through our hands.

How can you, my mate—
  Not hear, out of the echoes of the future,
  our descendants call?
  Not hear, out of the depths of history,
  our people's cry?

How can you,
  Still numb, pensive,
  let time pass by?
  Still waver, stand idle,
  waiting, waiting?

Resolve to get rid of shame and rancor.
Resolve to forget pain and injustice.
Resolve to give up the notion of your helplessness.
Resolve to clear away your confused and puzzled thoughts.

Look like a real warrior,
Open your sail and journey far!

For the sake of history and the future,
For the sake of the people and the revolution,
Please, give all you have
  to our beloved,
  our wounded
  homeland!

This poem remains unpublished. "Too revolutionary, too dangerous," is the verdict of the poet's seasoned spouse.
  Why, I ask? Why cannot a Communist poet publish this outpouring of commitment? Is it too soon? Too daring to express loyalty to socialism in nonofficial terms? Is there any truth at all in Ye Jianying's remark that "the policy of 'let a hundred flowers bloom, let a hundred schools contend' is a fundamental and long-term policy of the Chinese Communist Party"?

NOVEMBER 10 *Wei Jingsheng: slaughtering a chicken to let the monkey see*

Democracy is like rice we now get from Hankou—it takes time and costs money, but there are people who try to intercept it. Democracy is all the more difficult because it is intangible. (Mao Zedong, lecture, April 1937)

What is tragic is that in our people's republic only those who live like celestial immortals—with a full stomach—have the power to rule. How can the people help but have plenty of reason to wrest power from the hands of these overlords? (Wei Jingsheng, "The Fifth Modernization—Democracy," December 1978)

On October 16, Wei Jingsheng, one of the editors of *Tansuo* (Exploration), was condemned as a counterrevolutionary by a Peking court. His sentence: fifteen years in jail, then three more of political inactivity. His crimes, in the words of the *People's Daily* editorial the next day: "betraying the motherland" and "besmirching Marxism - Leninism - Mao Zedong thought." This news plunges me into my worst depression yet. My values are on the line in a way I'm not quite prepared for. I know the historical reasons for the absence of a legal tradition to protect the individual and for the lack of interest in freedom of thought. But cultural uniqueness explains too little now. It takes some weeks to make new sense of things. Hence this belated response in the journal.

The government's broadly acclaimed, conflict-ridden policy of Four Modernizations is showing its seams when challenged by a fifth, democracy. To safeguard the four, it has been necessary to silence the call for more freedom. China now looks "hungrier" to me. It has much less of the "rice" of democracy which Mao warned would be easily intercepted. Wei Jingsheng, too, warned that democracy would be conveniently forgotten by those who've had their fill.

I first heard about Wei Jingsheng's sentence at a dinner on Tuesday night. During dinner, all of us threw in different rumors we'd heard about the new legal system that is being instituted here. Some bits from that conversation: a surprisingly liberal sentencing (only a formal, verbal reprimand) for the "enlightenment" group in Guizhou province—a collection of strident, bitter youths who had raised the call for human rights far from the capital. It was found that they had legitimate grounds for their complaints against "autocratic authorities." The next day, the rumor is borne out by the *People's Daily* "truth": Wei Jingsheng has been condemned for fifteen years. Three headlines on the back page: "Peking Court Publicly Sentences Counterrevolutionary Criminal Wei Jingsheng," "Solemn and Just Sentencing," "Resolute Punishment of Counterrevolutionary Criminal." I read these articles more closely than anything else I have read in China. I don't recall being so upset by anything before.

Doggedly, I look up every character I don't know. I don't want to miss a single turn of phrase in these texts which say more about themselves than about Wei Jingsheng's crimes. Why does *"fandong,"* "anti-motion," come to connote such a vile offense in a socialist society? Is not the progress of history a matter of reason, not faith? (In English, *fandong* means "reactionary.") I try to calm my vague dreads about what all of this might mean for my friends and me. Wei Jingsheng, after all, was also accused of being a traitor. That is to say, he was too close to foreigners.

This panic lasts for a day or two. Then I begin to talk, at length, with everyone I find—friends at the university, cab drivers, study group members, passersby at the Democracy Wall. From them, I gather facts not mentioned in the *People's Daily*. Wei Jingsheng had been arrested on March 29. The same day, a Peking municipal ordinance limited the content and the location of big character posters and other nonofficial publications. As soon as it was announced that such writings must not challenge party leadership and the tenets of Marxism-Leninism-Mao Zedong thought, Wei was found to have gone beyond the pale. Was this a case of a law designed after the crime? Echoes here of the 1957 Hundred Flowers movement. It, too, spilled over and became the Anti-Rightist campaign when Mao Zedong redefined parameters of acceptable criticism *after* he had had an earful of the intellectuals' criticism of the party.

I have also been reading the courtroom transcripts, posted on Democracy Wall within days of the closed, "secret" hearing. A brave gesture. A hint here, finally, that cowardice and self-interest are not all that rules Chinese society in times of political upheaval. I'm forced to moderate my rage against those who did not speak out against the Cultural Revolution.

According to these transcripts, Wei Jingsheng was asked and answered in great detail questions about his contacts with foreigners. It seems that before and during China's February–March war in Vietnam, Wei Jingsheng approached some reporters about the human rights problem in China. Two British journalists subscribed to his journal *Tansuo* and offered further monies to support Wei's publishing activities. They turned down his request for a Chinese typewriter—a commodity not available for purchase by private citizens here. Then, during a casual encounter, Wei Jingsheng supposedly wrote out for them on a piece of paper the names of Chinese commanders at the Vietnam front. This is the essence of his traitorship, of his "selling state secrets to foreigners." It is still unclear whether that information was truly classified, even at that time.

This line of questioning raises urgent questions for me: Why did the news focus on his contacts with "certain foreigners"—an amorphous category that sends shivers through all relations between Chinese and foreigners? Who can tell just when that "certain" outsider can turn into an "enemy"? This lack of detail sets off—an intended result, perhaps—waves of private alarm. Why have none of the journalists involved with Wei Jingsheng been expelled or prosecuted if this indeed was a matter of treason?

The most nagging question in my mind, and in the minds of my friends, Chinese and foreigners alike, is this: Was the first charge concerning classified information used as a cover for prosecuting Wei Jingsheng on the second charge—counterrevolutionary activities? Had he stepped beyond the bounds of permissible criticism by naming the names of the culpable, the current leadership of Hua Guofeng and Deng Xiaoping? Had he doubted the validity of the "socialist system" in China today any more deeply than the newspapers that attack official corruption?

Reading the Chinese press, it is hard to know what landed Wei Jingsheng in jail for fifteen years. The published snippets are from the prosecutor's side. Then, a windfall: An American journalist turns out to have translations from "Beijing Unofficial Journals" Joint Publications Research Service (JPRS) #073421, dated May 10, which contains *Tansuo*'s last "Extra" of March 25; JPRS 023756, dated June 26, which contains the first issue of *Tansuo* and parts I and II of Wei Jingsheng's article on "The Fifth Modernization—Democracy"; and JPRS 073787, dated June 29, which contains part III of Wei's article. I get hold of these documents and flip eagerly through them. By now, they are "counterrevolutionary" propaganda.

Out of these documents, I reconstruct for myself the short-lived, muddy history of *Tansuo*. The journal was started in December 1978 at the height of Democracy Wall activism. This was a time when Deng Xiaoping encouraged people to voice their own opinions. Attacks on the followers of the Gang of Four helped him consolidate his power. In its opening publication statement, the new journal stated explicitly that it drew its sanction from the Chinese Constitution, which provides for freedom of speech, press, and assembly. From the beginning, the editors acknowledged officially sanctioned parameters and committed themselves to the amorphous project of "exploration." Their advocacy lacked focus from the start. All they knew was that they "could not recognize the absolute correctness of any theory." Pretty much what Deng Xiaoping was saying as well, in his own mild-mannered de-Mao-ification. He, too, was declaring publicly that Mao was not an infallible saint of the revolution.

In view of what happened later, *Tansuo*'s statement of purpose was hardly "subversive." The eight or so young people who got together to found the journal in December 1978 never asked themselves whom they really did or could represent. The crowds milling around Democracy Wall were not a reliable constituency. Youthful activists discovered their own marginality—the fact that they were isolated and open to repression—as soon as Deng Xiaoping had had enough of their irksome voices. The ultimate, tragic irony came in March 1979. Wei Jingsheng had to reach out to a foreign reporter to let the Chinese people know about the Chinese war in Vietnam. The "mass line" of *Tansuo*, as Mao would have said—their rootedness in society, not their sentimentality about the masses—was weak indeed.

By March, *Tansuo* was getting more strident. Something had happened. Fu Yuehua, a young woman who had been organizing out-of-town petitioners in keeping with a Central Committee promise to redress errors committed during the Cultural Revolution, had been arrested. Inquiries about her fate were met with hostility, especially from the police security personnel who had used "internal procedures" to detain her for investigation. The *Tansuo* editors pressed further. Hounded, the editors turned to bite those chasing them. They went too far, it seems, when their editorials started to name top leaders as objects of criticism. In the eyes of the authorities, the editors transgressed irrevocably when they wrote: "The people must maintain vigilance against Deng Xiaoping's metamorphosis into a dictator" (March 25, 1979).

So, I try to reconstruct for myself the historical background for the increasingly shrill tone of *Tansuo*. Then I take a few more days to read and reread Wei Jingsheng's long article, "The Fifth Modernization." It is too easy to excerpt theoretical indignations about Communism from his writings. These bits, quoted in the Western and Chinese press alike, are unreliable without some sense of his metaphors drawn from Chinese history and of his naive assertions about the West. Wei's "bad guys" are lordly types from *The Dream of the Red Chamber* (an eighteenth-century novel). His "good guys" are knights from the *Water Margin* (a fifteenth-century novel) and the long-haired Taiping (nineteenth-century) rebels. One turn of phrase which the government prosecutor found particularly incriminating (and which has been covertly savored by readers of the *People's Daily*) was the one in which he called Marxism-Leninism-Mao Zedong thought a "slightly fancier folk remedy than the stuff peddled by the Central Yangzi quack doctors," (my rendition from the *People's Daily*).

Even after reconstructing for myself this tragicomedy of *Tansuo*, I am no closer to answering the question I started with: What made Wei Jingsheng so threatening to the present leadership? Why did he have to be put away for fifteen years?

Perhaps they sensed the powerful appeal of his attacks to politically disillusioned urban youth. His writings are laced with a call to wake up, to see through outworn slogans. He is asking his generation to be on guard against being used again, as during the Cultural Revolution, by hungry rulers. This sounds like a Western liberal's attack on delusions fostered by totalitarian regimes. But from the mouth and pen of a Cultural Revolution activist, these outpourings have a different meaning. Wei Jingsheng was the leader of a Peking Red Guard group which ran into trouble early on with Jiang Qing, Mao's wife. Thus, he speaks to, if not exactly for, an entire generation of Chinese youth now in their late twenties or early thirties. These youths had followed Mao's line only to find themselves caught in the web of the machinations of older leaders.

Contrary to the expectations of Western critics, Wei Jingsheng's generation is growing up to rather than growing out of its politics.

Contrary to the wishes of the current Chinese leadership, they are unwilling and unable to forget the Cultural Revolution.

Where Ye Jianying declared the Cultural Revolution to have been a mistake, Wei Jingsheng calls the Cultural Revolution "the first occasion for the Chinese people to demonstrate their strength and their desire for democracy." What was wrong, according to Wei, is not the ideal of egalitarianism but the blind faith it generated among youth. He claims that the willingness of youths like himself to believe in a supreme leader made them vulnerable to Mao's whims. What comes through in Wei's appeal to those who shared his disillusionment is a call for more rather than less political involvement.

> Our young people are not "sick men of the East." They have sufficient courage to put up and to read posters and to discuss different views even though some of them are tabooed. They are not yet sure what is "truth" because the "truth" before them is no longer trustworthy. They want a new way of life. If anyone wants to deceive the simple-minded youth with old tricks, he is doomed to fail. They are by no means simple minded . . .

Why then was Wei Jingsheng locked up for fifteen years? What limits of doubt did he cross which so threatened the certainties propagated by the current regime? He talked about power and privilege concentrated in the hands of the "overlords." This week, the radio "study broadcast program" topic was "how cadres must not become overlords riding on the heads of the masses." Why was Wei Jingsheng declared to be a "criminal" if he only asserted as fact what the radio acknowledges as a "widespread mental tendency"?

The question of the parameters of dissent is becoming an obsession for me these days. I take it up with all my Chinese friends. They tell me that Wei Jingsheng acted stupidly in his contacts with foreigners. "He was too naive. He forgot that our leaders view all foreign journalists as spies," one young woman tells me. She shares my view that the charge about "selling state secrets" was a cover-up to get him on the "counterrevolutionary" charge.

I press these conversations further, unrelenting. Where did Wei Jingsheng go wrong? A young man tells me, "When Wei Jingsheng named Deng Xiaoping as a tyrant, he signed his own verdict. You see, you are never allowed to name a leader in China."

His explanation doesn't sit well with me. It's too thin, too easy, just a "line" somehow. Wei Jingsheng and *Tansuo*, after all, did not name Deng until March. Yet the implication is that their criminality began earlier. A young Communist Party member friend of mine puts it simply: "When you start to think in China, you have to be prepared to go to jail."

The consequences of doubt, then, are as severe as the consequences of active resistance? What is the difference between Wei Jingsheng and Zhang Zhixin—the woman heroine who defied the Gang of Four? To be sure, the "internal procedures" of the Gang were uglier. Her captors had tortured her, cut her vocal cords. They accused her of being against the Party, the People, and Marxism-Leninism-Mao Zedong thought. She died a Communist. Wei Jingsheng went to jail for making an amorphous call for human rights and because of his clumsy relations with foreigners.

She believed too much, he too little. Her resistance and his doubt were both labeled counterrevolutionary. But perhaps neither one was punished for a particular crime. They were once exemplary model work heroes, then they were damned as equally exemplary criminals. The power of models, whether to inspire or to admonish, has long been known and used in China. The *People's Daily* editorial the day after Wei Jingsheng's sentencing makes this appeal to models explicit: "To those who see counterrevolutionary criminals like Wei Jingsheng as 'pioneers of human rights,' or 'fighters for democracy'. . . we say to these people, you have added the abacus up wrongly. You'd better give up your fantasies."

I recognize the tradition, but continue to rage against it. Too much of what I value, of what my Chinese friends long for, is consigned to the realm of fantasies by the *People's Daily*. I don't like, don't accept their mathematics.

Other troubling confluences recently: Wei Jingsheng put away for fifteen years, food prices go up thirty to fifty percent. Students from the People's University down the road from us, at first officially encouraged to demonstrate against an army occupation of their school (which dates back to the Cultural Revolution), are now being accused of "anarchist tactics" and "covert support of the KMT." "Foolishly" they took their plea to the Central

Committee on October 10, the anniversary of the 1911 Republican Revolution, which happens to be National Day in Taiwan. A regulation has just been issued against the free circulation of foreign films. From now on, all foreign movies have to be first screened by three ministries (Foreign Affairs, Culture, and Education). In the words of a Chinese student friend of mine: "The senior cadres, with nothing better to do, will now get to see all the dirty movies, while we are deprived of study material." Two of my appointments with senior intellectuals in the Academy of Social Sciences have been canceled because of "poor health." Around Democracy Wall, discussions are heated again. On October 28, I hear a young worker read a position paper on Wei Jingsheng. He talks for four hours. More than three hundred people listen.

I continue to scavenge the JPRS translations for "news" unavailable in China. An article by Liang Yao, "The Deeds and Vices of Virtue Forest," from *Tansuo* of March 1979 catches my eye. So much I didn't see, had no way of knowing, in the spring. Then, all too caught up in my own settling into Chinese life, I missed its seamier side. Now, I am riveted by a description of Center Number 1, Peking's prison for political dissenters. An ordinary, ugly tale:

> When one enters this station's big hall one is first stripped and then searched. If one is slightly less than humble, he is subjected to abuse in minor cases or trounced and beaten in serious cases. Some 14 people live in a small, low-ceiling, cold, wet, dark room about 18 meters wide. Here they eat, sleep and discharge their waste. Therefore, when people enter this place it is as though they are entering a cottage that has never been swept or cleaned. Two people share a torn and lousy bedsheet, which has not been washed for a year. They sleep on a bare and rough floor. In these poor conditions, it is not unusual for people to become sick and die.
>
> Yuan Guoruo, a worker representative of the Lanzhou Railway Bureau, who was released from Virtue Forest on February 21st, talked to us about his personal experiences there.
>
> Yuan Guoruo was a former worker of the Lanzhou Railway Bureau. A certain leader had harbored a grudge against him and framed him because he had exposed the leader's mistakes. He was charged with being "an active counterrevo-

lutionary" and sentenced to two years' imprisonment. After being found not guilty, he was released. By then, his home was ruined, his family dead and his wife and children scattered.

After he was released he received no apology or compensation. Therefore he visited the central authorities. In addition to not solving his problem, the Ministry of Railways' Letters and Visiting Department detained him, sent him away and then jailed him. In collusion with Chen Shouyi of the Lanzhou Railway Bureau, Ministry of Railway Letters and Visits Department director Guan Shaoliang detained him in Virtue Forest 56 times and in the Lanzhou reception station 64 times.

Every time they detained him, they made many charges against him, such as trespassing on Zhongnan hai [the enclosed compound where Chinese Communist Party Headquarters officials live], trespassing on the Great Hall, mischief-making, holding up cars of foreigners, demanding money, trespassing on foreign embassies, and so on. It seemed that he had committed heinous crimes.

During his confinement he was brutally and callously tortured. They burned him with a poker, punished him with an electric current, and hung and beat him for as long as five hours. They beat him many times until he became unconscious, but he did not yield. He broke three pairs of handcuffs. They say Yuan Guoruo was very obstinate.

What links small-fry dissenters like Yuan Guoruo to Wei Jingsheng? Whatever they're accused of, it is their obstinacy that concerns me now. What makes them search out "trouble" over and over again? What sets them apart from the millions who have never set foot in, never heard of, Virtue Forest? Perhaps much less than the government hopes.

Yesterday, a Chinese friend drops by and tells me about how depressed his colleagues are because of the Wei Jingsheng sentence. An idiom slips out during our conversation: "Wei Jingsheng's case was the leadership's way to kill the chicken to frighten the monkey." *Shaji xiahou* is a complex, old idiom. It justifies many of the premonitions I have had for the past few weeks. Wei Jingsheng, then, was put away to warn people like my friends.

Yet I doubt this will work. Individuals like Wei seem too gutsy, or at least very clever. They're not unlike the proverbial monkey who created such havoc in the Jade Emperor's sedate, oppressive heaven.

NOVEMBER 12   *Finally, an*   An extraordinary breakthrough!
interview with a May Fourth   The opportunity to meet with a
intellectual, Zhang Shenfu   survivor of the May Fourth
movement has come, after months of intense frustration. The most eminent nearby personage of that era is Feng Youlan, China's foremost philosopher, now under house arrest because of his entanglements with the Gang of Four. I have been trying to see him for weeks. He lives less than two blocks from my dorm. The school authorities keep telling me that Feng is not feeling well. Same dead-ended response when I try to have an interview with Li Shu, head of the Modern History Institute of the Academy of Social Sciences and author of a particularly stimulating article on the problem of intellectuals during May Fourth. The line about Li Shu is that he is "too busy" to meet with me just now.

Then, a near accident. One day, scanning the list of members of New Tide (an enlightenment-oriented student society at Peking University, founded in 1919) I come upon a minor figure in my thesis, Zhang Songnian. I ask a Chinese friend if he is still alive. "Yes, I think he might be a researcher on the payroll of the Peking National Library. But maybe he's using another name." Some weeks later, another friend asks the Peking Library officials if there is indeed such a person, no doubt an old man by now, on their staff. Yes. He is known as Zhang Shenfu now, and he is willing to meet with me. For the next few weeks, I try to find as much biographical detail about Zhang Shenfu as I can. It's not very much. He seems to have been either forgotten or purged from history.

This afternoon, I arrive at the National Library at 2:15. I'm greeted by an educated, open-minded, aged cadre who tells me that the car sent for Zhang Shenfu should arrive shortly. At 2:30 sharp, the car pulls up and a young girl (Zhang's daughter, I learn later) gets out on one side, walks around to open the door for a short, well-dressed, infirm yet spritely old man. He walks with a cane. As soon as we're settled down in the reception room, tea

Zhang Shenfu, eighty-eight-year-old survivor of the May Fourth era, at his home, after our initial introduction at the Peking National Library.

before us, he's freed of his bodily limitations. A warm, wry smile plays on his face as he tells me I am the first foreigner he's been allowed to talk with in nearly twenty years. A great deprivation for a man who was, and still is, China's most ardent admirer of Bertrand Russell.

In the next two hours, Zhang Shenfu sketches for me the highlights of his public story, a story slowly coming into light again now that he has been rehabilitated. He was one of the foremost "rightists" in 1957. Born in 1893, Zhang was one of the three founders of the Chinese Communist Party in 1920, a leader of the December Ninth movement of 1935, a public spokesman for the democratic movement in the 1940s. Some of this I knew vaguely before. The bits that are freshest in retelling today are his impressions of the boisterous Lo Jialun, another Peking University student, who burst into the library on the day of May 4, 1919, to spread the news of the student protest. Zhang recalls the story unembarrassed by Lo's subsequent condemnation as a reactionary follower of the KMT. "At that time he was a progressive, thoughtful young man, even if brash."

The story of his own interest in logic comes out, scattered

between recollections of reading the British journal *The Monist* while in high school, of going to meet Russell in Shanghai in 1920, of continuing to propagate Russell's thought while a professor of philosophy at Qinghua in the 1930s. In between the tale of his philosophical explorations, bits of his romantic adventures. He was married several times (it is unclear to me yet just how many). His most noted love, then his wife, was Liu Qingyang, a May Fourth activist from Tianjin, whom he first met and with whom he began a turbulent love affair on the boat to France in December 1920. On that Marseilles-bound boat was also Peking University's controversial president, Cai Yuanpei, as well as other members of the New Tide society.

I want to know more about that boat ride! A chance here to hear his story firsthand, to delve into its unofficial crevices for a new interpretation of May Fourth. As we say goodbye today, I tell Zhang Shenfu I hope we can meet again. He looks at the Peking Library official and with a very clear, emphatic voice answers, "I hope so too. Very much. We must talk frankly. Time for telling truth is running out."

NOVEMBER 28   *Scholarly contacts opening, a meeting with Li Shu, director of the Modern History Institute*   After months of being told that he is busy, I have finally met Li Shu. Is it a coincidence that the appointment was set up the day after the delegation from the National Academy of Science visited Beida and heard my complaints about scholarly communications here? For weeks before, I had been told, "You are not eminent enough to have an interview with Li Shu" or "He's suffering from a cold." The day after the American delegation's visit, I get nine overdue letters from back home and an appointment with Li Shu.

He is a Hunanese man in his late sixties or early seventies. We talk at first about his own history, college in Peking before the Anti-Japanese War, an adventurous trip through Guilin and Hong Kong in 1948 before he could wind his way back to Peking and continue his work in the Communist Party's intellectual organs. He is thoughtful, funny, open. I come prepared with questions about his article on the "spontaneous" versus the "conscious" aspects of the May Fourth movement. I am hoping that he will clarify, expand his one-line commentary that May Fourth intellectuals saw themselves as *"Ubermenschen* [supermen, in Nietzsche's sense] who were the first to know and first to awaken from the feudal world view of traditional China."

Li Shu tells me openly that there is nothing new, "of a genuine historical substance in my article. I have not done any historical research for years." "Still," he continues, "it is worthwhile to pursue this line of questioning. Awakened intellectuals, then, as now, have their shortcomings, you know. A conservative habit of mind lingers on in all of us who have inherited the Confucian world view. Even after 1949, after landlords have been gotten rid of, feudal mentality has persisted, persists still in China today. If you want to investigate this further, you will need to talk to scholars doing actual research on modern intellectual history." As we say goodbye, he promises to set up meetings for me with Ding Shouhe and Li Zehou, researchers in the Academy of Social Sciences who, Li Shu believes, are doing the most important work in my area of interest.

NOVEMBER 30   *Digging in for a longer stay in China*   I have decided to extend my stay in China until June 1980. The decision has been germinating ever since I came back from the summer trip. Such a great change in my friendships and contacts upon return. Somehow, being away on the road and writing letters from China to Chinese friends has made them and me much more aware of our closeness, of the openings into each other's minds which these six months have begun. Back in Peking in September, the idea of leaving in February felt more and more ridiculous. All my work, thinking, writing was cramped by the imminent deadline. Choices about how to use my time were becoming harder also because of the sudden rush of introductions to people related to my research on the May Fourth movement.

Then, last weekend, a foreign friend left China after three years. I witnessed his wrenching departure in all its frenzied details. Seeing how much it hurt him to leave, I had to wonder how I would feel when time came for me to go. I consoled myself with the knowledge that this year is just the beginning, that I will be able to come back often. Openings here and my work-related reasons back home should help.

But these consolations don't work. I'm realizing, again and again, how much I am learning here, how many sources, how much information, and how many impressions I can gather just by letting present intimacies deepen. On Saturday night, a Western friend put it simply, "Why don't you stay until June. You'll never be able to come back as a student again, to live in a dorm, to pass your days relatively unnoticed, to be visited by Chinese friends freely, to go in and out of a Chinese residence hall without the cumbersome signing-in procedures required for visitors and experts."

On Monday I wrote to the Washington committee and asked for an extension. A week later, I mention my decision to the Foreign Students' Office at the university. Their only comment: "We wondered why you hadn't done it before. What's the matter, you don't like us?" As authorities? No. As people? Yes, more and more so in fact, as I start to live more informally here. Some informalities, I am discovering, are not dependent on official permission in China. For example, I am currently joining in preparations for the oncoming winter. The city is changing and I along with it. About two weeks ago, two days of sudden, icy winds. The Gobi desert is reannouncing its nearness after the long lull since the spring dust storms.

Along with the sharp, cutting air comes the roundness of bodily defenses. I watch and partake in a carefully timed, ritually observed layering: First, we put on the padded vests underneath regular cotton jackets. Next, we move on to long-sleeved *mian aos*, those typical North China jackets made of silk or cotton that are as effective against atmospheric invasion from the northwest as the Great Wall against human threats. With the *mian aos* come gloves and woolen scarves. Finally, on around the twentieth of November, we put on long, padded coats lined with padded cotton or sheepskin and padded cotton gloves. This synchronization of layers and dates might appear natural. In fact, it is a mysterious, arbitrary process.

One day, I turn up at the door of a colleague's house on campus. His wife is at home, and we chat for an hour. She apologizes about not seeing me off properly enough because she dares not to go out in her padded shoes: "It's just not time for them yet; everyone would talk." "Everyone?" I ask. "Yes, everyone. You see, neighbors are always commenting on one's daily demeanor." Sounds like interference to me. Then, I have to ask myself who suffers more interference: the Chinese woman noticed for unseasonable padded shoes or the American woman unnoticed unless her jeans are Calvin Kleins? "Mothers and nuns, both light candles," as Yeats wrote. For different reasons, with different consequences.

Winter in Peking: the chill and the residents of North China go well together. Bundled up, people just roll on. Underneath the visible slowing down of activity are increasingly spritely spirits. Cheeks are ruddier, hands and feet move more vigorously in place, conversations are louder in the bus lines, eyes dart about more playfully. Peking is somehow more cheerful, and so am I. A splurge of color to replace the leaves. Pomegranates abound in bright, soft, orange colors for a week or so. Followed by silk-clad babies. Parents' arms, which used to hold children dressed in dark green or muted blue sweaters, now flower with bundles of pink, yellow, red silk capes trimmed with fake white fur covering all of the baby except its face. On especially windy days, the top of the silk bundle is wrapped with bright gauzy scarves. Last Thursday on the trolley I saw a plumply wrapped woman carrying a scarlet bundle covered with a red scarf. Together, they looked like an ancient sculpture.

China can make anyone want to have a child, no matter how deep the doubts about Western families or how weighty the outward evidence of China's overpopulation. The quiet, enriching presence of children everywhere makes you want to give it a try.

I have also added some layers and relish the brush of desert cold against my cheeks. I ride my bicycle around the frozen lake where students are skating on the sliver of ice jutting out from still-flowing waters. They are having the kind of fun which, I gather from a cab driver, is denied to others. Ordinary working youth have no skating ponds. The driver grumbles on about having no place to go, nothing to do after work. "I have no room to put up a ping-pong table at home, no entrance permit to play basketball at the Workers' Stadium, no time to stand in line for rare movie tickets."

The student skaters on Nameless Lake are lucky. Complacent

A fully winterized Chinese child: layers of wool and silk, with only a face protruding. In the background, a quilt laid out to air during one of the few sunny days. Photograph courtesy of Jason Wolfe.

about their good fortune, they accept it as a natural reward for their success in the examinations. They swirl slowly on the ice. Solitary leaves hang stiffly on the willow trees. Among the brittle dots of green and brown, I can see the water tower pagoda gleaming across the lake. I feel at home here at Beida.

Less so, when I step outside the tiny northwest gate into the alley where kids play "jump ball." With a fist-sized roll of flour dough packed neatly between their heels, they kick across to the catcher. I ride past them to go on to some frozen rice paddies. Stalks stand imprisoned in the cold gray mud. I wonder if the frogs still chorus underneath.

We've been organizing for some action about hunger in Cambodia. Impossible to go on as if a people were not in danger of extermination in our time. I called Helen in Nanjing. I've started conversations around dinner tables here. A meeting of forty foreign students last week. Newly arrived Americans rather negative about doing anything collective. Other foreign students negative about American arrogance, callousness, and naivete. On this issue, I stand with the other foreigners. I hear rumors that one of my compatriots smirked as I chaired the organizational meeting last week: "She is not even an American." For once, maybe for the first time in years, this does not hurt me. Not too much, anyhow.

It's getting harder and harder to feel comfortable with my own kind in China. I catch myself wincing more and more as I near the Peking Hotel. If I have to go in for any reason, I brace myself. Each time I pass the bar, on my way to buy some instant coffee (an indulgence which I can now afford at $2.50, due to new Brazilian imports) or to mail some letters (since at the university, mail is more likely to be read), I shudder at the pack of hungry male eyes.

Last night, a colleague from Berkeley was shocked to see how instantly Western men focus on breasts and rear ends as women walk through the lobby of the Peking Hotel. He, too, is shocked by the men's looks. Then, an apparition in black sweater: embroidery over her nipples, belted into black pants, silk flowers down to her crotch, she hobbles in wearing hip-high platform boots. Suddenly freed from being looked at myself, I stand pained by the woman who invites the looks I hate.

I know these rituals of courtship well. But have forgotten them this year. I hear prostitution in the Peking Hotel is on the rise. Rumors abound about foreign women students going into "the business" for money and contacts. I try to forget.

It has been easy, perhaps too easy, for me to leave behind Western ways. To leave them behind, however, is not the same as reckoning with them. I have more work to do here. And I'm glad to have more time to do it.

CHAPTER 7

DECEMBER 2 *Interiors: some dwellings and some minds*

Staying on in China proved worthwhile promptly. As if the decision to stay itself precipitated the openings which evoked the idea of an extension in the first place. It all started with some interviews related to my May Fourth research. I am currently talking with an eighty-eight-year-old philosopher, two literary historians in their sixties, and four younger scholars in their forties. We are talking in their homes, a great privilege in this restricted society. We are learning to overcome the officially imposed line dividing foreigners from the Chinese people.

My experiences here at once confirm and run counter to the "head count" so fashionable among foreigners in Peking. There is constant competition about how many Chinese friends one has. The game is being played around the challenge, "How many doors have you overcome?" Bursting into Chinese homes has become a pastime for "brave" foreigners: an American journalist shows up at the door of a dissident editor, a French-Canadian student slips through the police network to spend a week with her roommate's family in Lanzhou, Gansu.

I am not in such a rush to get into Chinese homes. I have my reasons, excuses perhaps, for being less brave. My single room here in the dorm has provided plenty of opportunity for intimate, frank conversation. Also, political winds still rage across the acceptable kinds of contact between foreigners and Chinese. I am keenly aware of the consequences of our contacts for my Chinese friends.

Recently, a rather obvious realization. How many good friends does one have anywhere? I have about four or five in China. That seems precious enough.

Doors have, however, opened beyond the circle of my friends here. I have been to six homes in Peking in nine months. "Have you ever been in a new apartment building?" asked one of my foreign friends yesterday. "No." Thinking it over, I am struck by how similar were the homes I did visit. All are one-story houses in which privacy, plants, and books provide the dominant motif. These are the surroundings of newly rehabilitated, newly rewarded older intellectuals. Their specializations differ: from Buddhism to Bertrand Russell. Underneath this variety, a certain uniformity of tastes. These intellectuals spend their days writing or editing books. Many have children in college. There, however, the similarities end.

My friends' house nearest to my room is at the end of a footpath which runs along the sewage ditch. It has four tiny rooms and a yard full of rose bushes. Two middle-aged academics do their cooking, washing, and cleaning here. Their children are in college. The parents manage to write several articles a year at their back-to-back desks set alongside their bed.

Across town to the east, down a *hutong* (a Peking expression for alley, based on the Manchurian word for water-well), is the home of another middle-aged couple, nearly the same age as the first. They also have children at a university. These intellectuals have a small compound to themselves, a cook, and well-paid, secure positions at a government scientific institute. Whenever I enter their courtyard, in which flowerpots surround a gnarled little tree, whenever I am welcomed inside the spacious drawing room with its colored tiles, lace curtains, and an old piano, I feel I have entered the most Western world I know here in Peking. The conversation is inevitably light, general, and the food is always sumptuous. Last night's delicacies included Empress Dowager dumplings, and Green Mountain silk noodles. The good life prevails here unashamed.

Such calm is not the norm in the spacious compound of another older, more eminent intellectual family. Both husband and wife are survivors of the Cultural Revolution, researchers in the Academy of Social Sciences. He is in his mid-sixties, she in her late fifties. Both are urbane. Both had traveled and worked outside

China before 1949. The gate to their family compound is traditional black wood, engraved with a classical couplet in ancient golden characters. The cracked yellow script barely shows through the recently rubbed-off red slogans. Inside, a highly ordered tastefulness. Modest attention to old things is a passion for these traditional-minded *wenren* (literati).

Their drawing room is spacious. Dotted, but not crowded, with antiques. Its centerpiece: an original painting by Hu Jieqing (wife of Lao She, a famous modern writer who committed suicide during the Cultural Revolution). The subject of the painting is the family's cat, who still slinks around the couch in her aged, puffy whiteness. Hu Jieqing was, and remains, a family friend. She was tested by the same storms as my hosts.

All three were beaten during the Cultural Revolution, most of their books burned. What is left over today was salvaged by the clever ruse of younger colleagues. They organized themselves in a somewhat spurious Red Guard faction and posted the following notice on the front gate: "This house duly purged of the "four olds" (old ideas, old culture, old customs and old habits). Anyone else wanting to burn additional poisonous stuff must first contact Red Guard Unit No. . . ." Thus some of my hosts' things survived, furtively.

A more elaborate entrance but a more humble interior greets the visitor at the home of Zhang Shenfu, the eighty-eight-year-old philosopher, who is slowly becoming a friend. An old friend and mentor of Zhou Enlai, he was spared some of the worst excesses of the Cultural Revolution. Zhang Shenfu and his wife live at the end of a large courtyard occupied by four different families. Two carved stone lions stand guard at the gate, which faces an interior multicolored ceramic wall. Around these symbols of gentry living are the cluttered, shared spaces of three families thrown together by the Cultural Revolution. They share laundry, garbage, and bathroom facilities in the crowded front courtyard. In the back, in the innermost courtyard, are the capacious rooms of my host. It is winter now, so we talk in the middle room, in which there is a coal-burning stove. We always sit at the table near the window, my tape recorder plugged into the wall.

In the afternoon sun, I never seem to tire of looking at the impish glint in the corner of the old logician's eye. Zhang Shenfu is a lucid philosopher, clearest when he is talking about materialism and dialectics or about ideal norms of human behavior. His voice flutters and his eyes blink when I ask about the details of his turbulent political history. We always have mounds of delicious chocolate and fruit between us when we talk (I know that it costs the family a great deal to entertain me in such generous fashion).

Our talks make history come alive for me. We are just beginning. I am already overwhelmed by facts, events, and meanings I thought I knew. I feel my ignorance exposed every time I come to visit him.

Tenuously, slowly, I am becoming a historian for the first time. Even though much of what I thought has turned out to be unreliable, the themes of the past decade are helpful in shaping concerns I am pursuing here—concerns about the idealism and integrity of the Chinese intellectuals. Their integrity, I sense, is rooted in and limited by a grand ambition to undo feudal traditions. I find that the failure of the May Fourth movement is now more interesting to me than the fact that it happened at all.

May Fourth intellectuals like Zhang Shenfu came up with few answers to the lingering problem of feudal mentality in China. Yet, they have strewn, really mined, subsequent history with unsettling doubts about arbitrary authority. Each new generation of Chinese dissenters, of rebels, finds in May Fourth a model, an injunction against keeping quiet. This is, I believe, the source of the conscious echo between the April Fifth movement of 1976 and May Fourth movement of 1919.

More recently, another outburst of pained, self-aware modernity in an art exhibit at the Northern Sea (Bei Hai). Banned a few months ago as "too critical" of the present regime, "too bleak," and "too gloomy," the show has been allowed to be put up again. All of Peking is buzzing with the news. I get there around 4:15, just before closing time, and linger on as the crowd thins. I have a long talk with three of the artists. Among the many nude photographs, abstract blotches of black paint, and contorted pieces of wood, I am attracted by a small woodblock print of Lu Xun. Next to Mao and Zhou Enlai, Lu Xun is China's most official hero, the "brave, untiring proletarian intellectual." By now, many Chinese know that this is an exaggeration but find it hard to counter it. This print does that and more. It shows the underside of the "hero." Not only his mere-humanness, but his arrogance.

In the print: a vindictive figure with smug circles of cigarette smoke curling up past a sharp, houndish nose. A close echo here of official portraits of Lu Xun. But the artist has managed to capture a contradiction. The fierce, publicly celebrated revolutionary thinker is also prideful, bitter.

So many overblown, all-too-public myths are strenuously being exposed in China these days. It is not that the government line is entirely a lie. It is just that often it is used as a cumbersome cover for a more complex reality.

The artists I speak with confirm my sense that they try to see through the government line more than they aim to overthrow it. I talk about abstract art with a young painter on crutches, Ma Desheng, twenty-six. He points out that abstraction is not that foreign after all, how the earliest forms of Chinese painting were highly formalistic, how nonrepresentational forms can cut through an overabundance of particulars: "a realistic painting of a fat, complacent official hardly conveys the evils of bureaucratism. You need a symbol for that." His friend, Wang Kenian, thirty, a sculptor, speaks about the functions and limitations of "naive art." He dwells on his own lack of training, on his sudden, part-time discovery of his calling as an artist.

Wang describes how he extricated himself only recently from the fervent ideals of the Cultural Revolution. He tells me how, when he finished tinkering with a piece of scrap wood, he discovered its similarity with certain forms of African art. This forced him to think more deeply about the tribal function of art. He insists that an artist must "give voice to the common denominator of group experience."

He goes on to talk about his long-range goal: to use his talents to depict the feverish delusions of his generation. His major work in this exhibit: a statue of an anguished youth crucified between the red flag he waves in one hand and the red book in the other. Chinese viewers marvel at the gutsiness of these youths, at their willingness to delve into and to show the seamier side of their shared experiences. The artists themselves bask in the aura of this romantic image.

The exhibit strikes me as something less than great. The art lacks technical skill, even imagination. Borrowed techniques have not been mastered. They are merely flaunted around grandiose themes. The most recurrent title in the show is "Thought."

Various representations of reflection, rumination, gazing here. Part of an effort to probe the inner conflict engendered by living through and after the Cultural Revolution.

I talk to Qu Leilei (whose name means literally "crooked heap of stones"—too staunch a pen name for this questioning, uncertain young man). His series of four ink drawings called "Thought" is emblematic of the show. He gives me a set of photographic reproductions and explains the collage:

> First I used a large naked figure with his head bent towering over a globe nestled in his armpit. This shows the beginning of reflection, the questioner engaged in a problem with determined concentration.
>
> Next, through a bent figure under a scorching sun and with his breast marred by violently alternating EEG waves, I try to show how thought has become consuming, difficult.
>
> In the third image, through a contorted face, cowering underneath a frenzied mixture of thighs, fists, and nails, I try to show the unbearable turmoil of psychological conflict. The thinker is torn to shreds by his own insides.
>
> In the fourth print, I show a prone figure crushed by a huge blow. I bet you didn't notice the left hand. Most viewers see only the crushing, unresolved contradiction. They miss the determined effort in those arched fingers. The effort to get up and try again.

True enough, I had missed it. The arched figure, however, was noticed and painstakingly copied by a student from Qinghua University who had spent the day observing the drawings. (The Chinese tradition of disciplined emulation is still lingering here.) I asked this student why he likes these particular drawings. What meaning do they have for him? He smiles shyly and answers in halting English, "I just love them, that is all."

DECEMBER 9   *Bleak news: end of Democracy Wall and Cambodia protest*   I wake up to the sound of a fair outside my window. Blaring loudspeakers alternate commercial announcements with bad nineteenth-century waltzes. It turns out to be an exhibit of consumer goods by a local cooperative.

The "Thought" collage: *above left,* Incipient
Reflection; *right,* Hardships of Reasoning;
below left, Inner Conflict; *right,* Almost Crushed,
but Determined to Think Again.
Photographs courtesy of the artist.

The street is lined with furniture, pillow cases, bird cages, bottles of wine, plastic bags. Crowds of would-be buyers jostle each other for a look at things which are few and too expensive for most ordinary people: a beige corduroy-covered lounge chair, only 300 yuan. Nonetheless, the fact that these things are being shown hints at the promise of eventual ownership.

I doubt that this promise can be realized. A long talk with a Chinese friend a few days ago: "A very bad, rough year coming up for China. Factories are closing down all over the country. Products cannot be sold on the native market. They, also, fall below export standards. From Peking to Guizhou, locomotives, light industry machines are piling up. Shorter and shorter working hours for workers already strapped by huge rises in food prices."

The great unmentionable these days: the economic underperformance of the current leadership. Unable, or unwilling, to mobilize the population in the name of the political ideals of the Mao era, they stand by the notion of immediate profit. This makes them all the more vulnerable. They will have to do more and more to suppress those who point out that the emperor has no clothes. I hear that last night (Saturday, December 8) Democracy Wall was washed clean, totally stripped of all its posters. It is again a divider between the street and the buses parked behind. There is scarcity and repression in the air.

Last week mostly taken up with mobilizing foreign students in Peking around a petition on Cambodia. Tried to raise some money for the relief of the starving people there. By Thursday, we had collected 338 signatures from students from 47 countries and had raised $1,800 for the Swiss Red Cross. We presented the petition to the embassies of Vietnam, Thailand, the U.S.A., the U.S.S.R., to the Chinese Foreign Ministry, and to the United Nations. I chaired many of the organizational meetings and worked closely with Shanti, a woman from Sri Lanka, who has become a close friend.

We were photographed at the gate of the Thai Embassy, and welcomed by their political officer. We had a good, short reception from Ambassador Leonard Woodcock at the American Embassy. It confirmed my sense of his profound decency. A painful, brief altercation at the gate of the Vietnamese Embassy. I would never have thought ten years ago that we would be facing Vietnamese in such hostile circumstances. They were locked behind a chained gate. That gate was somehow a sign of fear, of culpability. The Vietnamese were so unlike the cool, suave Russians, who at least invited our delegation in for a long chat in their spacious consular room.

In the eyes of the Vietnamese man, who spoke perfect English and who kept telling us to go back to our studies and not to be "duped by American imperialism and Chinese propaganda," I saw the embattled exhaustion of a nation brutalized by three decades of nonstop warfare. I had to ask myself: What is pushing them on to fight? To kill? To be maimed? To be poor? Some of those with me felt the Vietnamese were just showing their "traditional cruelty." The traits of the "the Prussians of Southeast Asia," in the words of a Swiss student. I don't buy these generalizations about national character. But I have no other answers just yet.

I collapse with exhaustion on Thursday night. Late in the evening a phone conversation with a foreign friend who has lived in China for a long time: "Can I give you some advice? Don't throw yourself so much into this Kampuchea thing. Remember your body is a precious treasure, temporarily entrusted to you. Take my advice, get some sleep and don't get so involved."

Somehow this is the last straw. Unwittingly, my friend echoes the Vietnamese consul who told us to get back to study. He also echoes the unspoken message from Chinese officials. We had better "stick to scholarly pursuits." Being tired, I feel scared that my friend might be right. I weep for a long time.

The next morning, I ask myself. Why did I get so involved? I narrow the reasons. I had to do something, anything, so that the indictment against those who knew about genocide in Europe but did nothing would not stand so starkly in our time. We, I, who knew about the destruction of the Khmer people, came close to doing nothing. Then, we did. The Holocaust comes to mind, not as crushing guilt, but as awful, urgent precedent.

Also, I was glad to be able to help defuse conflict in this student effort in Peking. Caught between the bickering Americans and rather hostile Third World students, I found that I had to act as an American on behalf of something greater. This time I sense that my actions were not a flight from American identity but a building on it.

Finally, there is something irrevocably real about Asian people and their suffering here. Kampuchea is closer, more urgent, in China than back home.

JANUARY 27 *A visitor from home* Last May, for my thirty-second birthday in China, Jason sent me a test tube vase. It has two short husky cylinders joined by a thin, short channel. It holds two stalks of droopy hyacinths, one wilted rose, and a once proudly pink chrysanthemum. The thirst of any one flower affects the water supply of all. The connecting channel ensures that all get satisfied whenever I notice the level on the hyacinth side is becoming too low. This channel is impossible to clean. It is now a friendly gray-brown from seven months of Peking dust.

Jason just left after a twenty-day visit. We had a channel of words between us for nearly a year. It, too, had gotten dusty, cluttered. Now, we had a chance to connect more directly. We had many unrushed hours of talk as we tested the varieties of hot bean curd from Peking to Shanghai to Hangzhou. Things he had imagined me doing before, I could show him through visits with my Chinese friends. He brought my other, American, life here and thus made the prospect of my going home more real, my terror of it more speakable. I organized a special trip for us. Something like the one I hope he could do for me when I got home, a condensed view of what tourists never see: a dawn jog on the Altar of Heaven, a hard-class sleeper train ride on which we talk at length with a soldier in her sixth month of pregnancy, a drop-in visit to a primary school in an alley outside the dragon-walled mansion of a Ming official in Shanghai, a fancy opera about literati courtship in Hangzhou, a faded film about urban life before 1949 in Peking. In the end, I am surprised by how much more I received than I gave.

He brought a chance to see my China experience with fresh eyes. A cell biologist by training, he asked to visit scientific research facilities. These are institutions that I would have never been able to enter or see through expert eyes had I not accompanied him, translated for him. In Shanghai, we are taken through the Biochemical Institute, the Cell Biology Institute, Fudan University's Biology Department. In Peking, the Zoology Institute

With Jason at the Imperial Palace in the Forbidden City, Peking. We pose like Chinese visitors.

and the Peking University Biology Department. In all these places, we are given the usual not so brief "introduction." I'm used to all this since my own rushed tour in 1977.

But this time, we are traveling alone and have more opportunity to interact informally with our hosts. We ask questions together and have some leisure to reflect on the renaissance of Chinese science in the wake of the ravages of the Cultural Revolution. We take notes and debate the code meaning of *zuoyong*. It means "function" in biological research but is also used to justify slightly dangerous ideas in political discourse. We observe the remaining obstacles to scientific thought, ideological as well as technological. In most places, Jason is asked to give a talk about his own work on cell communication. I relish this opportunity to observe interactions among scientists. An expected opening, too, into Jason's own thinking, which back home I had assumed was perennially opaque to me. Here, in Chinese, I hear him less fearfully.

West Lake, Hangzhou on the first day of the new year, 1980. Photograph courtesy of Jason Wolfe.

We spent New Year's Eve in Hangzhou by the beautiful West Lake I had visited briefly in 1977 and have avoided since. Too laden with dead-ended romantic memories. Now that I live in China, I have gone beyond the optimism of that marathon of six cities in sixteen days. Then, I was looking so hard I had nearly forgotten how to think. This time, I walk back over that same ancient marble bridge more leisurely. A longer talk with a brigade leader of a tea commune near the one my group breezed through two summers ago. Now, I finally have time to pay attention to details.

In Hangzhou, I try to make some connections between the past I have outgrown and the present I am trying to create. It is not easy. For the first two days I try but cannot remember the name of a friend who had been my roommate during our 1977 group trip. I do recall that for her fortieth birthday I wrote a poem in Hangzhou. The day before Jason and I are due to leave, jogging alone with my furies in the rain, I remember her name. A few hours before beginning 1980, I write another poem.

Two and a Half Years after Lynn Traeger's
Fortieth Birthday in Hangzhou

West Lake is wetter now
shadowed by leafless willows.
They weep less now than when
we drank uncatholic doubts
into the dawn of your fifth decade.

More sober now than when
I wrote for you
of birds over a pink expanse.
More naked now than when
we shyly slipped
into forbidden waters.
Less poetry shields now
my germinal wishes.

The decade Orwell threatened
beckons in China.
A chance to birth ourselves
learning from peasants
who bend over the ancient bush
of dragon tea and reap the green
tips of their patient
everydayness.

December 31, 1979

Jason met my Chinese friends and thus I got to enjoy them anew. He asks them about the 1950s generation of Chinese scientists who came back to China, who gave up good jobs in the West and prestigious research opportunities, just to help the motherland. Those scientists could not have imagined that within two or three years of their return, in 1957, many would be damned as "rightists." That in less than a decade, during the Cultural Revolution, the rest would be punished as "the stinking ninth," bourgeois intellectuals deemed worse than traitors, capitalists, landlords, etc. And yet, with all that recent past not quite forgotten, another generation of Western-trained Chinese scientists is getting ready for the same kind of patriotic choice. What is it about China's misery and backwardness that binds the learned elite to its fate so much more closely than Russian intellectuals are bound to the U.S.S.R. or Indian intellectuals to India?

I have a certain friend whom Jason did not get to meet with all our rushing around Peking and Shanghai. He might have learned a lot from her about the problems facing younger, less eminent intellectuals. She is about to graduate from Beida, a member of the school's, and the nation's, last class of worker-peasant-soldier students. After Jason leaves, she comes to visit me. We plan some graduation fun. She puts on a cheerful face over her bleak mood: "My classmates and I have turned down the school's offer for a Saturday night music show for us. It would be hard to bear, given that they are telling us to scram, they are shoving us out." I don't get the verb she uses, *gundan* (literally, to roll an egg so fast that the rush allows no consideration of the fact that the egg might break). "We will, however, visit the new airport. Perhaps they'll let us see the nude wall paintings that have caused all the recent fuss."

The airport visit turns out to be the only group activity of this graduating class. Two days later there is an official meeting to tell the new graduates why it is right and noble to comply with the national job-allocation plan. On January 22, Tuesday, the school authorities announce the job placements. By the twenty-fifth, all worker-peasant-soldier students have to be out of the dorms and on their way to the assignments.

This is truly a swift "rolling out." No time for complaints. Although I doubt that this group would be contentious anyway. They feel such a cloud of damnation over their heads. No "good" unit wants them. They are assumed to be poorly trained "political hacks." I know from my friend that this group feels its own limitations keenly enough. They would have liked nothing better than a chance to get more training in the newly refurbished academic system . . . But there seems to be no room or time these days for this last of a generation which reminds the country of Mao's vision during the Cultural Revolution.

Yesterday, my friend left the university. All of her belongings were wrapped up in a quilt and one box. I give her a dragon-faced scarf and write out a classical Chinese poem about the courage it takes to enter Sichuan, an interesting, dangerous realm in the time of Li Bo. She gives me a collection of Cultural-Revolution-

With a recent graduate of Beida, winter, 1980. All her college belongings wrapped in front of us on the day of her "rolling out."

vintage oil paintings about Lu Xun. I take pictures of her old room, meet her younger brother, a factory worker with a lovely smile and shy, competent pronunciation of basic English. I want to take a picture of both of them. She refuses: "Brothers and sisters cannot take pictures together, you know. It might be misunderstood as a boyfriend-girlfriend relationship."

I snap back: "How much more feudal can you get? China will never be able to modernize with folks like you."

"Yes, that's right," chimes in her girlfriend who is off to an assignment in the hinterland of Southeast China. "What kind of materialist are you anyhow? Relationships are what you make them."

A strong bond of faith and hilarity between these two young women going off, relatively gladly, to where the party authorities tell them to go. They seem ready to do what must be done, no matter if they feel better suited for other tasks. My friend is lucky. Although she is going back to her old factory, she will be able to use her education in editing a newspaper for her co-workers.

I admire the trust and optimism that these remnants of the Cultural Revolution era still muster. Today, when it is fashionable, even sanctioned, to be selfish and cynical, they remain visionary, obedient.

My admiration, however, is wearing thin these days. I find myself fidgeting through the play we attended just before my graduating friend left. It is about vagrant youth "poisoned by the Gang of Four." I enjoy the hoodlum girl, who stands on a table hurling things at her loyal cadre father. But a wave of incredulity comes over me when she and her fellow gang members are shown "converting" to the good, inspired by a kind, blind old lady. This old lady is a prototype from the revolutionary soap operas . . . A few years ago I might have been moved by her story of pre-Liberation horror and post-'49 happiness. Less so now. I sense the disbelief all around me as well.

Not that the blind lady is lying. Just that the truths she speaks are overshadowed by so much that remains unsaid. There are so many unmentionable problems these days in China. These problems are corroding the praise lavished on the system by itself.

I am reminded of a poem written by a Shanghai friend at the outbreak of the Cultural Revolution in 1966. It speaks for and about a common woman, more credible, more compelling to me now than the virtuous heroine of the play.

> Not even a bell tolls.
> Whispers spread like broadcast
> That she has vanished in the night
> From all human sight.
> What her deeds, her faults,
> Her looks, her manner, her might,
> This I am led to feel—
> That the human flame is no more gold
> Than a buttercup
> That it blow out sooner than a candle
> At the slightest puff

These words made me sad when I first read them. They leave me angry now. I can't stop asking myself: Why didn't more people speak out against the Cultural Revolution? Why did so many vanish? Why were they beaten to death, while others watched or even helped in the beating?

I am reading about the feudal mentality these days, about slavish habits of loyalty, about the selfish maneuvering which centuries of autocracy bred into the Chinese character—habits despised and dissected by Lu Xun. I am beginning to grasp some of the details of a past that used to overwhelm me before.

I am running out of excuses for China in my mind. Maybe this is because I care for this country more the longer I stay. I sense myself ready to push through to some kind of understanding I could not have achieved or accepted before. Before this year, China mattered too much to me. I wanted it to answer to Western problems that I knew so well.

Now, with Jason here and gone, I know better where I come from and where I want to go back to. China matters to me now because I find it inspires, rewards, and punishes some of my finest friends here. To understand their attachments and commitments is a challenge I have assigned for myself for the rest of my time here. That challenge, increasingly fulfilled through historical research. Journal writing seems less germane than when I arrived here, almost a year ago.

JANUARY 29   *The problem of intellectuals: Ding Shouhe and Lin Ying*   Finally, the fruition of Li Shu's promise some months ago. With his sanction as the director of the Modern History Institute of the Academy of Social Sciences, I am able to meet with two scholars working on modern intellectual history, Ding Shouhe and Lin Ying. The third man, Li Zehou, was sick and unable to attend. I don't mind, since this means I'll be able to visit him at his home later in the spring.

Warmth and politeness mark our morning in the guest reception hall at the Academy compound. I sense a practiced, long-standing respect between Ding and Lin. It turns out they are neighbors in the same flat. Living upstairs from one another, they have long conversations, at times more furtively than others, about their own work and about their own impassioned concern with the fate of intellectuals. They are eager to talk with me about the broadest implications of their work. Perhaps they're using this encounter to talk with each other in new ways about the incomplete attack on feudal mentality begun in May Fourth.

Lin is calmly reflective. He is currently making his way into a new field, comparative religion. He asks me at length about Western views on Daoism. Ding, a more excitable man, seems to be in the midst of shifting from a more complacent, party-line historiography to his own critical interpretation. He tells me over and over again about the sanction of "true historical research" that is to be found in the regime's new slogan "search truth from facts."

We talk about what Chinese scholars mean today by "feudal mentality," a concept that has puzzled me for some time now. Ding and Lin agree that it embraces a longing for an authoritarian, patriarchical leader, a "family despot" presumed to be virtuous because he is powerful. "Then everyone can stop thinking, can abandon the responsibility for making choices for oneself." They agree that feudal mentality also includes a penchant for egalitarianism, "a lingering hold of the small-producers' mentality Marx criticized so rightly. May Fourth intellectuals, expecially Lu Xun, understood this well. They too were bitterly antagonistic to this mentality until they became deflected by the pressures of national salvation."

There is something very new, very complex for me in this discussion. How has China's feudal system endured for so long? Why has the twentieth-century rush toward modernity been nipped in the bud so quickly? My hosts explain that in the haste to build a strong, independent China—or rather, due to the constant worry that the nation might be wiped out by various external enemies—all new, modern ideas became instruments toward a nationalistic end. "Individualism of the 1910 period, the Marxism of the 1920s all became *shouduan* (mere means), toward *jiuguo* (national salvation). Thus, the scathing attack on *guo minxing* (national character, really feudal mentality) begun by Lu Xun was postponed. Lu Xun could and did dissect the ignorance, sullenness, passivity of the Chinese masses. The pressure of the Anti-Japanese War, however, transformed his call for saving humanity, *jiuren*, into national salvation, *jiuguo*."

Much here to think through. I will have to reconsider my all-too-ready admiration of May Fourth, my confidence in its long-range success.

FEBRUARY 8 *A conversation with a patriotic party historian, Li Xin* In the sitting room of my own dormitory, a meeting arranged by school authorities with Li Xin, senior researcher at the Modern History Institute of the Academy of Social Sciences. He is in charge of the party-sponsored Republican Period Biographical Project—and will supervise the evaluation of key personages, intellectual and political, in the period from 1911 to 1949. Li Xin has just returned from a visit to the United States, where he was sent to increase Western scholars' appreciation for Communist historiography.

Li Xin is effective at his task. He clearly merits the faith placed in him for such a delicate project. He knows the history of the republican era well and can distill its acceptable lessons readily. He is not particularly impressed with the role of intellectuals in history. "Sure, the May Fourth scholars [*xuezhe*, a term he uses with a slightly negative intonation] were unwilling to become bureaucrats, were not interested in getting rich. Some were even above lowly pursuits like sexual indulgence. . . . But they tended to give themselves such airs, you know. Take Hu Shi [one of the leading liberal lights of the May Fourth enlightenment], for example. When he became head of the Academia Sinica, he installed the phone number 5400 in commemoration of the event of 1919. To this day, we're stuck with it."

His version of the history of the 1920s and 1930s is rambling, anecdotal, judgmental. He gets most excited in telling me about a student demonstration against the KMT in 1946. "Those students were so much smarter, more experienced, than we were during the national salvation movement of 1935–36. They dared to beat up their opponents, they unmasked the naive, silly professors by throwing eggs and stones at them." The high point of the story comes when the "reactionary students" pull down the portraits of Sun Yat-sen and other democratic leaders. "This proved to one and all that the Communist Party and only the Communist Party represented the interests of true democracy in China." Is this historical proof, I ask myself?

Li Xin tells me of "new historical evidence" about another controversial May Fourth intellectual, Qu Qiubai, once head of the Chinese Communist Party, then condemned retrospectively as a renegade. Now that Qu is in the process of being rehabilitated posthumously, the historians are finding "new evidence" to prove that he was not so bad after all. Each new change in party line requires new historical evidence. I am getting to understand why survivors of that period like Zhang Shenfu, the old philosopher I am still interviewing, pose a problem for those who would generate only acceptable historical truths.

Yet, there is something in Li Xin's approach to history which I trust and value. Perhaps something as simple as his familiarity with details that I have no way of knowing, or finding on my own. Over lunch, he shares a tale of another younger enlightenment intellectual, He Ganzhi, who became a noted Communist historian. On the eve of Liberation, He wanted to get a divorce to marry his young love. He's "old lady" went to a committee made up of older May Fourth intellectuals like Cheng Fangu and Wu Yuzhang to ask them to be less "feudal," to go ahead and grant He's divorce so that he could go on openly with what he had been carrying on secretly. The older men, once ardent prophets of free love and intellectual emancipation, were hard to convince.

The story hints at the tradition-bound mentality of intellectuals I had assumed to be architects of China's enlightenment movement. The picture is getting more and more complex. Li Xin, unwittingly perhaps, aids in my confusion.

FEBRUARY 20   *Year of the Monkey*   According to the lunar calendar, on February 15 the Year of the Ram runs out and the new year, The Year of the Monkey, is ushered in. This ritual, which used to be called *Guonian* (passing the year), has been renamed in the People's Republic *Chunjie*, the Spring Festival. It is one of the three official holidays, along with May 1, the Workers' Festival, and October 1, the National Day Festival. It is a time to get off from work. For this holiday most workers get four days off, students get two weeks off, and unmarried youth in the labor force who are away from home or in the army get ten to twelve days to travel home. More and better produce is put on the market. In the store windows I see meat, oranges, household appliances, all unavailable before. Red flags are hung on official buildings and big red lanterns adorn official entrances. The most riotous of the folk festivals has been tamed, transformed. It is now a nationally sanctioned time for family gatherings.

I decide to stay in Peking for the holiday. Most foreign students are out traveling. My decision is shaped by the many invitations I received to join in *Guonian* celebrations. A teacher from school said to me months ago, "You must really come see how a clan like ours ushers in the New Year." Other friends and colleagues offer invitations daily. In all, eight families have invited me to come by, share a meal, join in the week-long celebrations that mark the coming of the Year of the Monkey.

I have been living in China for a year. A year ripe now with opportunities to share more deeply in the lives of my friends here. During the summer I had explored some Chinese places on my own. Now I am given a precious chance to step inside Chinese time.

As the holiday nears, I recall bits of *Guonian* in Taiwan in the spring of 1974. Four days and three sleepless nights, filled with the constant din of firecrackers—an energetic, deafening "cleaning off" of old ghosts from courtyards in our neighborhood, and especially from motorcycles and cars. The most common sight I recall is private vehicles ringed with firecrackers which were shot off for days unending. It was a way to avert future disasters by present trauma. I remember being exhausted by *Guonian* in Taiwan, by the unending noise, by the constant crowding. Everyone seemed to be out in the streets, circulating, undulating, pushing. I remember I could not stand to be outside for more than an hour or so. I did manage to get out to my teacher's house on the outskirts of Taibei, where we had dumplings and walked among the soothing hills.

With these memories in mind, I rather dreaded the coming of *Guonian* in China. I still find my threshold for *renao* (the Chinese definition for joviality, "creating heat" by milling around with lots of people in close quarters) rather low.

Chunjie in Peking turns out to be much quieter than *Guonian* in Taibei. Most residents here can't have private vehicles. There are few motorcycles and no cars yet to be exorcised. The regime's propaganda on behalf of disciplined atheism hardly explains the lack of din in public places, the absence of guardian demons on house gates, or the restrained greetings among mutual wellwishers. Back in the countryside, much of the old hilarity prevails, I gather. This year, even in the cities, the party has officially rehabilitated the traditional greeting: "Good luck and may you get rich." The reason: according to orthodox, "correct materialism," there is nothing wrong with wealth if it is not gotten through exploitation.

Peking is relatively calm, in spite of the intense crowding in buses and the stores. Lots of people from out of town are pouring in, vacationers are milling in the stores. This calm flows from relief, a delight in ordinary life. After years of "movements" which have wrenched people out of the family into society, there seems to be a general, gleeful settling back into normalcy. The New Year provides an occasion, an excuse for the return to the common and, until not long ago, scorned symbol of continuity in China: the family feast. This is a time for various generations to share a meal under one roof.

It takes me a while to grasp the obvious. At first I am taken aback by the widespread insistence among my friends here that they are going to do "nothing special" for the New Year. They tell me "Sure, there are some old customs about not using a knife, not sweeping the courtyard, during the first day of the festival. But we don't believe in these superstitions about gods of fortune swept away by mistake, or benevolent spirits who demand abstinence from labor." I hear myself arguing with them about the spiritual need to make some days different from others . . . When I stop arguing, I finally understand a little bit about how different it really is for most Chinese people to be able to bring their families together for a good, plentiful meal.

There is nothing outwardly extraordinary about the gathering of three generations at my teacher's house on Saturday night: a seventy-seven-year-old father with his second wife (the first one died during the Cultural Revolution), a younger brother with his wife and teenage daughter, a younger sister with husband and two little boys. My teacher's son is back home from school in Shanghai. This makes her family complete. It is hardly ordinary, however, or habitual for this extended clan to gather together.

Each family has brought a nicer dish than the next. No part of the clan could afford, in terms of time or money, to make such a feast alone.

Due to their joint efforts, we share a ten-course banquet, mostly meat. Meat is the greatest luxury in a country which still is so poor and where many foods are rationed. (I hear that pork from Sichuan is so plentiful just now that it is rotting. Officially prices remain high around the nation. Fish is rare, and chicken and duck can only be found at the free market.) We have a huge chicken which cost 10 yuan, and a duck which is so fancy that I hesitate to ask the price. The favorite dish is an old family recipe, a mixture of beans, fruits, and noodles, called "combination eight." Its round number suggests plenty, so that the New Year may be round in sundry ways.

Later, we stage a show in the courtyard. Each family outdoes the other in bringing firecrackers, shooting them high up in the air—devilish green whirling ones, short ones, overflowing with flowery sparks, and plain old boomers. For half an hour or so, everyone enjoys "blowing away the ghosts." Then, we regroup inside for a game of chance, another traditional *Guonian* pastime. Through this game, our luck is supposed to be divined for the next year. We throw six dice in descending order of ages from seventy-seven to seven. I am the ninth, after all the couples, before the five kids, and just ahead of my teacher's daughter who is twenty-six.

There are prizes according to "scholar-official's rank," a traditional sign of fortune. These range from candy to plates to cups, and the grand prize is a tin of butter cookies accompanied by the picture of the god of wealth. To my embarrassment and delight, I win the cookies. I donate the tin to the host family and gleefully take home the god of wealth.

Good fortune has already abounded this year. During the evening at my friend's house, I realize just how much. I feel grateful for this chance to share with her family the new, precious normalcy of the *Guonian*. This family, so ravaged by the 1957 Anti-Rightist campaign and the Cultural Revolution, now gathers for fun and relaxation. Their affectionate ways with each other can finally be shared openly. They have been giving each other covert support during the rough years when one or the other member of the family was in disgrace. I am also grateful to be able to share this evening in their home. Unwatched, unreported, I feel relatively unworried about consequences. A brittle kind of normalcy.

My friend's father was once a professor of English literature. Now, long cut off from the subject of his interest, he tells me about his time at Peking University in the 1920s, about how he walked for miles behind Sun Yat-sen's coffin in 1924 and again, in 1976, with his ardently patriotic daughter, for miles after Zhou Enlai's death. His stories center on intellectuals caught up in the most tumultuous half century of the Chinese revolution. The father's conclusion surprises me: "I am becoming a Marxist in my old age only to find that few people in China understand anything about what Marx wrote and what he meant."

My friend's younger sister hopes to go abroad for advanced study. She is a slight, shy, alert woman. Her older sister explains: "We had so little food to give her during the Anti-Japanese War that she couldn't grow very much. I carried her on my back in 1937 when we hid from the bombs." I had heard a similar story about the daughter, who was in her early teens during the Cultural Revolution when she was sent away to labor in Mongolia with little nourishment. This experience seems to have delayed her adolescence, stunted her growth, and may account for her still-irregular menstruation. I am taken aback by the natural harmony in this family so ravaged by history. All its members have been touched, in different ways, by the iconoclastic ideals of communism.

The traditions of *Guonian* seem to be slipping in through the "back door" of a normalized *Chunjie*. This year, I sense this through renewed expressions of respect for the aged. Given that a decade ago anything old was loathsome, especially during the height of the Cultural Revolution campaign against the Four Olds (old ideas, old customs, old habits, and old culture—anything old except Chairman Mao, of course), the change is quite remarkable. I join in the ritual of *bainian*, "paying respects," which takes place during this time of the New Year. This custom used to require the young to prostrate themselves on the ground in front of the old, to kowtow (*ketuo*), to knock one's head to the ground. Now, what remains of this custom are dutiful visits by younger people to the homes of the older people, relatives, teachers, etc.

I, too, go to *bainian* two teachers. Wang Yao, my adviser at Beida, has a full head of white hair and sparse teeth, browned by a pipe he smokes and battered by Cultural Revolution beatings. I find him ushering in a plentiful, active year. He is watching the color TV bought with royalties for his "rehabilitated" books on literary criticism. We chat about a recent commemorative essay he wrote on the leftist writers in the 1930s.

My older teacher is Zhang Shenfu, the philosopher. His family asks me to share a festive lunch. The two of us eat ten excellent dishes prepared by his twenty-two-year-old daughter and watched over by his garrulous, gracious wife. Throughout lunch, I try to serve him delicious morsels, relishing this time to chat informally after our weeks of interview work. I sense that this meal is a rare gift, an opportunity to be with him late in life as if we have known each other for a long time.

In fact we haven't. I am trying to catch up as fast as I can. This visit we try to keep free of the scholarly concerns which consume our other conversations. Still, he drifts into recollections of his European years. I take out my notebook and jot down: his salary . . . was 100 francs per month in Paris in 1921. He lost this stipend from the Chinese government due to political disputes among Chinese educational authorities in Paris. He moved on to a cheaper life in Berlin, lived in a working-class neighborhood, and translated Einstein's book on relativity for a living. It is in these two years, 1921–23, that he helped organize a small cell of the Chinese Communist Party in Europe and recruited into it the future leaders of the revolution Zhou Enlai and Zhu De, as well as his own lover (later his wife), Liu Qingyang.

This time, in the mood of trust and celebration of *Chunjie*, Zhang shares more details than usual about a train ride to Berlin in late 1921 with Zhou Enlai and Liu Qingyang, about Zhou's enduring concern for Zhang's material well-being. As the Communist Party's representative in Chongqing in the early 1940s, Zhou Enlai found him a job and a stipend, just when Jiang Jieshi (Chiang Kai-shek) had had his fill of Zhang's criticisms. Later, during the Cultural Revolution, Zhou again saved Zhang's life, by telling angry Red Guards that the old man was his own mentor, that without his guidance he would have never found his way into the Communist Party.

Interlaced in his praise for Zhou Enlai, vignettes about Mao Zedong's petty, enduring ire against Zhang Shenfu. "It all goes back to the May Fourth period, when I was supervising Mao's work in the Beida library. I found him making errors one day. I pointed them out to him and he became furious. That fury was unrelenting, never cooled."

Later during the *Chunjie* week, a dinner at the apartment of another Beida colleague. I meet his wife and get a glimpse of what kept him going during the Cultural Revolution disgrace. She is a beautiful, strong, articulate woman who tells me how she persuaded her husband not to commit suicide during the summer months of 1966 when he used to spend his days sweeping the sidewalks of the university with a blackboard hung around his neck, inscribed: "This is a filthy, counterrevolutionary element." She tells me what he can't or won't. That he was made to stand on a stool about twenty times per day and give little speeches about his crimes. There would always be a crowd, which was gathered from amidst the thousands milling around at the university: "You can't imagine the anxiety, the emotional pressure, of those years."

No, I cannot, but I am learning to appreciate the delicate normalcy which is coming over families like this. But the abnormal is not far behind in China, the past does not seem to be as definitely gone as one might suppose from the outside.

At another house, over lunch, a mischievous baby niece pulls off a curtain covering a bookshelf. Dozens of little red books of Chairman Mao's sayings spill out. The baby howls when the books are hastily put away into a drawer. This is a worker's family, the father is a low-level cadre who was not victimized by the Cultural Revolution (so unlike the "stinking ninth intellectuals" whom I had been visiting during the rest of the week). The host shows me a photo of his grandparents, peasants from Shanxi who came to Peking in 1968 on their one and only trip outside of their native village. They strike a formal pose, the way all out-of-towners still do, in the Forbidden City. In the photo, two tiny, cotton-clad, aged peasants are each holding a little red book. "Everyone in those days included Mao's sayings on formal occasions. It was a good-luck talisman or something," explains my host.

The past does not loom in the background of this family as it does in the injured psyches of my intellectual friends. It rests most openly in the eyes of my host's mother, a woman of fifty, who was illiterate until 1957. She had attended only a few literacy classes before she was swept up in the Great Leap Forward of

1958. She, like so many other uneducated urban housewives, was drawn into the newly established neighborhood factories. She plans to retire this year. "My mother still lacks any sense of culture," explains her college-educated son.

Guonian ends raucously for me. After all the fine meals, I spend a day watching folk celebrations at the Temple of Heaven. Hundreds of peasants from out of town are brought in for a show of traditional skills: dragon dancing, stilt walking, pole carrying, martial arts. Thousands fill the large park. Snow sharpens the outline of the trees which form the background of this overflow of color: green silk monsters with red tongues, men dressed in red silk portraying ladies of yore, lithe village youths indulging in feats of strength. All around, the din of cymbals and drums. I'm drawn by the face of an old man blowing a tiny horn. His ashen skin stands out against his furry brows and fur cap. From the gray tangle of fur and hair pour forth the merriest sounds I've heard in a long time. The day is truly *renao*. Tiring, yet still so unlike Taiwan.

CHAPTER 8

MARCH 9   *To Hong Kong and back*

On Friday, February 22—on the eve of the first anniversary of our arrival in China—I crossed the border to Hong Kong. Not that China had become too much to take. Nor did I have any urgent reason to go abroad. I simply wanted a break. I wanted to loosen some of my Peking habits, to challenge my pattern of fashioning days around historical research and the company of intellectual friends.

I also wanted—needed, really—to see China with fresh eyes. That, I know, requires distance and disjunction. Maybe this is a partial motivation for the mad rush of the Chinese to go abroad these days. Or is this a charitable interpretation for an affliction that has touched just about everybody I know here? As I reflect on what I have learned about my own culture this year in China, I am coming to see my friends' headlong pursuit of fellowships, visas, foreign connections, as something more than just a chance to get material advantages. Tape recorders, TVs, English enhance one's prestige in China. Study abroad is still the surest sign that one has "tasted Western ink," that one has surpassed the "hick scholars" nurtured at home. "Coastal eminences," scholars trained abroad before 1949, still rule Chinese academic life. And yet the hunger for foreign study is also a sign of the younger generation's quest for perspective. Enclosed in the People's Republic for thirty years, they want and need a perspective on their own experience which is unavailable at home. They prize and envy my travels abroad.

I expected Hong Kong to be jarring and my return to China to be rough. Neither turns out to be true. Perhaps the timing lessened the disparities in space. I crossed the border into the British colony on the day on which more than thirty thousand overseas Chinese were returning from New Year vacations spent with families in Guangdong. With business reopening on Monday, sons, daughters, cousins, and grandchildren of mainlanders were returning to the place in which they can make money. This enables them to come home to China regularly, well supplied with the goods of advanced industrial society. In that huge flow of humanity, the border becomes less distinct. On both sides stretch families with connections whose resiliency outsiders can hardly fathom. The endurance of these ties between Hong Kong and Canton, their primacy, threatens collectivist priorities in China as well as the individualism required and rewarded in capitalist Hong Kong.

There are no tickets for any means of transportation across the border the night I arrive in Canton. The direct Canton-Hong Kong train, the airplanes, and the hydrofoil are all sold out for at least two days. Overseas visitors, with clan-inspired foresight, have booked all tickets. Foreigners, straggling out of South China on personal business, are out of luck.

When I go to the China Travel Service in the East Hotel to plead for some way across the border, the clerks laugh. For once, the conveniences which Westerners in China take for granted are shown to be privileges dispensed only at certain times. As foreigners, we discover that we are extraneous to a more fundamental symbiosis between a needy China and its more trusted overseas Chinese kin.

A rhythm of help and solidarity between China and overseas Chinese began early in the nineteenth century and culminated around 1900. During the first decade of the twentieth century, immigrant Chinese workers in the United States and Southeast Asia financed not only family education and business ventures back home but also the revolution of Sun Yat-sen. This trust placed by China in relatives abroad antedates and supersedes all current claims of collaboration with Westerners in the project of modernization. In the future, I think we will see China rely more and more on overseas relatives for skills and resources needed to pull her out of the current backwardness.

As a student in China, I am somewhere in between overseas

kin and foreign guest. I have more options than American tourists, businessmen, journalists, or diplomats. Students are seen as more interested in Chinese society, more able to put up with its peculiarities and its hardships. The travel office representative, naturally enough, suggests that I run over to the train station and see if I can get on the local, hard-seat train to the border at Shenzhen. Most foreigners prefer, or are asked to take, the expensive, fast, through train to Kowloon.

Later, after some dinner, I return and find the train station jammed with Hong Kong students, day laborers, and poor relatives. All those who cannot afford or had missed out on the fancier conveniences across the border are crowding in here. I get into one of the long lines for tickets to Shenzhen, even though the sign says "No tickets for the next two days." At the window, the girl looks sympathetic. I sense some surprise and respect that I would stand in line with ordinary Chinese people. Before me, a young man buys seven tickets for the 4:30 A.M. train the next day. When the cashier hears my request for one ticket, an oddity in this queue of extended families, she unearths a seat on the 6:30 train. I wonder if it was foreigner's luck. A consideration dispensed to us in tight corners? I accept this piece of luck gratefully.

The next morning, before dawn, I walk ten blocks to the train station. The buses are few and crowded. The flow of humanity this morning in Canton is smooth, focused in the direction of the train station. I walk along with teenagers carrying backpacks, with young couples carrying their babies and pulling their suitcases. At the entrance to the station, the crowd thickens tenfold. Local families are here to see off relatives going back to Hong Kong. After last-minute advice, hugs, handshakes, baby pinching, there is a huge divide. Local Cantonese line up along the ropes set up by the security police, like a sea splitting apart to let heroes pass. They wave goodbye to the file of overseas Chinese disengaging from their midst. It is suddenly quiet in the cavernous walkway to the train.

In the compartments, the pitch of voices is high again. The jostling for seats begins. Although the seats are numbered, there are far fewer seats than travelers. Places for two or three turn out to be locations around which a whole family of six or seven organizes itself. Across from me, on a bench meant for three, are five people: a woman in her forties, two boys of seven and nine, as well as a young mother with a baby. Next to me is an older woman, called auntie by the mother of the boys. Two other girls are squeezed into a single space on our bench by an enterprising man, their father (also the father of the baby and of another daughter behind me). This thin, worn, carefully but inexpensively dressed man stands or squats next to us the whole way. Close by, a young man who seems to be traveling with the family. Between my knees and the lady with the baby are three huge string nets encasing clay pots with salted vegetables and dried fish. These are, I learn later, prized gifts from relatives in China in exchange for the TVs, tape recorders, clothes, watches, and calculators which pour in as New Year gifts from Hong Kong.

As we near the border, ties and jackets worn so formally among relatives in China are loosened. These Western clothes are a sign of respect for aged clan-heads in villages back home as well as symbols of the prosperity of lives abroad. Estrangement from the clan is not allowed to deepen. Babies are brought across the border each year to be introduced to older relatives in China. There is a commitment to make each new generation aware of its connections to older ones at home. This train, full of "better-off" relatives, is strangely quiet as we near the border. To leave behind the ancestral land seems far sadder than the tales of escape to freedom would have it.

Praise for the Western social system abounds in Hong Kong. Almost everyone I talk with, a cab driver with brothers in Canton, a fat shoestore proprietor who left Shanghai as a young girl and still wakes up with terrors of a Communist takeover, a young factory apprentice who left China a year ago to join her parents in "what seemed like heaven to those of us left behind," all speak of themselves as fortunate. The cab driver says he would be shot to death if he voiced critical opinions in China. I tell him I have heard my friends in China make similar critical remarks.

"Yes, in your presence, sure," he answers. "It doesn't count because you are an outsider. In our home village, the Communist Party boss would know exactly what I had said, thought, or done, and he would let me have it." The young woman who has been working in an electronics factory for the past twelve months tells me, "I am so confused now. I have come to see through the drivel dished out to us by the Gang of Four about the outside world. I had hoped that all was good, perfect here in Hong Kong. Instead I have found a different kind of hell."

Everyone who counts their blessings across the border from China, nonetheless, refers to the place up north as *"women de Zhongguo"*—"our China." There is a sense of belonging to China which is strikingly different from the nationalism of my friends in Peking. Among those up north, the word "China" has become more burdensome. With all the government's talk of backwardness and of the need to catch up with the West, many Chinese in China view the grinding poverty of their country as a drag on dreams of swift personal advancement. A few idealistic intellectuals and some orthodox cadres in China sometimes talk about *"wo guo"*—my nation. They still try to identify the aspirations of the self with the aims of the collectivity. A tougher and tougher task.

In Hong Kong, where personal benefit is pursued without adornment, "our China" looms as a remembrance of a community that was and might yet be. Here, there is a shared faith in spite of individualistic options. I witness this sense of "our destiny" during the showing of a film which is the rage in Hong Kong. *The Rising Sun* is a commercial American production about the Second World War, based on Japanese and American propaganda footage of the 1930s and the 1940s. It draws crowds four or five times the size of those at the most popular *gongfu* movie. Such films, full of martial arts, kicking, and bloody heroes, are the skilled specialty of Hong Kong filmmakers.

The audience is sullen during the first hour, which shows the fall of Shanghai, Nanjing, and Wuhan. This part dwells on rich Chinese who scramble into foreign concessions and board foreign ships, on the poor who are beaten into submission by native warlords pretending to protect them, on Japanese troops who rape, loot, and murder. During the second half of the film, American GIs are shown saving the world. The audience goes wild with cheers. *The Rising Sun* gives the audience a taste of a collective, Chinese, victory. Hong Kong viewers don't hear the film commentator, who insists that China was losing the war with Japan until America's valiant effort on its behalf.

For one young woman, a personnel manager for Levi Strauss Co., "our China" is the remembrance of a cause during her activist days as a student leader at a Hong Kong university. "Those of us who were patriotic (that is, pro-mainland) in the late 1960s performed a vital function. We spread information about a society in which we had invested hopes for a better future. There was so much ignorance and negative propaganda about China in those days."

By now, she has broken with some comrades from the student movement days. She's especially angry about those who chastised her when she refused to go along with the campaign to criticize Deng Xiaoping in 1976. "I didn't know if he was right or wrong. But I knew my comrades had poor reasons for criticizing him. It was being done in China, so we had to follow." Now, she puts on high-heeled shoes and fancy dresses to work at Levi's, "just so I can stay late at work and read through the bosses' papers. I want to learn about capitalism first hand."

For a young man who was only twelve when the Cultural Revolution spilled over into Hong Kong, "our China" evokes a future commitment. He is now a teacher at a night school for workers, attached to a leftist, patriotic middle school called *Xiang Dao* (Guide of the Masses). He wants to go to the United States to study sociology, then maybe go back to China. He doesn't share the older teachers' song-filled remembrances of the war against Japan. Neither does he share the disillusionment of his father, once a radical in the workers' union, who now urges his son to try his luck at the neighborhood gambling game. Raised in a family of thirteen in a two-room apartment without a kitchen, this friend of mine wants more than to get out of Hong Kong. He wants to be counted in. He has a stake in China's future.

"Our China" seems to be a raw yet familiar expression in the mouth of Li Yi, editor of *The Seventies*, a leftist journal that is coming of age after a decade of increasingly critical reporting on China. Li Yi strikes me as tired, aged, despite his casual, sporty looks. He articulates a position that has weight, if not exactly influence, among overseas intellectuals: China must be progressive in order to maintain popular support inside the nation and abroad.

Troubled by the squelching of the democratic movement, by the rampant corruption, by the privilege system within the bureaucracy, Li Yi refuses to be "patriotic" at all costs. Still, he is committed to work for and with China. He tells me excitedly about a letter to Deng Xiaoping planned by a group of Hong Kong intellectuals, himself included. They will ask for a reduction of Wei Jingsheng's sentence from fifteen to five years. Such a reduction, they believe, could be used to goad Taiwan authorities into giving a less harsh sentence to dissidents of the *Formosa* magazine now on trial in Taibei. They believe Deng's clemency would make the Taiwan government look bad if it gave its own dissenters ten-year sentences. Their letter warns Deng not to let the Taiwan government appear "more humane."

Their reasoning strikes me as naive. It ignores the shared dislike of dissenters both on the mainland and in Taiwan. And yet, I am moved by this persistent effort of overseas Chinese intellectuals to belong to, and to make a difference in, China. Perhaps this is the reason for the elaborate celebrations of the May Fourth movement among the Hong Kong intelligentsia each year. That celebration is their ritual of rededication to a shared history with China and to a potentially shared future.

This time in Hong Kong I manage to create some time to pay attention to local society. During my previous two trips—in 1974, exuberantly "free" after a year in Taiwan, and in 1977, gloomy after a too-brief tour inside China—I bought books and did nothing else. Now there is time to make new friends. The personnel manager for Levi's takes me to her home. She, her seven brothers and sisters, and their mother live in one room on the ground floor of a housing complex built ten years ago for squatters. In the front half of the room is a small workshop where the mother makes clothes. In the back half, a curtained bunk bed and two sofa benches. My friend changes her clothes behind the curtain on the bed. Ten people, including her grandmother, sleep in this room at night. The mother shares the lower bunk with one sister, two sisters sleep on the upper bunk, one brother on the work table in the store, two brothers on one sofa chair, my friend and her favorite sister on the other.

My friend is trying to help her younger siblings in their studies. Her sister is a high school math teacher who goes to night school to study advanced statistics and is preparing to take the examinations for entrance to the London School of Economics. "She is smart enough to go to London, you know. If only she gets the chance!" This, from a woman who herself managed to pass exams for college and graduate while holding down a full-time job. Here, as in the conversations with other Hong Kong friends, I sense a frantic, pervasive effort toward self-improvement.

A week later, I'm back in China. I exchange money in Canton at a bank counter. Seven young people are employed to do the work of two. I chat with them freely, glad to be back. With Hong Kong so close in mind and space, I can't help but wonder how capitalist competition releases individual initiative. My friend's sister in Hong Kong might never make it to college. Just by trying, however, she has experienced more autonomy than the idle bank clerks of her age across the border. Chinese youths expect to be assigned to jobs. Too often, they accept them as final.

I am beginning to see that in Westernized societies like Hong Kong one is challenged (perhaps compelled) to live more fully, to develop one's talents more than is possible or permissible in China today. To be sure, that challenge is fulfilled only rarely. And always with difficulty.

I arrive back in China on the day in which the Central Committee announces the official rehabilitation of Liu Shaoqi. On the same day, Chinese newspapers publish the Central Committee's recommendation to change the Constitution and abolish the *si da* (the Four Great Freedoms), the right to speak out freely, to air news publicly, to hold great debates, and to put up big-character posters.

While waiting for my boat at the Kowloon pier, I bought a local leftist daily which has a big red headline about the reversal of the verdict on Liu Shaoqi, archvillain of the Cultural Revolution. Below, the news of less democracy appears in smaller black characters. The inside pages feature an interview with Liu's daughter. Her mother, Wang Guangmei, was apparently not at home. (Wang Guangmei's own power and position seem to be increasing these days.) The daughter speaks about being relieved now that "justice has been done." She reasserts her absolute faith in the righteous judgment of the Communist Party.

Everything bad ever said about Liu Shaoqi has been overturned. He has become all good again. To my ears this sounds too much like the traditional pattern of praise and blame. Is this just another twist in the distortion of history? Of "facts" generated in the guise of "search for truth"?

Back in Peking, I ask about the abolition of the Four Great Freedoms. An attendant at a late-night cab station into which

I straggle from the airport tells me, "It is a good thing to get rid of that stuff. It says so right here in the paper." (The Chinese newspapers carry the whole text of the Central Committee communique on the abolition of the four freedoms in huge red characters. So unlike the small black news printed by Hong Kong sympathizers.)

"Maybe you don't understand," the cab driver tells me, "those four freedoms came into use in the old days, when the KMT was in power. Then, it was necessary to resort to such means to express dissent. Now, however, that the Communist Party has regained the full support of the people, we don't need such things as the four freedoms." Not convinced, I say nothing at all. I wonder if the cab driver knows that the constitution granting those rights was passed only after Liberation, in 1950, not before.

Among my friends at Beida, there is considerably more debate about the abolition of the Four Great Freedoms. Some of them suggest that big-character posters have a positive function. Their point of view runs counter to Deng's totally negative assessment of big-character posters, which were used often enough against him in the past. My friends at the university recall the example of the Tian An Men Incident of 1976. The Gang of Four was challenged through the kind of mass meeting that would be illegal under the new law. They also recall the positive effects of big-character posters in recent months at Beida. Through these posters, students voiced their complaints about crowded dorms, limited library seats, and short shower hours. As a result of the wall poster campaign, these "mistakes" got rectified within a week. How, then, can Deng Xiaoping claim that the four freedoms amount to nothing good and bring only harm?

No one I talk to in Peking expects to be able to do much to change the course of events. No one knows what to do to prevent the abolition of the Four Great Freedoms. Younger intellectuals, students mostly, are lined up firmly, fervently, behind Deng. He is a strong man now and his plans to nurture talent promise meritorious students a chance to go abroad and a greater share in ruling the country upon their return. Older, middle-aged faculty have other worries. They are upset by rumors that the Soviet path of development, branded as "revisionist" during the Cultural Revolution, is about to be declared to have been really "socialist" after all. They shudder when they describe to me a Soviet-style China.

My friends differ from the powerful and entrenched elite who view the early fifties as a "perfect" time, who crave a return to the pre-1957 conditions and power alignments. They insist that history cannot and should not be turned back. Many of them also argue that the Cultural Revolution was begun for good reason. That it was first and foremost an attack on privilege. I quote Hegel to humor away their dread of the Soviet model of modernization: "The first time as tragedy, the second time as farce."

A mood of regression, of wishing to turn time back, is spreading among those in power. Yesterday, March 8, was International Woman's Day, a very different kind of affair from 1979. Again, I go to the Great Hall of the People. I am hoping to see Wang Guangmei. She is not there. Fully rehabilitated, with a high position in the Party and in the Academy of Social Sciences, she no longer needs, it seems, the public exposure and support that she cultivated a year ago. Safe and secure, she is now remote again. No longer a hidden survivor but a center-stage figure, she too is helping to reverse and to erase the Cultural Revolution.

Last year the March 8 show opened with an extravagant ballet, Spanish style. It was followed by a satirical "cross talk" mocking the autocracy of the Gang of Four. Now, there is an endless stream of kids. A mediocre violinist of nine or so tries to do her best. I leave in the middle of a dance by kindergarten girls in pink dresses, with rouged cheeks and purple umbrellas, who saunter under blue plastic palms.

MARCH 30   *Research on intellectuals: no longer academic*   In the past couple of weeks the pace and content of scholarly conversations has increased dramatically. My language skills are now quite adequate to talk at length about the subject that matters to me the most: the legacy of May Fourth intellectuals. Worries about all that I have yet to learn about their personal lives and the contradictions between their advocacy of enlightenment and their revolutionary politics recede as I have more and more opportunity to talk to their descendants and their followers.

The history I thought I knew, its underside I came to study here, is growing more and more real daily. On the seventeenth of this month I finally met with Li Zehou, a noted philosopher of aesthetics and the author of the most interesting book on modern intellectual history to come out in China since the fall of the Gang of Four. He is also a man who, I gather, sees himself and is seen by many others as China's best hope for the revival of a genuine Marxist philosophy.

The meeting with Li Zehou is arranged through the Modern History Institute at the Academy of Social Sciences. In preparation for our conversation, I also read through Li Zehou's new book on Kant and critical philosophy. A Chinese graduate friend of mine alerts me that the postscript tells in simple, clear words how one intellectual survived the ravage of politics during the Cultural Revolution. I find the brief text. It is more elusive than I expected. Still, I translate it for myself because it contains such an unequivocal testament about the solace of thought in times that defy reason:

> Very early on, I developed an interest in Kant's philosophy. But I never expected to write about it. Then, in 1972, toward the end of the movement to send intellectuals down to the countryside, I, too, was exiled. I carried with me, hidden, Kant's *Critique of Pure Reason.* Down there, I found some leisure to look through it a few times and realized it had some salient points for our own dilemmas. That autumn, the Gang of Four was in full charge. Cultural life was suffocating. I had no way to work on aesthetics. They also mounted their rabid campaign against Confucianism, so there was no way to work on the history of Chinese thought. Thus I came to keep a low profile and write this book. With this I tried to lessen somewhat my own despondency and rage. Because of my poor health, the writing dragged on through 1976, until after the earthquake. In the temporary huts built at that time, I joined in earthquake relief work while also savoring the pleasure of writing this book.

I meet this author at his home, since the offices of the Academy of Social Sciences have yet to be finished. He lives in one room, shared by his wife and son. His wife is a dancer in a troupe belonging to the Mining Ministry. In his fifties, Li Zehou exudes extraordinary vigor and youth. His face is constantly alive, eyes full of a playful, critical intelligence. Often during our two-hour talk, he throws his head back and breaks out in sharp, high-pitched laughter. All this while he keeps telling me, inviting me, "Speak freely, don't be bound by empty, distorting formalities."

In this one room: a big bed, a smaller couch/day bed (on which I sit), a wicker chair pulled over from a desk (from which Li faces me). On the walls, a calendar with a Western nineteenth-century beauty and posters of Chinese movie stars. Books everywhere, his own books close at hand for reference during our talk. On the table, three little dishes of sweets prepared by his wife, a kind gesture that reminds me she cannot be here because of work.

We talk about Marxism, more seriously than I have with anyone in China this year. Li has read a recent article in the *New York Review of Books* about a new biography of Marx the scientist. He is remarkably informed and thoughtful as he criticizes nineteenth-century notions of evolution and authority, as he tells me his own appreciation of Marx "as a *philosopher* of history." He insists that the proper subject of philosophy of history is man—not the reified world of nature, so prominent in Stalin's theories. Li still believes in historical materialism but maintains doubts about dialectical materialism. He holds Kant in very high esteem, higher than Hegel, about whom he knows a great deal as well.

He is familiar with the work of the twentieth-century Western philosophers like Gramsci, Lévi-Strauss, Foucault, even Lacan. I am a bit incredulous at this. How did he get to read all these books? In what languages does he read them? The facilities and the relative freedom available to senior researchers in the Academy of Social Sciences don't explain it all. He has a passionate ambition: to distill all Western thought that might aid in the rebirth of genuine philosophy in China.

After a nearly breathless hour of talk on Western philosophy, we finally get around to the May Fourth intellectuals. Li's book on modern intellectual history concluded with a tantalizing generational scheme. It assigned this group the most creative, most important role in the development of Chinese thought and in the progress of the Chinese revolution. This scheme, and our conversation about it, reassures me that the old men, dead or dying, who consume my interest and energy these days are indeed a powerful influence on China today.

I am taken aback a bit when Li contrasts the lucky, creative May Fourth intellectuals with his own generation. He sees his comtemporaries as "ill fated," thwarted over and over again from realizing their potential. How could this man, so prolific and creative in his own work, feel that time has run out for his own generation? I sense a Confucian prejudice here, a belief that one's spade-work years are over by age fifty. Li's sentiment is widely shared by other middle-aged Chinese friends.

As we say goodbye, Li encourages me to keep the focus of my historical work on the problem of intellectuals. "There are only two truly significant issues in modern Chinese history: the problem of peasants and the problem of intellectuals. In recent history, the greatest tragedy has been the policy of making intellectuals more like peasants, sending them to the countryside, derogating publicly the knowledge that they had. What needs to be done now is to intellectualize the peasantry. On the day when most people will be intellectuals, Communism will be truly at hand." Some of this sounds arrogant to me. I tell him so. He doesn't mind. Invites me back for further conversation and debate.

Three days later, on March 20, I have a fine talk with Zheng Erkang and Wu Xiaoling, son and disciple respectively of Zheng Zhenduo, a May Fourth intellectual I had written about in my thesis. Zheng Zhenduo had been one of the few who was able to continue scholarly interests undisturbed in the decade after Liberation. He was even rewarded with a position in the Ministry of Culture. An ardent patriot, he was a loyal ally of the Communists who defended China's interests during the hard years of the Anti-Japanese War. In fact, he lost his prestigious professorship at Yanjing (Yenching) University in 1933 when he dared to sponsor leftists on the faculty. The details of that story come out poignantly during our conversation today.

Zheng's son, Zheng Erkang, is now at work on his father's biography. The new mood of intellectual emancipation sponsored by Deng Xiaoping is enabling him to take time off from work to travel and interview old associates of his father. The disciple, Professor Wu Xiaoling, an eminent older scholar of traditional literature himself, is also helping compile and edit his teacher's writings. An urbane, deeply scholarly mood here. We talk at length about the Confucian virtue of *qinggao*, the skill of staying above dirty politics—a virtue that informed Zheng Zhenduo's actions, even though he was a fellow traveler of revolutionaries. Again, as often before, I am surprised how deeply traditional the May Fourth rebels against tradition really were! This ideal of "purity" was important to so many of them.

Today, I press my hosts to tell me how one could be pure and committed all at once. I know that in practice, especially during periods of patriotic mobilization before 1949 and during mass movements since Liberation, this creative tension between intellectual integrity and social conscience broke down. But the idea of having both persists. My hosts explain to me that *qinggao* does not preclude negative commentary on the powers-that-be. "It is not only staying out of politics. It is an active dissatisfaction with reality at hand [*buman xianshi*]." During May Fourth, this idea of dissatisfaction with the present came into China along with evolutionist philosophy from the West. Intellectuals' dissent became seen as a positive force in pushing history forward. This was the same impulse that animated the intellectuals' criticism of party bureaucracy in 1957.

Zheng Zhenduo, I learn, died in a plane crash in 1958. Just in time, ironically, to avoid the criticism leveled against "bourgeois scholars" like himself in 1958–59 and to escape the beatings and persecution of the Cultural Revolution in the 1960s. His son and his disciple, on the other hand, were not spared the ravages of politics. In their revived commitment to critical scholarship, I glimpse the enduring power of *qinggao*. Unable to stay above the mess of the Cultural Revolution, they were prompt to recover the ideal of intellectual integrity as soon as chaos receded.

Yesterday, a fine talk with the son of another May Fourth intellectual, Zhu Ziqing, a man who is moving closer to the center of my work on the May Fourth enlightenment. His son, Zhu Qiaosen, is a shy, calm, inward man. Not unlike what I imagine the father to have been, from the few surviving photographs. As we sit in my dormitory room, the son is not anxious but full of a nearly painful diffidence. A living memorial to his father's painstaking honesty, to his persistent effort to tell right from wrong.

Zhu Ziqing was damned by many of the leftists of the 1930s and 1940s for being too liberal, too inactive. Then after he died in 1948 he was canonized by Mao. In one line, the chairman of the Communist Party praised this intellectual because "he died of hunger rather than accept food handouts from American imperialists." Whether this was fact or lore didn't matter. To be patriotic was enough. That was all that could be said about Zhu Ziqing until recently.

His son has been coming back to the father's legacy circuitously. He co-authored a recently published, excellent biography of Li Dazhao, the May Fourth intellectual who helped found the Communist Party and whom Mao regarded as a mentor for the rest of his life. From this "safe" standpoint, Zhu Qiaosen is now slowly beginning to work on his father's biography. Unlike Zheng Zhenduo's son, Zhu does not have public sanction for his project yet. Zhu Ziqing's literary work is too complex, too moody to be easily subsumed in the "progressive" category.

He was, as his son explains to me, a "conscientiously self-dissecting petit-bourgeois intellectual." He never pretended, never wanted to be anything else. He knew and confessed publicly his fear of violent politics—that thrill which kept his more revolutionary detractors going in the bleak years of the White Terror of 1927–35, and the Anti-Japanese War of 1937–45. And yet, as the son demonstrates to me with textual detail, the father was a ceaseless critic, "perennially dissatisfied with the status quo." An echo here of the *qinggao* ideal. No wonder. Zheng Zhenduo and Zhu Ziqing were close friends all their lives.

The petit-bourgeois intellectual's sympathy for the common people becomes more and more real to me as the son fills in the details of his father's life. Zhu Ziqing's enduring commitment to the May Fourth legacy was the cause of some tension with Communist intellectuals who also shared the formative experience of May Fourth during their student years at Peking University. One fellow student that Zhu did not lose contact with, who remained a beacon of political inspiration, was Deng Zhongxia, a labor organizer for the Communist Party in the 1920s.

Today, the son clears up a small but critical mystery in my historical research. I have been concerned about the identity of the hero-subject of Zhu Ziqing's 1924 poem "To A.S." The poem is a poignant description of an activist by a scholarly admirer. "It is really about Deng Zhongxia. My father had met Deng on the shores of West Lake that summer and was deeply moved by his fiery fellow student.

After Zhu Qiaosen leaves, I translate the poem "To A.S."

Your hands are like torches
your eyes like waves
your words like stones.
What could have made me forget? . . .

You want to build a red heaven on earth,
on an earth full of thorns
on an earth full of sly foxes
on an earth full of the walking dead.
You would make yourself into a sharp knife,
a sword able to cut down thorns.
You would be a roaring lion
to set the foxes running scared.
You would be a spring thunder
to startle into awakening the walking dead.

I love to see you ride . . .
I imagine you as a sand- and rock-stirring tornado
that aims to blow down entrenched palaces of gold.
Blow on. . . .

Last year, I saw you on a summer day.
Why did you look so drained?
Your eyes were parched,
your hair too long.
But your blood was burning.

I, who had been wallowing in mud,
was baked by your fire.
You have the fragrance of a strong cigar
You have the power of hard brandy
You burn like red pepper.
How can I ever forget you?

Out of marginal details like the identity of "A.S.," I am now
slowly reconstructing the history of May Fourth. The distinction
between "hard" and "soft" intellectuals, so sharp in Chinese and
Western scholarship on May Fourth, is becoming less and less
meaningful. What matters to me now is not what each contributed
to a retrospectively successful revolution but how they managed
to stay in touch, how each helped the other preserve the ideals

of a cultural enlightenment in the frenzied years of political, nationalist revolution.

APRIL 8 *Easter in Datong: Buddhist caves and abandoned class struggle* Eight hours northwest of Peking, after a train ride which goes along the Great Wall and cuts across the dull yellow hills of Shanxi province, lies Datong, a small mining town. Its name means "Great Peace," and it was the capital of the "barbarian" Wei dynasty founded by the Toba clan in A.D. 386. Deeply moved by the simple, imaginative Wei-period wall paintings in Dunhuang last summer, I wanted to see more of their art: this time, the grand undertaking in sculpture at Datong.

I'm making this visit to the center of early Buddhism in the middle of the Passover season. Just before leaving Peking, I gave a lecture on Marxist approaches to religion to future foreign correspondents at the *People's Daily* Journalism Institute. I was invited by one of the foreign experts, who heard that I take religion seriously in my own life. After the formal talk, hastily prepared, a surprisingly open conversation about Zionism with the Chinese students. To my surprise, many have read *O Jerusalem*, a journalistic account of the struggles that led up to the founding of the state of Israel. Well supplied with reading matter by the institute, they were openly sympathetic to the plight of the Jewish people.

This trip to Datong is possible because of a brief Easter vacation granted to us by the Education Ministry. Consideration for "foreigners' religious beliefs" is increasing here. What about the Chinese people's religious beliefs? The morning after I get into the rain-drenched mining town, I take the local bus to Yun Gang, the Cloud Hillock Caves of the Wei dynasty faithful. The rough ride takes about forty-five minutes.

The time passes quickly in conversation with an engineer. She is on her way to work, shy yet curious. In a soft voice, persistently, she conducts a conversation with me on behalf of the fifty or so other riders. She asks about wages, work hours, rents, and unemployment in the U.S. Whenever (which is often enough) American facts sound opulent compared to the situation in China the bus ripples with a nervously envious "Ohhh." When we talk about aspects of American life that breed insecurity, competition, and tension in daily life (no one on the bus could quite believe that the U.S. government does not provide job security for everyone), bus riders turn to each other, with an excited "Ah, you see."

A sense of relief all around. When fellow riders find out that socialism—which they are expected to believe is better than capitalism— seems, in fact, to provide more humane consideration of basic necessities, they relax. Our conversation becomes more personal, full of freely shared facts about local life. The engineer boasts about the heating costs for winter in this coal-mining area: "Five to eight yuan! Less than 10 percent of an average worker's monthly salary is enough for a winter's coal bill. So much less than in Peking, you know!" No, I didn't. In Peking, I hadn't thought to ask.

The Buddhist caves are a disappointment at first. Perhaps I have been too spoiled by the intense, well-preserved colors of Dunhuang. Perhaps the day is just too cold and windy to allow for leisurely savoring of stony detail. Whatever the reason or the excuse, these caves strike me as tattered, gaudy. Having pored through a beautiful, recently published book of photographs about Yun Gang, I am not prepared for the poor and ravaged condition of the place. Westerners who came in the 1910s, 1920s, and 1930s marked with chalk those statues they liked and bargained with local dealers. During two months in 1930, according to one Western art historian, more than one thousand statues were taken from the caves.

Now, the evidence—the absence, really—is everywhere. Missing arms, heads, and countless bullet holes deface these fifteen-hundred-year-old monuments. How much the Cultural Revolution contributed to this ravage is unclear from the upbeat talk of the local guides.

What remains today is mostly what was too huge and too firmly anchored into rock to be looted or ripped apart. There are twenty or so hulking Buddhas carved into the mountain side. Stark, severe, immobile testaments to a faith that required and created awe. Before Buddhism, Chinese culture had known only the intimate scale of ancestor worship (name tablets of deceased relatives, for example). Buddhism's arrival sparked a yearning for something much greater than the self, the family, or the clan. The

Datong: stone carvings from the Yun Gang caves (Wei dynasty, 534–557) and a wood sculpture from the Huayan temple (Liao dynasty, 916–1125).

sheer size of these statues was meant to convey, especially to the commoners, the power of a godly savior.

Walking around the huge toes, gazing up at the broken elbows of these stiff deities, I find myself uncomfortable. I'm surprised by my own instinctive sympathy for the Confucian prejudice against Buddhism. I recall its source: a seventeeth-century description of Yun Gang by a literati visitor: "They [the Wei] were afraid that the statues were too small, and that they would not be noticed; as a diameter of one cubit was not enough they wanted to make it several cubits; as several cubits did not always answer their needs, they did all they could to make diameters of several dozen cubits, and to produce a work which would last, they . . . carved Buddhas by the hundreds and thousands in the rocks. The people whom they sent to look at the carvings were impressed; they therefore thought that they had reached the heights of wisdom, little thinking that they had reached the heights of folly. The way of the Duke of Zhou and Confucius has been followed for thousands of years, but does it need illustrations such as these?" ("Memoir of the Buddhist Carvings at Yun Gang," quoted in *Nagel's China* [New York, 1968], pp. 878–89).

I don't want to go away with this Confucian-inspired impression. So, I walk through the caves a second time. I start to notice side-images. A flurry of heavenly musicians and earthly demons crowds around the still Buddhas. On their faces I can make out playful smiles, faint echoes of plump delights promised to the faithful after enlightenment. In these barely distinct images, I rediscover the mystery of Wei Buddhism, its unique combination of joy and fear, solemn prayer and exuberant dreams.

After Yun Gang, I spend the next few hours gazing at a Liao-period (916–1125) monastery in town. Looking at postcard renditions of the Huayan temple, I had been struck by gilded images in a harsh green light. These pictures conjured up loud, imperious deities. In reality, the remains are dark, silent, reserved. Created more than six centuries after the sculptures of Yun Gang, these images testify to a more refined, domesticated piety. The Huayan statues have been protected surprisingly well from the ravages of weather and war as well as from the blight of Ming-Qing restoration, which was marked by a mania for the livid blues and greens, that the late imperial clergy deemed important to common worshipers.

There are seventeen statues on the main dais. Three Buddhas, each one flanked by two monks and surrounded by six Boddhisattvas. The entire grouping is guarded by demon-slaying soldiers. The main hue of this silent gathering is gray-green. Layers of age over gold are interrupted in a few places by a shiny cheek, a radiant chest. The corner of a smile brushed clean by a worshiper long ago. With the gold so muted through time, the shapes are allowed to speak more starkly. Each Boddhisattva wears a different crown. These symbols of earthly power here transcend their mundane models by an irregular, uncluttered fancifulness. These crowns adorn the awesome. Two standing Boddhisattvas among the six are draped in flowing scarves. The folds do nothing to hide a lithe, sensual waist as it joins a full torso to a swaying hip.

Each of the seventeen statues stands apart on a pedestal of its own. This arrangement has bequeathed restraint, silence to each. They look very withdrawn, these creations of the spirit. As if they had endured for so long only by overcoming emotions which link, bind, tear humans to and from each other. The Buddhist message—that attachment breeds suffering—is inscribed forever in the quiet spaces between these perfect works of art.

Another kind of message about suffering and the process of its abolition is inscribed in the Class Struggle Education Exhibit attached to the Grave of Ten Thousand in the mining village of Mei Yu Kou outside of Datong. A Chinese friend who made a pilgrimage to Mei Yu Kou during the Cultural Revolution suggested that I visit the place. He recalled that the scene was moving in spite of its heavy-handedly didactic intent. I decide to take the one-hour bus ride mostly to see more of the countryside around Datong. I'm hoping for some perspective on more recent history after the charm of Datong's distant past.

A nine-hundred-year leap from the Buddhas of the Liao dynasty to the Japanese atrocities in North China in the 1940s. Datong has been a mining area for a long time. Its destitute peasants, driven off the land by natural disasters and exorbitant rents, have for over a century found alternative means of subsistence in the coal pits of this region. The harsh circumstances of their labor under Chinese rulers, however, pales by comparison to their slavery when the Japanese occupied Shanxi. Planning to increase the amount of coal extracted in Datong from 3 million tons in 1941 to

8 million by 1945, the Japanese resorted to concentration camp methods in this area.

They first cajoled native populations into labor camps by promises of pay and food. Eventually, miners were rounded up, put underground, and, after they had collapsed from exhaustion and hunger, discarded. Their bodies were stacked into a mass grave along a secluded mountain path.

The burial ground outside Datong was discovered in the early 1960s during the Socialist Education Campaign. In the heat of that mass mobilization, surviving miners took youths to the pit, which they had kept secret out of dread of ghosts and political retribution. Curiosity about and interest in the mass grave spread quickly. More and more visitors came. In 1966, plans were laid for paving the path up to and around the grave. In 1968, a large restaurant at the foot of the hill where the bones had been stacked was converted into the "Grave of Ten Thousand Class Struggle Education Exhibition Hall."

Today, the big building stands isolated and deserted at the top of a mud alley. Mei Yu Kou itself looks like a thriving mining village. I am surprised to find the museum open on a Sunday morning. It is a cavernous, solitary place, plastered with quotations from Chairman Mao. It reminds me of the exhibit hall dedicated to the Chairman in Changsha, Hunan. Yet another awkward remnant of past political fervor. That fervor becomes more and more outdated each day as portraits of the Chairman are removed from Tian An Men Square in Peking. The excuse in the capital is "restoration of the Forbidden City." Rumors are also spreading that statues of Mao have been taken down in other cities as well. His sayings have already been washed off street placards and are being replaced by paintings of "modernized" traffic flow. According to a recent Central Committee communique, fewer museums are to be built to living or recently deceased political leaders.

It strikes me as unfortunate and unfair that the history museum at Datong should suffer the same fate of oblivion as the Cultural Revolution monument in Changsha. After all, the bones of the miners killed in Datong in the 1940s are more solid evidence of history as it happened than the "eternal wisdom of the Helmsman" enshrined in Changsha in the 1960s. And yet, both historical museums stand abandoned today by the public, by the very masses they had been meant to instruct.

I walk through the Class Struggle Education Exhibit for two hours. Accompanied by a knowledgeable curator, I keep asking myself why the project of a museum about "class education" failed. The quotation from Chairman Mao at the entrance of the museum seems, in retrospect, an insightful warning: "Young workers who have no experience of oppression themselves need education about class struggle more than anyone else, lest they forget the world mission of the proletariat." In Peking, now, Western clothing fads flourish among young workers more rapidly than among any other group. Many have already procured bell-bottom pants, hair permanents, tinted glasses, and Hong Kong pop music tapes. These young "proletarians" are often outspoken, wistful, in their praise for the "good life" in Taiwan, Hong Kong, and the United States. Perhaps Mao was foreseeing something too complicated, too thorny for China to acknowledge just yet.

Mao's prophecy has been borne out. But the reasons it has are hard to fathom. The myth of Mao himself certainly deadened the sense of history that might have nourished the consciousness of young proletarians. The exhibit is full of slogans. Over and over again, bold red placards insist on insights about a past that should have been. The facts of oppression are here in ample evidence. In the ragged cloth sandals that miners were made to pay for as "leather" shoes, in the slivers of bone they used to wipe off the sweat because rags were too expensive, in the length of the leather belts which they used to haul hundred-pound chunks of coal out of the mines, in the carge map, spread wide, showing the location of the mass graves throughout North China.

These bits of history are drowned out by the slogans. The "proof" they proclaim is too emblematic, even when true. Take, for example, the identification tag of a miner from Anhui province. This body is the only one that could be named positively in the mass grave. The name, age, height, and weight of the worker are exhibited along with his bloody fingerprint, his preserved skeleton, and a large photograph of his aged wife, who was somehow located in the 1960s. An enlarged placard of the dead man's tag is hung alongside a blowup of his wife's letter congratulating the museum on the project of Class Struggle Education. "Chairman Mao's eternal wisdom will never be in doubt."

In the darkened rooms of this museum, pieces of the ragged

past are displayed next to, and imply equal validity with, huge contemporary oil paintings representing what the suffering must have been like. The center of each room is bulging with a massive, contemporary sculpture of laborers in distress.

Toward the end, we come to a brightly lit section entitled "Under Oppression There Must Be Resistance." In these rooms, the slogans claim that the arrangement of the bones in the mass grave, and some holes in some of the skulls, "prove" that the miners had died fighting against their Japanese overseers. A fancy electronic display provides an overview of forms of resistance in North China during the Japanese occupation. Along with labor slowdowns, these included filling coal trucks with rocks covered with a thin layer of coal, destroying equipment, exploding rail lines, destroying power lines, blowing up bridges. The final room is brighter than all the rest. It contains a painting of a happy peasant with a blue bandanna around his waist, a photograph of Datong on the eve of Liberation, May 1, 1949, and a large reproduction of Mao Zedong.

The exhibit is meant to convey an upbeat message. Perhaps it succeeds so well that it has to fail. Perhaps its unblemished optimism about class struggle makes the past it seeks to commemorate no longer pertinent to the "bright" life of today. Perhaps, too, the fact that the public has abandoned such museums is not accidental. After all, Chairman Hua Guofeng has declared officially that "class struggle is over" in socialist China. Historians today, under the inspiration of the new slogan, are carrying on a public debate about whether class struggle was ever the moving force of history. The implication of this controversy is that in considering the past, as now, emphasis should be placed on the forces, not the relations, of production.

I walk up the hill with the curator, past some village boys playing on the path. We come to the iron door of the mass grave. An old man has been informed of our visit during my two-hour tour of the building down the hill. He is there with keys in hand, takes off the lock, and we go in. The curator turns on the light. We spend a few minutes peering down a valley in which lie the bones of seventy or so miners. We are both quiet, say nothing.

Walking down the hill slowly, we start to chat about today's young people. My guide complains about their lack of interest in this message of the past. He seems worried about the shaky foundations of socialism among contemporary, doubt-ridden youths. I tell him they must be understood, not blamed. He agrees, and explains that the best method is "to make friends with them and then to lead them to the right path through affectionate concern."

We part warmly, exchange addresses. I tell him that some day I'd like to bring my American students back to this historic site.

On the bus back, I find myself contrasting the Yad Vashem Holocaust Memorial in Jerusalem and the Grave of Ten Thousand in Datong. Certainly the scale of events and their implications are starkly different. Still, both are meant to instruct against forgetfulness. Both intend to use the horror of killing to inspire better ways of living. Two statements from the Datong exhibit stick in my mind: "Four Chinese died for every thousand tons of coal which the Japanese extracted from North China" and "In the old society all of China could be likened to a Grave of Ten Thousand." These two statements might have been woven into a more memorable tale without the glossy new paintings, without the bronze model mines, without the lighting effects. And with fewer quotations from Chairman Mao, perhaps.

Understatement strikes me as the main achievement of Yad Vashem. Its black and white photographs, its emphasis on the words of those who went through hell rather than those who came to inherit the land after them. Nonetheless, an ironic parallel between the nationalistic message at the end of Yad Vashem— that the modern state of Israel is somehow the logical and necessary result of the Holocaust—and the brightest, last room in Datong. The Maoist revolution is also shown, too easily, to be the logical and necessary result of the history which murdered the miners of Datong.

Proclamations about the inevitable seem to me to rob history of its quieter, more disconcerting truths about process and will. It takes time and painstaking effort to defeat imperialism, racism, and class oppression. The present is poorly served by "shoulds" about the future based upon a romanticized reading of the past. To immortalize the heroic, or only the heroic, is, in the end, to make contemporary, ordinary people beside the point to the struggle at hand.

What if, on the other hand, one were to try to reckon with past sufferers in all their fallibility? Would not our tasks in the present then be more compelling and more possible?

Ye Junjian at home in Peking looking through a copy of his 1947 novel, *Mountain Village*.

Over Easter vacation in Datong, I read an early novel by a new Chinese friend, Ye Junjian, better known in the West as Chun-Chan Yeh. He went to England in the 1940s to present a fairer picture of life in China than was available in the works popularized by Lin Yutang. He came back to China before Liberation, worked as a translator of children's stories, and is now returning to his own fiction after the harsh years of the Cultural Revolution.

Ye Junjian's early novel is called *Mountain Village*. He wrote it in English and published it in London in 1947. It describes the rural background of the Chinese revolution through warm but realistic evocation of destitute peasants caught in the flux of incomprehensible events. The author is remarkably honest about the superstitions, the doubts, and the opportunism of the "oppressed." He is also unflinching in his descriptions of young revolutionaries who idealize the poor and, as a result, serve them clumsily.

A conversation in this novel between a fugitive Communist intellectual and the mountain villagers who hide him for the night is particularly memorable. I reread it in light of my impressions of Datong:

> "Good stuff! You're really my comrade, you're really so understanding!" He became talkative and lively. . . . "My birthplace is not far from here. It is in the next county."
>
> "How exciting!" my mother cried. "It is the county where the first What-you-call-it- President or Emperor—of our republican Dynasty was born?"

Talking about the local landlords, the young revolutionary reassures Uncle Pan, a local peasant, that he need not worry about calling the exploiter "a tiger who bites right into the bone." The young man declares: "I'm not going to denounce you to the old tiger, because I'm not his 'running dog.' " Then, he concludes: "Uncle Pan is absolutely right. He is a real proletarian, with an instinctive hatred for the exploiting class."

When Uncle Pan does not denounce the young man to the police who come looking for him, the Communist intellectual is even more convinced about "real proletarian" Uncle Pan. That conviction is put to the test when the "revolutionary dynasty" comes to power briefly and tries to make Uncle Pan some sort of "mandarin" by appointing him head of the Peasant Union. In the end, Uncle Pan tries to walk back to his ancestral village with his "daughter," the beloved calf he helped birth. The revolutionaries stop him, put him into a reform camp, and take his one and only "love" for public use.

The novel ends with the defeat of the revolutionary uprising. Nonetheless, the reader comes away with a sense of the permanently altered mountain village. Old ways of living have become untenable even though nothing new or conclusive has emerged. On the last page, the narrator, his mother, and the watchdog Laipao are off to the faraway city to find a father gone long before as secretary to a foreign company: "So we started out, I went in front, my mother behind me, and Laipao behind my mother, innocently wagging his tail. He did not know that it was *going to be a long journey.*"

I underline the last words in Ye Junjian's novel and think back to the Grave of Ten Thousand. Why can't something like this be the central theme of monuments meant to instruct about past suffering? Why can't museums convey the message that the path will be long and twisting? That each generation must chart and choose its liberation anew lest the past circle back and choke those who would forget?

MAY 10   *Yet another early May in Peking*   I remember the excited specialness of May Fourth a year ago. The night before, I had gone to see the movie *Song of Youth*, a fictional version of the Beida legend. The legend of intellectuals' heroism in moments of national need. I remember crying, despite my efforts to remain just an observer and critic of the legend. In the end, I lost my distance from the sentimental girl in white, and from the long-gowned men who love her, fight over her and for China.

That night, I had gone for a midnight bike ride around the lake. Slowly, I told myself that I had overidentified with China, with the May Fourth movement. To be here at Beida, for the sixtieth anniversary of the event, was an unending thrill. Ten years of engagement with something abstract finally became more concrete. A gift, really. On the day of May Fourth itself, I remember sitting restlessly in the sports stadium, near, but not yet in touch with, the old men of the May Fourth generation.

A year later, May Fourth is a rather ordinary day. I spend the morning working on a tentative chronology of the life of Zhang Shenfu, the eighty-eight-year-old philosopher of the May Fourth period who had been peripheral to my dissertation. I want to work on his biography, a project which I expect will take up the next few years. I write out eleven pages in Chinese. I am not as embarrassed by my language limitations as I was a year ago. I hope that some of the factual questions on chronology can be answered during our Monday talks.

As I jot down what I want to ask him before I leave in June, I glimpse the many problems left. He has already told me much of what he remembers of his early childhood, of the circumstances of the founding of the Chinese Communist Party, how he came to study Bertrand Russell, how he met the fierce young activist who became his lover in Paris in 1921 and was to remain his wife until 1948. I still have to work out the connections between his philosophical interests and political activity, between his iconoclasm against tradition and his deep respect for Confucius, between the revolution he helped to create and the revolutionaries who denied him a voice in politics after 1949. I finally sense that I have a book inside me. A work of real history which I hope will change how Zhang and his times are viewed inside China and abroad as well.

The night of May Fourth: a dinner at the house of another friend, a sixty-eight-year-old sociologist. He studied in France and Germany in the 1930s and came back to China in its moment of need, during the Anti-Japanese War. He was damned for his bourgeois thought early in the 1950s, then declared a "rightist" in 1957. He has done little research in the past twenty years. Today, his health is good, he rides his bike, his cheeks are flushed, especially after he has indulged his taste for fine wine from Shaoxing. He is getting ready for a conference in the United States and has completed a book on the history of social science in the West.

I try hard to understand the resiliency of spirit that animates so many of my Peking friends. This is not, as some outsiders have called it, a "yo-yo" snap-back phenomenon.

These intellectuals have a certain inner dignity, a high-mindedness nurtured over many centuries by the scholar-literati tradition. Their predecessors had long experience coping with ruthless aristocrats. Yet, there is also something new in the intellectuals' resiliency: patriotism. No longer just defenders of China's cultural greatness, my friends have a passionate commitment to make some dent in the poverty and backwardness of China.

Although I admire their passion and commitment, I am still nagged by one question: Why did these intellectuals not speak out against the Cultural Revolution? Certainly, they would have suffered a worse fate. Certainly, also, their shaky voices would have carried little weight in the din of mass hysteria. Still, I keep thinking of the fate of Russian dissidents who, in spite of persecution, continue to bear witness against the present so that the future might be better. Chinese intellectuals, by contrast, are more compliant in the hands of the powerful. Why?

Monday night, the fifth of May, a bonfire dance to celebrate the May Fourth movement. Rumors of the celebration had come through the grapevine early. It becomes official when the students' class representatives are called in to learn the "group dance" which is to be performed, allowed really, at the bonfire. Just in case anybody gets notions about rock and roll, or something.

A Chinese friend, down the hall in our dormitory, is eager to teach me the group dance. She takes her responsibility seriously, learning the steps well herself. Then, one noontime, during the rest period, we decide to practice in the hall. I learn quickly enough, being able to dredge up some waltzes from my Romanian memories. She shows me how to curl the fingers of my free hand upward—"It is more graceful, don't you think?"—and how to bend slightly forward while swirling. "It creates a more harmonious movement."

These feminine graces have nothing girlish about them. My friend is a young woman steeled by the austerity of manual labor in the grassland province of Qinghai. Yet she loves music, and the feeling of movement. After our practice session, not shy nor coy, she asks me how to dance rock and roll. I can't explain so I try to find some music to let her hear the rhythm. All I can find is some Israeli pop music on a birthday tape sent by my nephew from back home. We relax after our May Fourth bonfire preparations by swinging to the latest disco hits from Tel Aviv.

On Monday night (the bonfire was postponed one day because of winds) the main fire is lit by Yang Hui, an eighty-six-year-old May Fourth veteran. A professor in the Literature Department, he has never retired. Yang makes some brief, hoarse remarks about the flame of May Fourth, and the Beida tradition to be handed down from generation to generation. After him the school's Communist Party secretary explains that the flame is Communism. After his speech, model-student representatives take the torch from Yang Hui's hands and run to light the other three fires on the athletic field.

The program for the evening begins with some choral singing. First, a group of veterans of the Anti-Japanese War student movement who are now instructors in their late fifties. Then, some members of the teachers' and workers' union, including some recently rehabilitated "rightists," middle-aged remnants of the visionary young men and women who had spoken out about party bureaucratism during the Hundred Flowers movement, who had called for a new May Fourth in 1957. Some were jailed, some demoted, all deeply shaken. Now they sing soberly, as if on command.

In the far right corner a group from the Chemistry Department hums a melody, accompanied by hand cymbals and a tin lunchbox filled with sand. Hauntingly simple sounds. A young man gets up to orate a poem about youths' quest for love and beauty, a grandiose message delivered in Peking-opera style. The dancing is about to begin. Just in time, in the dark and milling crowd, I find the friend who taught me the group dance. She is ready to line up with a curly-haired boy (from Guangxi, she told me shyly later). As soon as she sees me she grabs my hand and draws me into the circle of their class. I feel more awkward, more reluctant than I had expected. Too old, too un-Chinese for this lighthearted experiment that echoes my pioneer days in Romania.

The loudspeaker is playing a Hong Kong version of the theme song from a recent Chinese movie. A tune called "Our Life Overflows with Brightness." It celebrates, at once, romantic love and revolutionary ardor. On this Monday night there are no words, just the tune, familiar yet new. Next to the fire of the Literature Department, I find the orderly circle of the Economics Department. Couples are moving gracefully in a prearranged pattern. Calm, just as they have been taught, with hardly a smile. Yet there is a quiet, confident enjoyment. Then, a loud groan when, after twenty minutes of dancing, the loudspeaker announces the end of the party. "For the sake of everyone's protection, rest, and successful study," the voice in the box claims, "the fires will be doused and the lights turned off."

Four days later, I turn thirty-three in China. Another birthday in this country of unharassed aging. People around me are marked by bitter Peking weather and a barely balanced diet. Yet, no matter how gaunt a face, or how worn a body, age here is not as difficult or embarrassing as back home. My birthday unfolds in a sluggish way. First, a longer than usual run around the lake. Then, a morning of reading 1921–22 newspapers in the library. In three hours of work, I turn up three short articles by Zhang Shenfu written during his year in Paris.

Later, dinner with a friend from Sri Lanka, who lends me a book comparing Buddhist and Freudian psychology. The night ends with a study group discussion of COMICON, the agency for economic collaboration and planning set up by the Soviet Union for its allies. I ride my bicycle home in the soft wind of the Peking spring, wondering what Albania is doing now with the cobalt it used to sell to China in the 1960s.

EPILOGUE

JUNE 24 *Kathmandu, with China in mind*

It is a mild, cloudy day in Kathmandu. The house of my closest friend from America, Jan, is here to welcome me, to help me heal. It is large and beautiful. Looking over terraced fields, farmhouses, and across the street to a prince's mansion, I sit down to write this last of my China journal entries.

Nepal lies before me, backward but not poor. Such a change from China. The simple fact of population is suddenly, stunningly apparent. On the roads here, an ambling, sparse pace. Large farmhouses are built of brick or clay. Rice paddies are spread out on convenient land, not carved out of a hostile environment as in Sichuan. In the crisp mountain air the fields are strangely silent after the din of frogs in the muggy heat of Peking. Here, there is no smell of human excrement, the constant aroma of cultivation in China. A popular king rules over satisfied peasants and somewhat restive urban workers and intellectuals. The day I arrived, the socialists had been defeated in a general election. The walls are still covered with Equality, Fraternity, Liberty, even though the advocates of these slogans have slipped across the borders to India for safety.

I arrived in Kathmandu four days ago. A long, cumbersome trip out of China. Thwarted many months ago in my request to come into Nepal through Tibet. Chinese authorities explained: "You cannot be the first American, especially a woman, to go out of our country alone (not in a tour group) on the treacherous bus ride down the mountain from Lhasa into Kathmandu." So I book a flight through Burma. My only piece of good luck: As I ready to board the plane from Peking to Rangoon, I meet two Nepalese doctors. They have just finished their studies in China.

On their way home after five years away, they turn out to be warm, expert companions for this ordeal. They have been through Burma before, know a good cheap hotel in Rangoon we can stay at when our Chinese flight to India gets delayed for a day. After a fine nighttime tour of the haunting terraced temples of Rangoon, we board the flight to Delhi. Some twenty hours later, they deposit me by taxi at Jan's house.

We had been planning this reunion for over a year. This is the first time we have both been in Asia at the same time. Her work on Tibetan Buddhism has brought her close to the refugee communities in Nepal and India. We had argued about Chinese policy toward Tibet before. Now I come just to be with her, to be comforted by her nearness, by a voice I have relied on so many times in the past. I arrive on the eve of Shabbat. Jan knows my rituals well. A fine table is set, candles in place, wine and a delicious dinner. Tired in body and mind, I accept and delight in the services of her cook, Kanchi, and the errand boy, Laxman.

After the ceremonies we know from home have been consummated, she finally asks me about China. I tell her a few anecdotes about the lives of my friends there. The Cultural Revolution looms large in their lives and in my memory. Jan's response: "It sounds so awful. How could you stand it?" "But it wasn't awful, you see. There was something so inspiring about the spirit of those survivors. Their lack of bitterness I can't figure to this day." In fact, I can't figure very much at all. I just stop talking. In the dusk of this Friday night, we sit in her garden, and I cry. I guess this is what I came to Kathmandu for. To cry. All the pain of leaving China, leaving my friends there, is pouring out. Across my tears, I see Jan's eyes. The most trusted friend I have says nothing, holds my hands, and smiles.

Yesterday, we went on a trip to Laxman's village. After two hours on a bus, half an hour on a jeep, and a two-hour walk, we come to his two-story clay house. It is the home of the two wives of his older brother and his own fifteen-year-old wife. His mother makes us a fine lunch of curried potatoes and fried wheat dumplings. We climb down a mountain to swim in a gorge and hike back out of the quiet, quaint villages into the noisy town for our motorized journey home.

In China, I could not have hopped on a bus, then a jeep, and walked to the village home of a friend. I would have had to negotiate with the concerned authorities for months. Permission would likely have been denied. "Insufficient cause" for my curiosity and because there was no personnel available to guide and to watch me. In China I could not go where I wished, either to a commune to work on or to Lhasa. I could not pay my own language tutors the way Jan does. I could not luxuriate in private housing or in the services of hired help. It seems strange, but here in Kathmandu I realized how little I minded those privations and frustrations. My needs had diminished according to circumstances. My single room at Beida became the height of luxury I longed for. I achieved it. My desires, I now see, had been satisfied beyond my expectations.

The pull toward China is stronger now that I realize how delicate and how tenuous the contacts, the communications I had there. Over sixteen months I was able to savor a very shy, slow intimacy with China. From this distance, the fact that it happened at all is precious indeed. The last month before my departure, the pace of sharing suddenly so intense, I had no time to write in this journal at all. I kept my diaries, however. From those, I now extract some memorable moments, my meetings with the aged survivors of the May Fourth generation, the elaborate ritual of send-off, parting words of encouragement and criticism for my work on intellectuals, and finally, the departure on June eighteenth.

APRIL 2　*A conversation with* An Austrian student working on
Zhu Guanqian May Fourth literature heard of
my work on Zhu Ziqing. She suggested a meeting with Beida's most famous literary historian of that generation, Zhu Guanqian. He is an eighty-two-year-old philosopher of aesthetics and literary scholar, a close friend of Zhu Ziqing. I had heard stories about how he used to run around the track every day before the harsh beatings of the Cultural Revolution. Today, a short, bowed, frail man greets me. His teeth are missing, his eyes are sunk deep but curious. An active, pro-

ductive mind, so unlike the unfocused ruminations of Zhang Shenfu, the May Fourth survivor I have come to know best.

Not fortunate enough to die early like his friend Zhu Ziqing in 1948, Zhu Guanqian became prey to the forces of violence and irrationality around him. Yet he continues to bear witness to the cosmopolitan ideals of the May Fourth enlightenment. In poor health, he is hard at work on a Chinese translation of Giambattista Vico's *The New Science*.

We talk at first about his interest in modern psychology, a curious link I am finding among many of the enlightenment-oriented students who were at Beida around 1919. He tells me of its origins, for him, in literature, of how he used psychology as an angle to familiarize himself more with contemporary European thought. He received a Ph.D. in France based on a thesis on the psychology of despair.

Later he became interested in French psychological explorations of "idées fixes," then in Jung, eventually in Adler. His presentation of this is like an oration, a neat formula showing how literature, psychology, and philosophy combined to shape his work on aesthetics. That work, damned frequently both before and after 1949 for its "bourgeois idealism," he now can reclaim proudly as his own. He rambles on about the accord between traditional Chinese views of art and Croce's notion of "lyrical expression." He remains convinced that there were no grounds for his work to be labeled anti-Marxist. "Perhaps it was not Marxist as such, but it was crucified needlessly by my opponents obsessed with abstract categories of materialism and idealism."

We then talk of his friendship with Zhu Ziqing, whom he knew well since middle school. "Both of us were followers of an anarchist math teacher, you know." I also did not know that Zhu was responsible for inviting Zhu Ziqing to teach at Qinghua University, where already Zhang Shenfu and Feng Youlan, two other May Fourth intellectuals, were in the Philosophy Department. Nor did I know the ins and outs of the Kai Ming book store founded by Zhu Ziqing, Zhu Guanqian, and another May Fourth intellectual, Ye Shengtao. "We organized around the slogan 'freedom for education,' a conviction we all shared into the 1940s when we defended for the last time the freedom of art, its right to some distance from politics. . . . If you get to talk to Ye Shengtao while you are here and he's in good health it would be helpful." I will try, I promise.

As we say goodbye, Zhu Guanqian brings the conversation around to the development of his own Marxism. "I'm still struggling with the debate over superstructure and ideology. If you have a chance, do read my new introduction to a recently published book, *The History of Western Aesthetics*. You see, I really believe in Marxism now. Not the simplistic distortions so prevalent among younger people in China. Too bad that those of us who can really read Marx and understand him are so few!"

This remark has been reiterated by almost every intellectual over seventy whom I have met here! A strange, resilient faith they are creating for themselves in their old age. So unlike the dutiful mouthing of party slogans by younger, more vulnerable intellectuals in their forties and fifties.

APRIL 15　*A conversation with Feng Youlan*　　Finally! After months of letters back and forth I am able to meet the eighty-five-year-old philosopher, China's most noted, most controversial survivor of the May Fourth era. His house is less than three minutes from the dormitory that I have been in all year! A beautiful, quiet courtyard across from the house of Zhou Peiyuan, the president of Beida. A spacious, unadorned living room. The daughter, a noted writer in her own right, greets me and calls her father in. Feng comes in, holding a cane. He is stocky, with glasses, and a youthful woolen cap on his bald head. Remarkably well-preserved after the many attacks leveled against him as foremost representative of "bourgeois thought." Most recently, ironically, he was damned as an ultraleftist because of his association with the Gang of Four.

He practices *taiji chuan* every day. He seems determined to outlive or at least to disprove his countless detractors. The tone of our discussion is quiet, unrushed. He answers me directly, without prepared notes. He is unvengeful about what happened to him. Yet, he, too, like other aged men of the May Fourth generation I am meeting, wants to set the record straight, to have some say to posterity. Perhaps through me.

We talk of the history of his involvement with the New Tide

Philosopher Feng Youlan, 85, at home on the Beida campus.

student society active at Beida during the May Fourth movement. "Since I graduated in 1918 I could not have joined the society in China. It was really only in the United States that I was contacted by other Beida graduates, like Fu Sinian and Lo Jialun. I joined from abroad by writing a couple of articles on the philosophy of Bergson." A story of accidental, circumstantial association that forces me to rethink the cohesiveness, if there ever was any, between the New Tide group members.

He answers, though not exactly eagerly, my questions concerning Zhang Shenfu, his fellow colleague in the Philosophy Department at Qinghua in the 1930s. Feng hired Zhang, but, in retrospect, clearly does not think much of his achievement as a professional philosopher. Feng insists that with another Western-trained logician, Jin Yuelin, they did set "a unique tone in Chinese philosophy at the time. You see, we were the only ones to be interested in, to teach problems in philosophy. Other established departments, most especially Beida, only did conventional, Chinese-style history of philosophy. We probed issues in logic, epistemology, even dialectics. These areas had not been taught by professional philosophers before. To be sure, Zhang Shenfu's interest in materialist dialectics developed much earlier than mine. No matter what others might have said, or even myself at times, I became interested in Marxism only after Liberation. And even then, for a while, it was a spontaneous, uninformed curiosity. Only in recent years have I deepened my understanding of Marxist philosophy. But our country has too few genuine Marxist philosophers."

Again, the nearly self-righteous indictment of younger colleagues by a man who was himself often tempted by ideology but has somehow maintained a philosophical course distinctly his own. How? Generational timing explains as much as anything else.

Educated abroad in the early 1920s, Feng Youlan, like Zhang Shenfu and Zhu Guanqian, has some ground of thought to stand on that is thoroughly his. They all developed their own questions about tradition, long before they were forced to parrot politically acceptable answers.

Yet there is something especially secure, refined about Feng Youlan. More than the other old men I have met, he seems tougher, healthier. His mind is clear in spite of the battering. What was it that enabled him to survive it all better than the others? More intelligence? Probably not. More cleverness in dealing with authority? Too often younger scholars call Feng Youlan a *zhengke*, a political meddler, whereas Zhang Shenfu, isolated, nearly forgotten, remains a model of the *xuezhe*, the disinterested scholar.

MAY 7   *A conversation with Sheng Cheng*   Today, I was taken by a Belgian friend to visit this eighty-year-old poet friend of Romain Rolland, Paul Valéry, Hemingway, and Picasso. He lives in two small, crowded rooms at the Language Institute. He came back to China last year, after a prolonged sojourn in France, Taiwan, and the United States. We speak of his early friendship with Zhou Enlai before the May Fourth movement. Together they had organized railroad workers, then went off to France together. He knows little about Zhang Shenfu's years in France. Instead he tells me his own story: how the vocation of poet hit him "from the blue" while reading Goethe in Padua. "And so I left behind the study of biology and agricultural science I was doing in France for the sake of China's modernization. I chose another path to help my native land. I became a poet so as to bring home modern ideas, a critical spirit my country had lost since that first Enlightenment, the Dong Lin movement of the end of the Ming dynasty in the early seventeenth century."

The story of Sheng Cheng's journey from native son to cosmopolitan revolutionary has been recorded in his autobiography, *Ma Mère et Moi à Travers la Première Révolution Chinoise* (My Mother and I in the Midst of the First Chinese Revolution). He gives me the book today as a gift, after three hours of fine conversation in his beloved adopted language, French. The introduction to the 1928 edition of the autobiography was by Paul Valéry:

> The ambition of our author is remarkable. He wants to touch our hearts. It is for good reason that he flatters himself that he illuminated China for us. He has awakened our interest intimately. He has evoked a gentle, inner glow which renders transparent the organism of Chinese family life. It shows us its customs, virtues, grandeur and misery. This adventurous Sheng Cheng has written his book in French. He's tried nothing less than to probe the living depth of an abyss which we have known before only through the reports of observers too much like ourselves.

Valéry's words, written more than half a century ago, are apt today. Sheng Cheng is still fired by the same ambition: to evoke the spirit of his people in a language foreigners might understand but which they cannot mistake as their own. He continues to write poems in French. Today he reads to me in an impassioned voice from his latest collection, *Du Pineau Nouveau dans le Cannette d'Antan* (New Wine in Old Bottles). It is a mimeographed pamphlet full of his rambling ruminations about Greek mythology, friends in France, and socialism in China. He writes out for me a quatrain he wrote last April to commemorate Zhou Enlai: "You'll understand it better than many of my countrymen."

> CERTES, du quatre mai vient le cinq avril
> Voilà deux printemps, deux mouvements symétriques,
> Deux révolutions, deux dates historiques!
> L'Eternel féminin et L'éternel viril.

I translate the poem for him. Encouraged to abandon literalness, I write, next to Sheng Cheng's quatrain:

> No doubt! From May Fourth comes April Fifth.
> Look, twice springtime, twice movements synchronize,
> Two revolutions, two dates in history.
> The female and the virile timelessness.

Sheng Cheng is a thorough modernist with a passion for his own tradition. Especially Daoism remains a powerful source of inspiration in his daily life and in his poetry. With a glint of romance in his eyes, he quotes me from another of his collections, *Souffle des années folles* (The Sigh of the Years of Madness): "Je suis un quand elle est une" (Literally, I am one when she is one). "I am whole when she is whole, or rather when whole with her," the poet explains to me. "You see this is what draws me to Daoist mysticism to this day. The promise of wholeness, which I find sorely missing in the bitter, fractured vision of the modern West."

Before leaving, Sheng Cheng insists on giving me the names and addresses of his Paris friends. "They will take you into the corners of the artistes' world you'd never know otherwise." As we say goodbye, I am struck once again by the tenacity of tradition, by the love of classical culture most alive in these aged cosmopolitan intellectuals flung so far from the center of the peasant revolution led by Mao.

JUNE 4   *A conversation with*
Ye Shengtao

Another member of the New Tide. Feng Youlan and Zhang Shenfu had shared with me the philosophical beginnings of May Fourth. But Ye Shengtao is my first living source concerning its literary significance. I had read his early novel *Schoolmaster Ni Huanzhi* many times as a source book on the psychological and political maturation of the May Fourth generation. Today, at eighty-six, Ye is a sweet, gentle-mannered man. Even before I met him, I heard stories of his even-tempered benevolence. This enabled him to survive many of the political trials before and after Liberation more graciously than other May Fourth intellectuals. His lack of rancor has been recognized by the Communist Party, which appointed him vice-

Novelist-educator Ye Shengtao,
86, at his home in Peking.

minister of education in 1954. He is coming back to public life
these days with ceremonial addresses on educational policy. Ceremonial as the occasion might be, the depth of his concern and
his skill in finding an official hearing for his views are quite striking!

Ye has a shaven head, very kind, warm eyes, and a polite
manner. Thoroughly Confucian. He is more open than the other
octogenarians I have been meeting, more at peace with himself.
In his recollections of old friends like Zhu Ziqing and Zheng
Zhenduo, he refers to them as *xiansheng* "Mr. so and so." He calls
me *nin,* a soft, yet distancing usage of "thou" that I haven't heard
since my days in Taiwan.

He retells the story of how he entered New Tide without being
a student at Beida. "I was too poor to afford the 300 yuan per
year tuition." A close friend of Gu Jiegang, the man who became
China's foremost critical historian, Ye heard about the student

enlightenment movement and was eager to contribute to its experiments with vernacular language fiction on the forbidden topic of family repression. He wrote his first stories about the love and pain of young men and women caught in the web of the old society for the *New Tide* and was thus made a corresponding member.

He also tells me of his long politicizing involvement with the Commercial Press in Shanghai in the years between 1925 and 1927. "We had no idea that there was any difference between the Nationalist Party and the Communist Party at that time. We just had a vague, incomplete hostility toward imperialism and an equally vague, yet passionate interest in women's liberation. Words like 'freedom' and 'liberation' were like dirty swear words for some people at the Press at that time. So it was even more important to use them, however poorly we understood it all."

Such a different tone here from the "progressive versus reactionary" history recorded in Chinese texts. It is not that Ye Shengtao's version contradicts party history. It is just that it acknowledges twists and turns, moments of doubt, wavering, and the prolonged tortuous process of commitment for intellectuals. In his writings and those of Zhu Ziqing, I see, for the first time, a new criticism of the May Fourth movement, one that has been eluding me for many years now. The months after my return home will tell whether bits that I have heard in China, the privileged openings into the lives and thoughts of these aged May Fourth luminaries do, in fact, amount to a new understanding of their would-be enlightenment movement.

JUNE 15   *Celebrating Zhang Shenfu's eighty-eighth birthday*   He is really eighty-seven. Today's occasion is thoroughly traditional, a celebration of his eighty-eighth *sui*. The Chinese reckoning of his birthday according to the lunar calendar makes him one year old at birth. This Sunday is a festive gathering. After months of conversation, I feel truly part of the family. The day made more moving because of the reunion between Zhang Shenfu and his younger brother Zhang Dainian, an eminent professor of philosophy at Beida who has had his own share of political persecution. At lunch, too, is Li Jian-

Toasting Zhang Shenfu's eighty-eighth birthday. Photograph courtesy of Chris Gilmartin.

sheng, the widow of Zhang Bojun, an old political associate of Zhang Shenfu from their days in Berlin in the early 1920s. Li Jiansheng herself has only recently been rehabilitated, because of her husband's reputation as one of the most notorious rightists of 1957.

A brittle normalcy around the birthday table. Each guest there has paid more than his or her share of political dues. Beneath the pain and worry of recent decades, I sense an even deeper attachment to each other, to China, and to their vision of what culture might yet become. Their loyalty to each other and to China, though shaken by recent events, remains unbroken. I try to fathom its sources, its tenacity, but I know that it will take years to understand.

A biography of Zhang Shenfu is becoming more and more feasible. We have been meeting monthly for the past half year and every week during this last month. So many small, unexpected facts coming up during our conversations. Zhang was on the periphery of every major event, from 1919 through 1957. He has been touched by history, although his impact was small. The connections between his philosophical interest in mathematical logic, his political activism, and his womanizing remain elusive.

But the prospect of working them out, ferreting them out from the hundreds of articles I have collected here, becomes more and more intersting to me. A chance, for the first time, to do genuinely historical research. Unlike the loose, frustrating project on May Fourth ideas, this has the coherence of one life. I will need a long time, though, to find the right form, the literary style that will evoke this marginal life compellingly.

JUNE 25   *Kathmandu: after the old men, what?*   Talking with Jan about the Zhang Shenfu project, about the problems in oral history she is facing in her current interviews with Tibetan refugees. I had arrived in China thoroughly unprepared for oral history: a lousy tape recorder, poor-quality tapes, and total ignorance about methodology. I hadn't thought about how to filter out the subjective distortion in all remembrance, especially in those of a man so wounded by history as Zhang. Yet he, like the others of his generation, did not speak to me because he had been injured, or because he needed redress from posterity. Rather, a very simple (too simple?) desire to set the record straight. Zhang especially was free in admitting his own frailties, his own errors of judgment. The appeal of piecing his story together is so great that I am tempted to drop or postpone the May Fourth project altogether. Jan suggests I wait until I get home, let some dust settle before resetting scholarly priorities.

She wants to hear more about my time in China. The details of my departure are sharpest and most painful. A consummation of slow-ripening intimacies. I describe for her my send-off, an elaborate, precise ritual in Chinese culture. My friends are intellectuals, heirs to the tradition of the Grand Historian of the Han period, Sima Qian, and of Li Bo and Du Fu, poet-friends of the Tang dynasty. They are artists in shaping time, in accentuating the delicate pleasures of friendship and the sorrows of parting. They prepared, crafted really, occasions, gifts, words which made my final days exquisite and meaningful, not simply exhausting and hectic.

The most precious gift was time itself. A long, leisurely conversation is part of the Chinese way of saying goodbye. This began to become clear when one of my friends, a busy educator who kept politely insisting on seeing me off at the airport, turned up in Peking the week before I left. He came over for a long chat, bringing a gift, a silk-covered, inscribed diary. He shared stories of his youth in the Communist movement at Ya'nan, news about a historiographical conference for Chinese, Soviet, and Mongol scholars in Ulan Bator last year. He also shared worries about new tension between Han and Tibetan in China.

This conversation was only the first among many. Always, we talked before or after festive meals. These occasions were shaped by friends so we could relax together. While at ease, finally, we cement our friendship. These are times to say what could not have been said before. My friends thus sow seeds of questions they intend me to ponder after I leave China. They are, in effect, setting the agenda for my work on intellectual history. They urge me to continue it.

A scientist in his late sixties dwells on a story about the show of faith which the Party demanded from progressive, leftist professors in the 1950s. "We were asked to make up lies about our 'bourgeois background,' to make up stories of complicity with the KMT. The point of these confessions was to prove your devotion to the new China by berating yourself. The intensely personal confessions of older scholars like myself were solicited by our own fierce younger students. We tried to hear and to reproduce the unified voice the Party deemed acceptable. Thus, we forgot our own."

My friend tells me this story with an impish, accepting smile on his face. He encourages me to pursue my research on May Fourth intellectuals. He demands that I document their commitment to the revolution against feudal culture before 1949, before their more recent, forced political stammerings.

A similarly challenging smile is on Zhang Shenfu's face when he takes the opportunity of our ceremonial goodbye lunch to set me straight about the difference between his principle "rather break than bend" and the "mistaken, silly" Confucian ideal of "pursuing a goal even when you know it cannot be achieved." He explains to me that his own contentious sticking to the truth is nothing like the muddle-headed, weak-willed way in which the traditional literati upheld moral ideals while collaborating with autocratic rulers. His words are meant to incite me to work harder, to have something more substantive to ask about when I return.

Our lunch is part of my gift to him and to his family. I have no other way of letting them know how precious their openness has been for me. My gift to them turns out to be a gift to me: an unexpected chance to savor Peking's novel opulence through the eyes of some of its aged, house-bound residents. This is Zhang Shenfu's first outing in two years. His wife has not been past their block for four years now. As we drive to the restaurant, both of them bubble over with pride for their city. Its broad avenues are lined with flags in honor of Argentinian-Chinese friendship. (The president of Argentina is due for a state visit today.) The restoration of Tian An Men Square is also news to them. From the sixth floor of the restaurant, they point excitedly to the tall buildings that now stand on the old muddy riverbed they recall from their youth. Zhang Shenfu delights in introducing Western food to his young daughter. The tastes and the memories of his time in Europe well up.

We are all very quiet on the ride home. I am leaving soon and it hurts. Before I leave, they give me a flower-scroll painted by a Manchu woman painter, a friend of a friend of the family. Two bursts of red chrysanthemum, inscribed simply "For Shu Hengzhe."

I receive other gifts as well. A modern painting of a would-be goddess. Inscribed with a poem by friends in the Literature Department, the scroll shows a dancing girl in red holding high a Middle Eastern lute above her head. A playful imitation of the Buddhist art from Dunhuang that I had admired so vocally. A poem by Yuan Liangjun, the scholar with whom I have argued the most here. It is a warm tribute to the values we share beneath our disparate views. The last line, a confident hope for our meeting again. It almost stills my worries about the changing political winds of the future.

On my last night in China, I take my plants over to the house of my closest friend. I can think of no gift more personal, nothing else that I have nurtured as patiently over our sixteen months together. She gives me a tiny box. In it, a gift inscribed "For your daughter." A jade button that has been in her family for many years. It speaks of her wish that I marry, that I have what I most want, a child.

Retelling all this to Jan in Kathmandu brings back too clearly the sadness of parting. Not to slip into debilitating melancholy, I reread my diaries from the last weeks in China. I realize that my departure started early, that I became as premeditated in my ritual of leave-taking as my friends were in their send-off. In the symmetry of our rituals I see how much I had become at home in China.

MAY 24   *A rainy morning at Beida*   It is nice to be able to lie in bed for a long time. Soothing drips of water on the leaves outside my window. Very nearby. My room is small, small enough that I have domesticated it without much effort. I am now taking down things from the wall. As I have so often since leaving Romania. Each time I have to leave a home, a country I have to come to love, I have to disrobe walls. I am taking down the blue folk embroidery I found in a peasant market outside of Xian. A fierce pain shoots through me. It has to be done. I'm tired. The feeling is too, too familiar.

Too, too many books to pack. I collected books randomly through this year. As much out of interest as out of guilt about being unprepared for study in China. Maybe someday my students will want to use them, the way I slowly read through and enjoyed the books my Stanford teachers had collected during their studies in Taiwan. I'm glad I've saved money enough for the huge shipping bill this will amount to.

A gladness about this leaving emerged yesterday, suddenly, for the first time. I'll be glad to see Jan, glad to be heading home through Romania to see my aunt there, then Paris, then folks in the States. Glad, too, to begin a different kind of work.

It is clear that my "freedom," from a teaching schedule, from family, from ongoing responsibilities back home, is ending soon. I must store up some energy, some calm on which to rebuild my other life. The deep peace of mind I have gained here endures in spite of the many hassles and frustrations, the million things that are going wrong during my departure.

Beida Literature Department graduate students and faculty, with Yue Daiyun, Wang Yao, and Yuan Liangjun in the center (*front row*).

JUNE 5 *The day after the*
Literature Department farewell

Yesterday morning, I gave my lecture on Lu Xun, Brecht, and Sartre. After weeks of preparation, my faculty adviser and friend, Yue Diayun, translated the article into Chinese. The Literature Department made copies for graduate students and faculty. My language tutor, Mrs. Zhao, has been going over the half-Chinese, half-English outline with me. A young student friend tapes the Chinese version of the article so that I can practice pronunciation. I want to avoid the embarrassment of a year ago, when, in giving a talk on Western approaches to Chinese literature, I mispronounced the word for structuralism, *jiegou zhuyi*, so that it came out something like "link-dogism." Two different tones for *gou* make all the difference. In the rush of last-minute errands I find I can only spend one day practicing the talk.

I intended this lecture to be my parting gift to colleagues in the department. I hope to raise issues they cannot yet explore. I want to introduce them to comparative methodology, which they are so eager for yet intimidated by. I hope to create an atmosphere of genuine discussion, of an intellectual exchange. In my room, one on one, we had this often. In public, seminars remain rare in the aftermath of the Cultural Revolution.

The talk goes well. Responses are more formal than I expected. There is an order, a ritual, in the discussion period. All in the room are silent until the most senior scholar has spoken. He is far more honest than I or others there had imagined possible in such a public setting. He praises the paper as offering a "grand vista" on the problem of intellectuals and revolution. By using the word "grand" he points out how much has been trimmed out of research on this topic by ideological requirements in China. He concludes, "I know that I have been an object for your research work this year. Yet I don't mind a bit. You have been mine as well. I am glad for the opportunity." His truthfulness leaves me grateful and speechless.

The somewhat younger chairman of the Modern Literature Section comments next. Although we have not met before, clearly he is not addressing me as an outsider (as a friend points out with surprise later). He takes my paper and my presentation seriously, not to be dealt with by polite platitudes. He lets me and others know how it affected his own sense of the problems of intellectuals directly. His response is pointed, critical. He warns me not see history too narrowly, and therefore falsely. He points out that the Cultural Revolution was not a "tragedy of the intellectuals" but a "tragedy for all of Chinese society. Everyone suffered. Just because writers and scholars are more articulate, and more obsessive about their own tribulations, the plight of others is not diminished."

Another senior member of the department whom I had not met speaks at length after the chairman. His is the only old-style ideological "rap" of the morning. He tries to "prove" how correct the Communist Party policy has been since 1942, in spite of "troublesome deviations" to the right and to the left. He takes issue with my view that revolutionary intellectuals who consciously, willfully betray their class are hateful to the bourgeoisie they've betrayed and also to the proletariat. He insists that Mao's praise of Lu Xun in Ya'nan in 1942 "proves" that the "proletariat" indeed has always "trusted" Lu Xun. I take up each one of his criticisms in turn. With respect, but without fear, I try to respond.

At the end of the discussion, my friends on the faculty respond to the paper. Their comments are a mixture of praise and criticism.

In that open, exposed setting, we explore and express our differences about necessity and reason in history. In my view, necessity is the result of choice and cannot be equated with reason. My friends listen to me and seem to hear, for the first time, that I take will and accident to be more important than reason and necessity. This is not a very Marxist interpretation of history. In that public setting, they go on to tell why they can't and don't share my point of view. Tested by much turmoil since Liberation, they speak about a commitment to and confidence in the "scientific necessity" of the dictatorship of the proletariat. They know and mention aloud the fact that this commitment and confidence is something I lack. In front of all those other people, we agree to discuss our differences further over the years.

That night, my goodbye party for the Literature Department. At a small local restaurant I have reserved a room, and I have been planning the menu for days. I arrive with some fine bottles of Seagrams, still in their Christmas packaging. I greet my teachers, now my friends, as they arrive one by one or in couples. For the next few hours, while we sample various dishes, there is a lot of warm, open hilarity. So many bonds of friendship and apprenticeship around the table. These people have been with each other for so much longer than with me. Yet, there is something novel in their pleasure of sharing a simple social evening together. After the self-incrimination and mutual accusations of the past decades, plain scholarly banter is a great relief.

The most touching, awkward moment of the night comes when two husbands are persuaded, to be honest, forced, to toast their own wives. Public expressions of personal intimacy are even more delicate than those of professional respect. Confucian culture, after all, runs deeper in these scholars than the memories of the Cultural Revolution.

JUNE 18 *At Peking Airport, alone after sixteen months in China*   At 6 A.M. this morning, all the graduate students in the Literature Department and all the officials from the Foreign Students' Office are waiting outside the dormitory gate to see me off. The school has arranged for a car to take me and my bags to the airport.

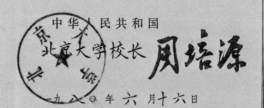

进修证明书

学生 维拉·施瓦支

系 美利坚合众国 人，于一九七九年 三月至一九八〇年 六 月

在本校 中国语言文学 系 文 学 专业进修。特此证明。

中华人民共和国
北京大学校长 周培源

证件号码（京留进）第 80005 号 一九八〇年 六 月十六日

Certificate of Advanced Study. It reads: "This is to certify that the student Vera Schwarcz, from the United States of America, was enrolled in the Peking University Language and Literature Department, specializing in literature, from March, 1979, to June, 1980." It is stamped with the signature of Zhou Peiyuan, President of Peking University.

In the car, there is room for only one representative of the Foreign Students' Office, a friend from Sri Lanka, and a Chinese friend. The others line up and shake hands ceremoniously. It is not a time to be sentimental. One is expected not to burden others with the weight of sadness. My friends try to follow the decorum for leave-taking. So do I.

During the ride out to the airport, my Chinese friend and I continue our debate about reason and necessity. She keeps worrying about the implications of unbridled will, since she just finished a long article on Nietzsche. I answer by pointing out the differences between Nietzsche's omnipotent "I" left over after the death of God and the anxious, responsibility-ridden self left over in the philosophy of Sartre and Camus. I promise her to return to China with more solid information about how modern Western science is calling into question the categories of reason and necessity.

She takes hold of my hand and wonders out loud whether we will ever see each other again. I look into her eyes and suddenly realize that I have the same worry. With twenty minutes left in the ride to the airport, we just hold each other's hands, look out of separate windows, and try not to cry.

Later as we say goodbye in front of others, we shake hands for a long time. After I hug my friend from Sri Lanka, I turn to hug her. The woman I have come to feel closest to in the last sixteen months holds me off. She smiles shyly, "Let's keep it Chinese through the end."

INDEX

An asterisk (*) has been used to mark all Chinese pseudonyms.